ArtScroll Judaica Classics®

הגות בפרשיות התורה

STUDIES
IN THE
WEEKLY
PARASHAH

הגות בפרשיות התורה

STUDIES

Published by

Mesorah Publications, ltd

ARTSCROLL / ארטסקרול ירושלים בע״מ
JERUSALEM, ltd.

IN THE WEEKLY PARASHAH

The classical interpretations of major
topics and themes in the Torah

by

Yehuda Nachshoni

translated from the Hebrew by
Shmuel Himelstein

FIRST EDITION
First Impression . . . August 1989
Second Impression . . . January 1991
Third Impression . . . January 1993
Fourth Impression . . . December 1998
Fifth Impression . . . December 2001

Published and Distributed by
MESORAH PUBLICATIONS, Ltd.
4401 Second Avenue
Brooklyn, New York 11232

Distributed in Europe by
LEHMANNS
Unit E, Viking Industrial Park
Rolling Mill Road
Jarrow, Tyne & Wear NE32 3DP
England

Distributed in Australia & New Zealand by
GOLDS WORLD OF JUDAICA
3-13 William Street
Balaclava, Melbourne 3183
Victoria Australia

Distributed in Israel by
SIFRIATI / A. GITLER — BOOKS
6 Hayarkon Street
Bnei Brak 51127

Distributed in South Africa by
KOLLEL BOOKSHOP
Shop 8A Norwood Hypermarket
Norwood 2196, Johannesburg, South Africa

THE ARTSCROLL JUDAICA CLASSICS ®
STUDIES IN THE WEEKLY PARASHAH
Vol V: Devarim
© Copyright 1989, by MESORAH PUBLICATIONS, Ltd.
4401 Second Avenue / Brooklyn, N.Y. 11232 / (718) 921-9000 / www.artscroll.com

ISBN:
0-89906-941-x (hard cover)
0-89906-942-8 (paperback)

Typography by CompuScribe at ArtScroll Studios, Ltd.
4401 Second Avenue / Brooklyn, N.Y. 11232 / (718) 921-9000

Printed in the United States of America by Noble Book Press Corp.
Bound by Sefercraft, Quality Bookbinders, Ltd. Brooklyn, N.Y.

✌ Table of Contents

ספר דברים

Devarim

Devarim – דברים

I.

The Book of Those Who Inherited the Land?

The nature of the Book of *Devarim*, the *Mishneh Torah*, is a basic question among the *rishonim* and *acharonim* on this *parashah*. *Ramban* opens his commentary on *Devarim* by stating:

The subject of this Book is known, it being a review of the Torah — *Mishneh Torah*. In it, Moshe explains to the generation which will enter *Eretz Yisrael* most of the *mitzvos* of the Torah, which Israel will need. It mentions nothing of the laws of the *kohanim*, and nothing about the actions of the *kohanim*, nor about the ritual purity of the *kohanim* and their deeds, because [Moshe] had already explained these to them. As the *kohanim* are diligent, they do not need to be warned time after time.

As to [the rest of the people of] Israel, [Moshe] repeats time after time the *mitzvos* that affect them, sometimes to add an explanation, and sometimes merely to caution Israel with all types of warnings. Thus we see in this Book, that there are many warnings, one after another, in regard to idolatry, with [Moshe] rebuking the people and instilling fear in them, in order to make people fear punishment and not transgress these laws. This Book also adds a number of *mitzvos* that were not mentioned at all, such as *yibum* (levirate marriage) and the laws of slandering a virgin bride, of divorcing a woman, of conspiring witnesses, etc.

These were not written in the first Books, which addressed those who left Egypt, for these *mitzvos* may not have been in force except *in Eretz Yisrael*, even though they are *mitzvos* dependent upon the person [as opposed to those dependent on land]. In this they resemble the *mitzvah* of *nesachim*, the drink offerings [which is also dependent on the person, and yet is mentioned (*Bamidbar* 15:2) in connection with *Eretz Yisrael*]. Alternately, this was because they are not common, and were therefore only mentioned to the generation that would inherit the land.

In this introduction, *Ramban* mentions most of the special features of *Mishneh Torah*. He notes the fact that this *chumash* repeats a number of *mitzvos* found in previous *chumashim*, but also brings others that had not been mentioned before. He also notes that there is no reference here to the sacrifices.

According to *Ramban*, this *chumash* was meant for those who inherited the land. Here the Torah came to warn them to observe the *mitzvos* and to explain what needed explaining, to caution them where this was necessary, and even to teach them those *mitzvos* which had been given to Moshe at Sinai, but which only took effect once they entered *Eretz Yisrael*, or *mitzvos* which were of immediate concern to the generation that would take possession of the land.

Thus, according to *Ramban*, *Devarim* is a utilitarian volume for those who were about to conquer the land, and there was nothing new in it that had not been given at Sinai. There are nevertheless some *mitzvos* in *Devarim* that were not written down until the need to do so arose for the generation which was given the task to conquer and inherit *Eretz Yisrael*. The conditions were such that a separate Book was necessary, one which would offer the people spiritual guidance.

Abarbanel does not accept *Ramban's* thesis as is. He asks a number of questions about it, for this Book itself is a mixture of warnings and of *mitzvos*, with both intermingled together. One cannot say that the purpose was only to teach the Jews the *mitzvos* or only to serve as a warning to the Jewish people, because the learning itself is a warning, and the warning is a learning experience.

According to Abarbanel, it is difficult to accept the view that Moshe remained silent for forty years before teaching *Bnei Yisrael* certain *mitzvos*, and waited to teach them to those who would enter the land. It is true that *Ramban* mentions the *mitzvah* of drink offerings (as an example of a *mitzvah* which took effect only in *Eretz Yisrael* — "when you come into the land of your habitations" — even though it is not a *mitzvah* dependent on land), but this is no proof, for it is already mentioned in *Bamidbar*, in *Parashas Shelach*. In addition, many of the *mitzvos* given in *Vayikra* are only in effect in *Eretz Yisrael*, such as *shemittah* and *yovel*. Many *mitzvos* mentioned in *Mishneh Torah* are very common indeed, and one cannot imagine that they were never needed until the time the Jews entered *Eretz Yisrael*.

Abarbanel therefore holds that *Devarim* is neither a book of warnings nor a book of instruction, but was meant to explain those matters about which doubts had arisen in the minds of the Jews, and thus needed a special explanation. The warnings were meant to strengthen in the people's hearts the belief in reward and punishment, and in Hashem's *hashgachah*, Providence, over all of Creation, a belief which had been weakened among them by the harsh punishments which they had received, and which might otherwise have instilled in them a feeling of despair. So too did Moshe repeat here matters, beliefs and *mitzvos*, over which the people had developed doubts, as a result of certain events.

Abarbanel uses this idea throughout his commentary on *Devarim*. Whenever the Torah repeats any law in this Book, Abarbanel explains the reason for it, just as he explains why the Torah repeats certain beliefs and *mitzvos* which are found in other books of the Torah. All of Abarbanel's commentary on *Devarim* is based on the fundamental principle that this Book is meant to explain beliefs and instructions which Moshe had been given at Sinai, but which were improperly understood, or where an incorrect view had developed among the Jewish people.

Gra ("Gaon Rabbenu Eliyahu" — the Vilna Gaon) has an interesting view on the divisions within *Devarim* and on its nature. This interpretation of *Gra* is brought by *HaKesav VeHaKabalah*. According to this view, the first five verses of *Devarim* serve as an introduction to the entire Book. This introduction refers to three separate areas: (a) "that Moshe spoke" (*Devarim* 1:1), (b) "Moshe spoke to *Bnei Yisrael*" (ibid. v. 3) and (c) "Moshe began to explain" (ibid. v. 5). *Devarim* is thus divided into three parts, each with a different content. From the beginning of this Book until the *parashah* that begins, "And Moshe called," just before the Ten Commandments (*Devarim* 5:1), are only words of admonishment, and these are referred to by the phrase, "that Moshe spoke." From that point on, until the blessings and curses, are the *mitzvos*, which "Moshe spoke to *Bnei Yisrael*." This section concludes with *Devarim* 27:8, where we are told, "And you shall write upon the stones all the words of this Torah explained well" (בַּאֵר הֵיטֵב). That is referred to by the third phrase, "Moshe began to explain" — הוֹאִיל מֹשֶׁה בֵּאֵר.

It is interesting that *Gra* points out that all three sections begin with the words that the books of *Sh'mos*, *Vayikra* and *Bamidbar* begin with. The first of the three begins with אֵלֶּה הַדְּבָרִים — "these are the words"

(*Devarim* 1:1), and that parallels וְאֵלֶּה שְׁמוֹת — "and these are the names" (*Sh'mos* 1:1). The next section begins with the word *Vayikra*, וַיִּקְרָא — "He [Moshe] called" (*Devarim* 5:1), of course paralleling the beginning of *Vayikra*, and finally, the third section begins with the words וַיְדַבֵּר מֹשֶׁה — "And Moshe spoke" (ibid. 27:9), paralleling וַיְדַבֵּר ה' — "And Hashem spoke", in *Bamidbar*. When *Chazal* in the Midrash tell us that "*Vayikra* is full of *halachos* and *Devarim* is full of *halachos*," the reference to *Devarim* is to the second section, which begins with the word *Vayikra*, and which is indeed full of *halachos*.

This explanation clarifies the question with which we began, as to the nature of the Book of *Devarim*, but it doesn't answer why only certain *mitzvos* are repeated here, and why certain *mitzvos* are mentioned here and nowhere else.

⋙ The Shechinah (Divine Presence) Speaks from His Throat

In *Ohel Yaakov*, the Dubno Maggid mentions that he asked *Gra* what the difference is between *Mishneh Torah* and the previous four Books. *Gra* answered that for the first four Books, the voice emanating from Moshe was Hashem Himself speaking, whereas in *Devarim*, it was like the words of the prophets, where the prophets merely repeated what they had heard from Hashem.

Yerios HaOhel, a disciple of the Dubno Maggid, remarks that he did not find this statement anywhere in *Gra's* works, but found it in *Tiferes Yisrael* by *Maharal*, ch. 43. *Maharal* there explains the words of *Chazal* (*Megillah* 31b) that the first curses (*Vayikra* ch.22) were said by Hashem, whereas those in *Mishneh Torah* "were said by Moshe himself." This seems very strange. Would Moshe himself have said these on his own? Rather, says *Maharal*, throughout the Torah, Hashem placed His words in Moshe's mouth, as we see in *Sh'mos* 19:19: "Moshe would speak, and Hashem would answer him in a voice." With *Mishneh Torah*, though, Moshe spoke *by himself*, as a messenger of Hashem, and that is what is meant by "Moshe himself said them."

The Midrash in our *parashah* is surprised at Moshe's ability to express himself, after he himself had said (*Sh'mos* 4:10), "I am not a man of words." The Dubno Maggid, basing himself on the interpretation given by *Gra* above, answers this question by stating that Hashem had specifically given the Torah through Moshe, who was known to have a speech impediment, so that all of Israel would see and hear that the words coming from Moshe's throat were those of Hashem Himself. Now though, in the Book of *Devarim*, after the first four Books had been completed, Moshe was healed of his affliction, so that he could pass on Hashem's message to Israel as a prophet, in a way that the Jews would listen to him.

Mekor Berachah gives another answer to the appearance here of Moshe as a "man of words," who knew how to give admonishment in a proper fashion. According to him, Moshe never had a speech impediment, but had simply claimed that he was not sufficiently talented to be able to appear before kings. That needs a special skill, as David said (*Tehillim* 119:46): "I will speak of Your testimonies before kings, and will not be ashamed." We find the phrase which Moshe applied to himself, כְּבַד פֶּה — "slow of speech" — referring to the ability to speak properly and to phrase matters in the correct fashion. Thus we find in *Yechezkel* (3:5):

> For you are not sent to a people of a strange speech and of a hard language (כִּבְדֵי לָשׁוֹן), but to the House of Israel.

It is possible that Moshe did not want to go to Pharaoh as he had already forgotten how to speak Egyptian, or that he felt he did not have the skill to talk to kings. At the same time, though, Moshe was a speaker who was able to rebuke the people when needed, with a talent to move people spiritually through his oratory.

As we mentioned above, *Maharal's* view is that in the first four Books of the Torah it was the *Shechinah* speaking from Moshe's throat, whereas in *Devarim* Moshe was a messenger of Hashem, just like all the other prophets. The Lubavitcher Rebbi, in his *sichos* in 5724 (1964), goes in an entirely different direction. He notes that *Rashi* says in *Megillah* 31 that in the first four Books Moshe appeared only as a messenger. In *Mishneh Torah* on the other hand, says the Rebbi, the *Shechinah*, Divine Presence, united, as it were, with Moshe, and spoke from his throat. When *Chazal* tell us that Moshe spoke "by himself" in the book of *Devarim*, it refers to the fact that here Moshe spoke in the first person on behalf of Hashem: "and *I* will give" rain, "and *I* will give" grass in your field (*Devarim* 11:14-15). This was Hashem speaking through Moshe's throat.

Of course this view is the exact opposite of that of *Maharal*, but one can find a similar idea in *Zohar Vayikra*, where it states:

> The curses in *Mishneh Torah* he said from his own mouth (מִפִּי עַצְמוֹ). It does not say "by himself"(מֵעַצְמוֹ), but "from his own mouth." The one means from Hashem's mouth, and the other means from his own mouth, from the voice that united with him.

What *Zohar* wishes to tell us is that the words were not those of

Moshe but of Hashem, coming forth from Moshe's throat in the first person. Based on this, though, it is difficult to understand why *Chazal* rule that one is permitted to make a break between *aliyos* in the middle of the curses in the Book of *Devarim*, because Moshe said them "from his own mouth." According to *Zohar* above, "from his own mouth" should be the highest degree of Hashem's transmitting of material to a person, where the person gives the message as if he himself is saying it. Thus, the curses given "from his own mouth" are really the words of Hashem, and why should one be permitted to make a break in the middle for *aliyos*? This question requires further study.

◆§ "These Are the Words Which Moshe Spoke"

Or HaChayim makes an inference from the first word of *Devarim*, the word אֵלֶּה — "these" — using a well-known rule: Wherever the Torah states "אֵלֶּה" it is to distinguish the following passages from those that came before. What the Torah wished to stress, then, is that only *these* words were said by Moshe, without his having been commanded to do so, whereas the first four Books were said by Hashem Himself, including every single letter and detail.

Os Chayim VeShalom is vociferously against this view. He says: "The heart of each person who reads this should tremble to suppose that the words as written came from a great *gaon*, a holy one of Hashem, with *Ruach HaKodesh* (Divine Inspiration), *Or HaChayim*." How can one say that Moshe said the words on his own, asks *Os Chayim VeShalom*, for a person who says that the entire Torah is from heaven except for a single verse is referred to by *Chazal* as "having dishonored the word of Hashem" (*Sanhedrin* 99). *Os Chayim VeShalom* therefore explains *Or HaChayim* based on the ideas of *Maharal* and *Gra* which we brought above, that in *Devarim* Moshe passed on the words of Hashem as His *messenger*. The only difference was that in *Devarim*, Moshe was never given a specific order by Hashem to say what he did when he did. Instead, he relied on Hashem's earlier order to him, in which Hashem told him to teach the people Torah and *mitzvos*, and to warn them to observe the *mitzvos*. Moshe's mission was to transmit the words of Hashem, as told to him by Hashem with all the details. *Os Chayim Veshalom* is unsure whether this is what *Or HaChayim* said, and even quotes a certain great *talmid chacham* and Kabbalist that *Or HaChayim* was punished because of this by erring dreadfully later in his interpretation of *Parashas Vayelech*. In the latter, *Or HaChayim* explained why a certain verse states that Hashem spoke *all* (כָּל) these words, even though the word כָּל simply does not appear in that verse.

Os Chayim VeShalom does not mention who this great *talmid chacham* is, and he, of course, rejects this view and justifies *Or HaChayim*. The statement that Moshe said certain verses "by himself" nevertheless remains surprising.

Kli Chemdah deals at length with justifying the statements on this topic by the different *rishonim*, especially *Ramban*, which were attacked by those who did not understand them fully.

Radvaz Part 6 repeats Abarbanel's questions on *Ramban* which we quoted above, and adds more of his own. He is surprised how it is possible to say that Moshe suppressed his prophecy for forty years and left a number of *mitzvos* unsaid until the people were ready to enter Canaan. He also notes that certain *mitzvos* which are only applicable in *Eretz Yisrael*, such as *shemittah* and *yovel*, were already mentioned in earlier Books of the Torah. So too is he surprised when *Ramban* states that the *mitzvos* in *Mishneh Torah* are infrequent ones, and were not needed until that time, for one of the *mitzvos* is (*Devarim* 8:10), "you shall eat and be satisfied and bless," which refers to the *bircas hamazon* after meals, and that surely is a frequent *mitzvah*. So too are the laws of divorce used frequently. *Radvaz* therefore concludes that he does not understand *Ramban*. According to him, one simply cannot ask questions or explain the wishes of Hashem in arranging the Torah and its *mitzvos*.

Kli Chemdah justifies *Ramban's* view completely. There is no doubt that the entire Torah, with all its details, was given to Moshe at Sinai, but only when specific *mitzvos* became applicable were they revealed to the people. An example of this is the laws of inheritance, which Moshe only mentioned after the daughters of Tzelafchad came and asked him. By the same token, the laws of *shemittah* and *yovel* were mentioned before the spies were sent to *Eretz Yisrael*, at which time the people were about to enter the land. The fact that the spies caused the people to remain in the desert an additional forty years is irrelevant. It is true that Hashem knows everything in advance and was obviously aware that the people would sin and would remain in the desert, but that fact does not contradict man's free will. As to *bircas hamazon*, the people were not required to say it until they entered *Eretz Yisrael*, and proof of this is that Moshe instituted that the Jews recite a blessing over the manna.

In summary, *Kli Chemdah* brings his own view. The first four Books of the Torah were given to Moshe *by Hashem*, just as Hashem said them, but in *Mishneh Torah* (*Devarim*) Moshe expanded on the explanations of some of the *mitzvos* by himself. Afterwards, Hashem commanded him to write the entire Torah down, including Moshe's direct words, his explanations and his warnings. *Kli Chemdah* claims that this is what *Or HaChayim* said. He quotes *Ra'avan* to explain the view of R' Yehudah, that throughout the Torah one does not expound *semichus* (i.e., using the fact that two *parashiyos* are adjacent to one another to deduce a *halachah*), but one does so in *Mishneh Torah*. The reason is that the first four Books of the Torah were given by Hashem Himself, and one cannot say that one *parashah* precedes another, but *Mishneh Torah* was arranged by Moshe, and he had specific intentions in placing the different *parashiyos* in the order he did. Afterwards, Hashem agreed to the order in which Moshe had arranged the laws, and they were written down in accordance with Hashem.

II.

The Inheritance of Edom, Ammon and Moav

In our *parashah*, the Torah warns Israel not to pass through three specific lands on the way to Canaan: that of (*Devarim* 2:4) "your brothers the sons of Esav, who live in Seir," that of the desert of Moav (ibid. v. 8-9), and that of the land of the sons of Ammon (ibid. v. 19). Here, the Torah refers to Esav as "your brother," and later too, the Torah tells us (ibid. v. 8), "We passed by our brothers the children of Esav."

Ramban says that Israel's *yichus* (genealogy) is derived from Avraham, and that all of Avraham's descendants are called brothers, "because they were all circumcised." Only the children of Avraham's concubines — Yishmael, Midian and all the children of Keturah (*Bereishis* ch. 25) — were not part of this brotherhood, "because from Yitzchak will your seed be called" (ibid. 21:12).

Many commentators are surprised at these words of *Ramban*, for we are told in *Nedarim* 31a:

> One who says, "I vow not to have any benefit from the seed of Avraham," may have benefit from other nations, as it states, "because from Yitzchak will your seed be called" — *from* Yitzchak, but not *all* of Yitzchak.

We thus see clearly from this *gemara* that all the other nations, including Edom, are not considered to be related to Avraham, and have no brotherhood with Israel. In fact. *Ramban* himself writes in *Parashas Lech Lecha* (*Bereishis* 17:6) that (the descendants of) Esav do not fulfill the *mitzvah* of *bris milah*, and were not commanded to do so. Thus, we see clearly that Esav is not considered "the seed of Avraham." In addition, Yishmael was circumcised, as the Torah tells us clearly. This question requires further study.

Or HaChayim HaKadosh explains that the brotherly relations with Esav are due to the fact that Esav acted in a brotherly way with Israel, and sold the people water and food. This we see when Moshe sent messengers to Sichon the king of Cheshbon: "Sell me food for money . . . as did the children of Esav, who live in Seir, and the Moavites that live in Ar" (*Devarim* 2:28-29). This explanation, though, is also a difficult one, for this verse states that not only Esav sold Israel food and water, but Moav as well, so why should there only be brotherly feelings for Esav and not for Moav? This question too needs further study.

The verse, "as did the children of Esav, who live in Seir, and the Moavites that live in Ar," is also an unclear one, and the commentators discuss it, for it implies that the Moavites did supply food for money, yet we are told in *Devarim* 23:4-5 about the Moavites, that "even to their tenth generation they shall never enter into the congregation of Hashem; because they did not meet you with bread and with water in the way, when you came out of Egypt." That same question applies to the children of Edom, of whom we are told (*Bamidbar* 20:21), that "Edom refused to allow Israel to pass through his border," and there is no mention of Edom selling Israel food.

Rashbam differentiates between "the children of Esav, who live in Seir" (*Devarim* 2:29) and "Edom" (*Bamidbar* 20:21). The latter were a more wicked tribe than the one which lived in Seir. According to *Rashbam*, it is possible that the children of Esav did indeed sell Israel their needs for money, but they simply refused to allow the Jews to pass through their country, and that is why the Torah says that "Israel turned aside from him" (ibid.). Israel did not pass through their land without permission, but did do business with them.

Ibn Ezra, though, discards this possibility, for the Moavites who lived in Ar also traded with Israel, and yet we are told, "because they did not meet you with bread and with water in the way." Ibn Ezra therefore has a new interpretation, that the phrase, "as the children of Esav . . . did," refers to what the Jews asked from Edom: "Let us pass through your land" (ibid. v. 17). The children of Esav did give the Jews permission to go around Mount Seir and pass through their border, except that the king came out to meet Israel with an army (ibid. v. 20) and did not permit them to pass through his capital, which was close to the land of Canaan.

Ramban, on the other hand, says in *Parashas Ki Seitzei* that this interpretation is incorrect. Israel did not cross the border of either Edom or Moav, and there is no logical reason to differentiate between the capital city and the other cities. Nor does *Ramban* accept *Rashi's* interpretation, that "as they ... did" (*Devarim* 2:29) refers to the fact that they sold food for money, while the words "because they did not meet you" (ibid. 23:5) means (as *Mizrachi* interprets *Rashi*) that they did not give them food for free.

After all, asks *Ramban*, what is so terrible if one sells food to an army? He therefore explains that the Torah excluded the Ammonites and the Moavites for two different reasons, in both of which they were guilty of showing ingratitude to the descendants of Avraham. After all, it was Avraham who had saved their father Lot from the sword and from captivity, and it was due to Avraham's merit that Lot was saved from the overturning of S'dom and Amorah. As *Ramban* explains, "because they did not meet you with bread and with water in the way" (ibid.) refers only to the Ammonites, who neither supplied food and drink nor even sold it; while "because they hired against you Bilaam the son of Beor of Pesor of Aram Naharayim, to curse you" (ibid.) refers to Moav. Thus when our *parashah* speaks of "the children of Esav, who live in Seir, and the Moavites that live in Ar" (ibid. 2:29), it does not mention the Ammonites, for both Esav and Moav did supply food and drink. That is why the Ammonites are to be excluded from marrying into Israel. The Moavites, on the other hand, even though they did supply food and water, are nevertheless not permitted to marry into Israel because of another sin — for having hired Bilaam to curse Israel.

HaKesav VeHaKabalah has an original explanation of this topic. When the Torah stated, "as did the children of Esav" (ibid.), it does not refer to the bread and water which the people of Edom and Moav gave, nor even to the request to pass through their lands. Rather, Moshe asked Sichon to permit the Jews to pass through his land, and promised that no damages would occur. Moshe was afraid, though, that Sichon would claim, "Why am I any worse than Edom and Moav, who did not permit you to pass through their lands, and to whom you did not do anything?" By the same token, Sichon implied that Israel should not do anything to him for his refusal. Moshe therefore warned Sichon not to err by thinking that way. It was true that Moshe was asking for permission, as was proper and polite, but if Sichon refused permission, the Jews would go through his land by force. This is what Moshe meant when he said, "Let me but pass through on foot as did the children of

Esav . . . and the Moavites" (ibid. v. 28-29); namely, "*if* you act to me as did the children of Esav and the Moavites, and refuse to allow me to pass through your land, then I will do so by force." Moshe did not want to say openly, "if you do what they did," because he wanted to imply that he did not suspect Sichon of not allowing such a small favor. The word "כַּאֲשֶׁר," which we translated "as," is meant here to be understood as "if": "if you do as they did," I will have to use force. The use of אֲשֶׁר in this sense is seen clearly in the phrase (*Vayikra* 4:22), אֲשֶׁר נָשִׂיא יֶחֱטָא, which does not mean "when" a *nasi* sins, but rather "if" he does so.

Abarbanel too explains, "Let me but pass through on foot," as against your will, but he does not continue with this line of thought to the continuation of the passage, "as did the children of Esav."

✂ Esav, Ammon and Moav

Once the Torah tells Israel not to vex the children of Esav, Ammon and Moav, it goes on to tell us how it happened that we nevertheless inherited their lands. In order to do so, the Torah gives a detailed history of the region: In earlier times, the Chorim had dwelled in Seir, and the children of Esav had taken their land from them (*Devarim* 2:12). In Moav, the original dwellers had been Emim, known as the "Refa'im," but the Moavites had known them as Emim. The Refa'im had also dwelled in the land of the Ammonites, where the Ammonites had referred to them as Zamzumim (ibid. v. 20).

All of this seems to be superfluous, and it seems hard to understand what the Torah wishes to tell us. If the Torah wishes to tell us that Esav, Ammon and Moav inherited their lands, from people who were stronger than them, with the help of Hashem, and therefore we should not take their land from them, why did the Torah have to stress that the land had belonged to the "Refa'im," whose land had been promised by Hashem to Avraham? What is more surprising is the verse: "And as for the Avim who live in open cities up to Azah, Kaftorim who come from Kaftor destroyed them and lived in place of them." Who were these Avim? What do they have to do with the matters here? And why do we need to know that the Kaftorim took their land from them?

According to *Rashi*, the reason for this verse is to calm down Israel. The special protected status of the land of the children of Esav, Ammon and Moav will not detract from your inheritance in the land. It is true that the land which they inherited was once held by the "Refa'im," but that is not the same land of the Refa'im that Hashem had promised to Avraham. On the other hand, Hashem promises to give Israel the land of the Avim, who are one of the Philistine nations (see *Yehoshua* ch. 23).

Hashem in essence tells Israel here: Avraham's oath to Avimelech (*Bereishis* 21:23-24) would require you not to conquer their land, but I brought the Kaftorim upon them and it was they who took their land. Now you are permitted to conquer it from the Kaftorim. The problem with this interpretation, though, is that the main gist of it is not found in the words of the Torah.

Malbim explains that the Torah wanted to say that the children of Esav and the children of Lot, who are the nations of Ammon and Moav, also inherited their land as a result of Avraham's merit and his inheritance, and therefore their inheritance should not be taken from them. The Torah now tells us that when Hashem promised the land of the Ten Nations to Avraham as an inheritance, He immediately prepared the ways to transfer the land to Avraham's inheritors in the future. At the time, this inheritance had belonged to the children of Shem. Hashem therefore arranged that the Canaanites would conquer the land from the children of Shem, so that Israel would be able to take it later. This idea is seen in *Rashi, Parashas Lech Lecha*, on the verse, "The Canaanites were then in the land" (*Bereishis* 12:6). At the time, the land of Edom, Moav, and Ammon were under the rule of mighty men — the Refa'im and Anakim. Hashem arranged matters in such a way that Kedarla'omer and the kings with him vanquished the residents of the land and destroyed the Refa'im living there, as we see in the verse (*Bereishis* 14:5-6), "And in the fourteenth year Kedarla'omer came and the kings that were with him, and they smote the Refa'im in Ashteros Karnaim," which is the land of Og, that being the place where the Refa'im lived at the time. "And the Zuzim in Ham" — these were the Zamzumim, where the Ammonites lived later. "And the Eimim in Shoveh Kiryasayim" — this later became the land of Moav; "and the Chori in their mountain of Seir." Thus we are told that the land where Moav now lived was the one where "the Eimim had lived previously," these being the people who were considered to be "Refa'im," or "giants." As to Se'ir, the Chorim had lived there first, in other words before Kedarla'omer defeated them. Afterwards, the children of Esav inherited the land from them, "as Israel did to the land of its inheritance which Hashem gave to them" (*Devarim* 2:12). That was the reason why Israel was not to take Esav's inheritance.

According to *Malbim*, the "Avim" were one of the nations of Canaan (in accordance with *Ramban's* view, which we will bring below). The Kaftorim inherited the land from them, but they were part of the land of Canaan. Hashem did this because the Avim were a strong nation that lived in open cities. By having the Kaftorim conquer the Avim, Hashem made it easier for Israel to conquer the Kaftorim later, just as Hashem did with Edom, Ammon and Moav, whose lands had once been settled by the Anakim. These lands then passed over to weaker nations than they, and then passed over to the seed of Avraham.

Rashbam, though, holds that the verses come to tell us that Hashem will keep His oath and will give the Promised Land to Israel, for Hashem had strong nations uprooted by weaker ones, who were of the seed of Avraham's relatives. This would be all the more true with Hashem's promise to uproot large nations to make way for the seed of Avraham himself.

S'forno holds that the Refa'im here were the same Refa'im whose land Hashem had promised to Avraham (see *Bereishis* 15:20). Legally, they should not have inherited this land which had been promised to Avraham's seed, but Hashem nevertheless gave it to them. *Or HaChayim* has a similar interpretation.

ܟܒ Refa'im, Avim, Kaftorim

We have brought a number of views as to whether the Refa'im referred to in "the land of Refa'im" (*Devarim* 2:20) are the same Refa'im mentioned to Avraham (*Bereishis* 15:20), or whether they were a different nation by the same name. As we mentioned, *Rashi's* view is that this was not the land of Refa'im promised to Avraham and his descendants, and therefore Israel had no claims against the land of Ammon and Moav, which, even though it was considered Refa'im, was not the original Refa'im.

Ramban, as does *S'forno*, holds that this is indeed a reference to the original Refa'im, and disputes *Rashi's* interpretation. *Rashi* himself states in regard to the land of Se'ir, that Hashem gave ten lands to Avraham, including the Keni, Kenizi and Kadmoni, and these three were inherited by the sons of Esav, Ammon and Moav. If that is so, it means that Esav, Ammon and Moav did indeed inherit part of Avraham's inheritance, and why couldn't they also have inherited the Refa'im? Why should the Refa'im be different from the Keni, Kenizi and Kadmoni? In addition, the Torah states, "the Refa'im lived in it previously" (*Devarim* 2:20), namely, that this was the land of the Refa'im before it was transferred to the hands of others. It is true that Refa'im was part of Avraham's inheritance, but the Torah stresses, "I have given it to the children of Lot as an inheritance" (ibid. v. 19). *Ramban* therefore explains this exactly opposite from *Rashi*. The Refa'im were one of the nations that Hashem gave as an inheritance to Avraham. The children of Esav also inherited from the Chorim, and that too was from Avraham's inheritance, being the land of Chivi, the sixth son of Canaan. In the war of Amrafel, who fought against the kings of S'dom, Amorah, Adma and Tzevo'im, who were the kings of Canaan, the Refa'im were defeated at Ashteros Karnayim, and the Chorim in their mountain, Se'ir; both the Refa'im and Chorim were descendants of Canaan. Hashem gave the land of the Chori — which was the land of the Chivi — to the descendants of Esav, whereas the land of Refa'im was a large one, and was inherited by Ammon, Moav, and Og, as in the verse: "they smote the Refa'im in Ashteros Karnayim" (*Bereishis* 14:5). In *Yehoshua*, too (ch. 17), the Perizi and Refa'im are mentioned, but once Ammon inherited their land, they gave them different names. Thus we see that Avraham's relatives also took part of his inheritance, and this land was not to be taken from them unless another nation had taken the land in between, as we see in the statement of *Chazal* that Ammon and Moav were purified by Sichon, meaning that since Sichon had taken the area from Ammon and Moav, Israel was permitted to take it from Sichon.

Tur, too, states that the land of Ammon and Moav "is considered the land of Refa'im" (*Devarim* 2:20), namely the original Refa'im, that derived from Avraham's inheritance. This is a sign that Hashem wanted them to inherit the land, and it was forbidden to take it from them.

Abarbanel says that this story comes to teach us two things: a) that the inheritance of these nations came to them from Avraham's inheritance, just as in the case of Israel's inheritance, the only difference between the two being that Israel was granted a Godly light. As to inheritance, whatever Avraham's relatives inherited remained theirs. b) This story was meant to serve as reassurance for Israel, that just as these nations inherited their land through Avraham, though large and powerful nations had lived there previously, the same would apply all the more to Israel, and it too would receive the land it had been promised, even though strong nations dwelled in the land right then.

As to the Avim, *Ramban* gives a number of interpretations: a) the Avim had once lived up to Azah, which was the border of Canaan, as we see in *Bereishis* 10:19, "And the border of the Canaanites was from Sidon, as one comes to Gerar, up to Azah." The Kaftorim, who were of Egyptian descent, inherited the land from them. Therefore, even though the Kaftorim were not included in the seven nations whose land was promised to Israel, Israel nevertheless inherited their land, as the Kaftorim had taken it from others. b) The Avim (עַוִּים) were the Chivi (חִוִּי), and there are a number of words where the letters ח and ע are interchanged. Esav inherited the land of the Chivi (as mentioned above), but after the Kaftorim destroyed them and settled the land instead of them, the land could now be owned by Israel. c) *Chazal* in *Bereishis*

Rabbah 76 tell us that the Chivi too were Refa'im. *Ramban* bases this on the fact that Chivi — as he shows — means a snake, which burrows in the ground, and those who are hidden in the ground are called Refa'im, as in the verse (*Iyov* 26:5), "The Refa'im (i.e., the dead) are confined in the compartments of Gehinnom underneath the waters." The Chivi multiplied greatly and inherited large countries, and members of this one group became known as the Refa'im, the Chorim and the Avim. Avraham referred to this nation as the Refa'im, whereas Moshe (*Devarim* 7:1), in listing the seven nations of Canaan, used the word Chivi instead of Refa'im. Here, the Torah tells us that part of the Chivi land, the part which was the inheritance of the Avim, was permitted for Israel to inherit, while other parts, taken by Esav, Ammon, and Moav, are forbidden to Israel.

On the other hand, *Ramban* does not accept *Rashi's* view that the Avim were among the five Philistine lords, and even though Avraham had sworn to Avimelech, Israel was nevertheless permitted to inherit their land, as the Kaftorim had annihilated the original inhabitants. As proof, we see in *Yehoshua* Chapter 13, where the five lords of the Philistines are mentioned, that it notes the Avim in addition to them. Thus we see that the Avim were not part of the five. Furthermore, *Ramban* asks, according to *Rashi:* Who permitted Yehoshua to conquer the five Philistine lords, since the Torah had only permitted conquest of the Avim?

Va'eschanan – ואתחנן

I.

Moshe Desires to Enter Eretz Yisrael

Chazal, in the Midrash, and various commentators discuss Moshe's plea to enter *Eretz Yisrael*. According to *Ramban*, this *parashah* is a *tochechah* — a rebuke — from the beginning to the end. Moshe rebuked Israel for having been the cause, by their deeds, of his inability to enter the land, which was so precious to him.

Ibn Ezra, on the other hand, holds that the main purpose of this *parashah* was to endear *Eretz Yisrael* to the Jewish people. If the people would be understanding enough to appreciate the land in the way expressed by Moshe's prayer, they would be sure to keep the *mitzvos*, in order not to be exiled from their land.

Yalkut has a similar interpretation. It says:

> Could Moshe have asked Hashem to enter *Eretz Yisrael* after he had been told, "You will not pass this Jordan" (*Devarim* 3:27)? This is analogous to a mortal king who had two servants, and ordered one of them not to drink wine for thirty days. The man said, "What did he order me: not to drink wine for thirty days? I won't taste it even for a whole year." And why did he say this? In order to lessen the effect of the words of his master. The king then ordered the other servant not to drink wine for thirty days. The man responded, "Can I then live without wine for even an hour?" And why did he say this? In order to show how much he respected his master's word. Similarly, with Moshe [he said this in order to show how much he respected the words of Hashem].

Thus Moshe's prayers were not for himself, but were meant to stress the great loss involved, so that the people would appreciate *Eretz*

Yisrael. As a result, they would not sin — as Ibn Ezra states — so that they would not lose the land as Moshe had done.

◆§ The Torah Preceded Eretz Yisrael

According to Rabbenu Bachya quoting *Rashba*, the importance of *Eretz Yisrael* is expressed in the very first words, "You have begun" (*Devarim* 3:24). It was Hashem who through Moshe began to give "Your greatness," namely the Torah and the *mitzvos*, through which He showed His glory and greatness. "Your mighty hand" — this refers to what we read about Hashem's giving of the Torah, where we are told, "You heard His words from within the fire" (ibid. 4:36). "For which god is like You in the Heavens?" — as we see in the verse (ibid.), "Out of heaven He made you to hear His voice, so that He would teach you; and upon earth He showed you His great fire." "For which god is there in the Heavens who could do anything like Your deeds and Your might?" After all of this, it was only proper that Israel should also receive *Eretz Yisrael* from Moshe, for there is no Torah without *Eretz Yisrael*, and the one who begins a *mitzvah* should be the one to complete it. Therefore, "Let me please pass over and see the good land" (ibid. 3:25).

Chasam Sofer explains that Moshe argued that after all the major and difficult preparations that had been made to enter the land, he wished to complete the task, in order to fulfill the aim of the Torah.

Avnei Shoham expands on this idea. Moshe saw how many miracles Hashem had performed for Israel in order to redeem them — the ten plagues, the splitting of the Red Sea, the war with Amalek, the manna and the quails that fed them — and all these were meant to be no more than a prologue to the great deeds of the conquest of *Eretz Yisrael*. Moshe thus thought, and rightfully, that had he crossed the Jordan, and had he brought Israel into *Eretz Yisrael*, the miracles that occurred later in the wars against the 31 kings would have had an entirely different dimension, and Hashem's revealing Himself to Israel by His deeds would have been infinitely greater. Not only would these miracles have had an entirely different dimension, but even the miracles which had happened until that time would have been appreciated differently, and would have been understood much more readily as Hashem's *hashgachah* (Providence) of the world. Hashem's mighty hand would also have been more obvious, for whoever lives outside *Eretz Yisrael* is like one who has no God (*Kesubos* 110), and is unable to sense the might of the *kedushah* emanating from Hashem.

There is a specific verse, though, which explains why Moshe wanted to enter *Eretz Yisrael*, when he exclaimed (ibid.), "I pray You, let me go over, and see the good land that is beyond the Jordan, that good mountain, and Lebanon." On this, *Chazal* tell us (and this is also brought in *Targum Onkelos*) that "Lebanon" refers to the *Beis HaMikdash*. Moshe desired greatly to see the *Beis HaMikdash* in all its glory. He saw the receiving of the Torah as only a beginning, and now begged Hashem to allow him to see the end as well. It was that place which was the ultimate fulfillment of the Torah, and that was why Moshe longed so much to enter it.

Shaloh, too, says that this *parashah* begins with the virtues of *Eretz Yisrael*, for the air of *Eretz Yisrael* makes one wise. It is there that one achieves the crown of Torah, for "out of Zion shall Torah emerge, and the word of Hashem from Jerusalem" (*Yeshayahu* 2:3). By the same token, it is from *Eretz Yisrael* that one ascends to the Jerusalem on High which is the World to Come, as in: "And Your people will all be righteous; they will inherit the land for ever" (ibid. 60:21). This is why our *parashah* begins and ends with the topic of *Eretz Israel*, with the giving of the Torah in the middle.

Abarbanel, at the beginning of the *parashah*, wonders why Moshe tried so much to enter *Eretz Yisrael*. Didn't he know that when his soul left his body it would be in the world of souls, where it would enjoy bliss so great that no human body can comprehend it? Why did he choose physical life over eternal life in the world of the souls? To this, Abarbanel offers four reasons, some of which are given by *Chazal*:

a) *Chazal*, in *Sotah* 15, state in the name of R' Simla'i:

> Why did Moshe Rabbenu desire so greatly to enter *Eretz Yisrael*? Did he then need to eat of its fruits or be satisfied from its good? Rather, Moshe said, "Israel were commanded many *mitzvos*, and they cannot be fulfilled except in *Eretz Yisrael*. I wish to enter so that they will be fulfilled by me."

Thus Moshe wanted to enter *Eretz Yisrael* in order to observe those *mitzvos* which are dependent on the land.

b) Every person desires to achieve his life's aim. Hashem gave His chosen land to His children, and gave over His children to Moshe so that he would refine and prepare them to enter *Eretz Yisrael*. Moshe endured all the problems caused by the people for forty years, and he therefore wished to bring them into *Eretz Yisrael* and thereby to achieve the goal of all his efforts.

c) The spies spoke *lashon hara*. Israel was taken in by their words, and did not believe what Hashem had said, that it was a good land. Moshe therefore longed to see the land, so as to verify what Hashem had said, and to tell the people: "Today you see the land, and it is a good one, as I told you."

d) Moshe wanted to pray at Mount Moriah — where the *Batei Mikdash* would eventually be built — and to tell the people that that was the place that had been chosen. Moshe prayed to Hashem and asked to see "the good mountain and Lebanon" (*Devarim* 3:25) and, as *Chazal* tell us in *Yoma* 66 and in *Sifri*, it is called Lebanon (לְבָנוֹן) because it makes white (לָבָן) the sins of Israel.

Abarbanel includes in his summary above all that is mentioned in the Midrash and the commentators on why Moshe so desired to enter *Eretz Yisrael*. On the third reason above, that of attempting to prove to the people that the spies had been wrong, the Midrash states that Moshe was afraid that the people might say that he too was like the spies, and just as they did not have the merit to enter *Eretz Yisrael*, he too did not have the merit. According to *Midrash Tanchuma*, Moshe claimed: "Lord of the Universe! Are all equal before You? Do you destroy both the pure and the wicked?"

Pa'aneach Raza sees this argument as the basis of Moshe's plea. He says that Moshe claimed that people would say that his fate was the same as that of the people who had died in the desert. Just as they had not had the merit to enter *Eretz Yisrael*, Moshe too did not have the merit. Hashem then told him, "I will show you the land," as it states in the verse, "Lift up your eyes. . .and see" (ibid. v. 27), whereas those who died in the desert did not have the merit even to see the land. This we see in the verse (*Bamidbar* 14:23), "neither shall any of them that provoked Me see it," therefore there was no reason for concern on Moshe's part that people would think that he was the same as those who had died in the desert.

As to the question asked by the *gemara* in *Sotah*, "Did he then need to eat of its fruits or be satisfied from its good?" there are *acharonim* that ask: We know that the text of the blessing that is made after baked goods or the fruit of the "seven species" (i.e., the *berachah mei'ein shalosh*), as ordained by *Chazal*, states, "bring us up to it (*Eretz Yisrael*) and let us rejoice in its rebuilding, and we will eat of its fruit and be satisfied from its good." Thus we see that we do ask for those very things that the *gemara* said Moshe did not even desire. From this, we can see that our character traits are not the same as those of Moshe. We want the material benefits of the land, and seek to enjoy its blessings, whereas Moshe, in his plea, was primarily interested in the spiritual components of the land. If it had only been for the physical benefits, he would not have pleaded so much with Hashem. He was willing to forgo the material benefits, but he did not want to forgo the *mitzvos* that can only be performed in *Eretz Yisrael*, and which are dependent on the sanctity of the land.

⋙ Moshe's Prayer Was Not Accepted

Abarbanel, *Ikarim* and a number of other *rishonim* attempt to explain the reason why Moshe's prayer was not granted. Is it then possible that a prayer, and especially one by Moshe, should not be accepted? The *rishonim* note, that according to *Chazal*, Moshe's prayer was in conflict with an oath taken by Hashem, who had said, "Therefore you will not bring this congregation to the land that I have given them"(*Bamidbar* 20:12)." The word "therefore" (לָכֵן) is considered to be an oath, as we see in *I Shmuel* 3:14, "therefore (לָכֵן) I have sworn unto the house of Eli." Moshe's prayer could not annul Hashem's oath.

Chasam Sofer, though, holds that Hashem did indeed listen to Moshe's prayer. We have a rule that under certain circumstances prayer accomplishes *half*. Moshe prayed, "Let me please pass over and see" (*Devarim* 3:25), and the prayer was answered in that Hashem told Moshe, "See with your eyes, for you will not pass over this Jordan" (ibid. v. 27). Hashem answered the part of the prayer regarding seeing, but not that part regarding entering the land.

Ohel Yaakov, by the Dubno Maggid, explains this along similar lines. It is interesting that *Chazal* themselves say that Moshe's prayer was accepted. Thus we are told in *Berachos* 32:

> Prayer is greater than *gemilas chasadim*, because there was no one who was more involved in *gemilas chasadim* than Moshe Rabbenu, and he was only answered through his prayer, as it states, "Let me please pass over and see the good land," which is followed by, "And Hashem said, 'Go up to the summit ... and see.' " (ibid.).

On this, *Rashi* comments, "I was appeased by this prayer, to show [the land] to you." Thus we see clearly that Moshe's prayer was answered in having Hashem allow him to see the land.

Tzror HaMor explains that when Moshe said, "I beseeched Hashem at that time, to say" (ibid. v. 23), he meant to convey a message for all generations, that a person should not despair regardless of the circumstances, and that he should pray even when a sharp sword is at his throat, just as in the case of the decree against Moshe.

Rashi, though, quoting *Chazal*, states that Moshe did not consider his situation impossible. As it was he who had conquered the lands of

Sichon and Og, which are the eastern part of *Eretz Yisrael*, he believed that Hashem's oath had been canceled.

Gur Aryeh, by *Maharal*, explains *Rashi's* words, which appear to be surprising. After all, how could Moshe think such a thing when the oath by Hashem that Moshe not enter the land was still in force? According to *Maharal*, the land of Sichon and Og was part of the inheritance of the Patriarchs that had been promised to Avraham, as *Rashi* states on the verse, "That was called the land of Refa'im" (ibid. v. 13). The reason that Moshe was permitted to enter that territory was because Reuven and Gad had not yet requested that this land should be theirs, and thus it was not considered *Eretz Yisrael* at the time. If Reuven and Gad had not asked for the land they would not have received it, and, as *Ramban* explains in *Parashas Chukas*, the land would then have remained desolate. Thus, allowing Moshe to enter into the land of Sichon and Og was not a violation of Hashem's oath. Afterwards, when Reuven and Gad asked for the land and it became part of the settled *Eretz Yisrael*, Moshe thought that the fact that he was there might mean that the oath had been annulled. He was nevertheless unsure of his position and prayed and pleaded, for it was possible that the oath had not been annulled. Furthermore, he prayed because he was afraid that even if the oath had been annulled, his punishment had not.

According to *Kli Chemdah*, *Gur Aryeh's* words cannot be in keeping with *Ramban*. *Ramban* states in *Parashas Matos* that Israel was not commanded regarding the laws of *hag'alas keilim* (a process whereby non-kosher utensils are made kosher) in the war against Sichon and Og. As Sichon and Og were kings of the Emori'im and their land was part of the inheritance of Israel, and as in the battles for *Eretz Yisrael* all forbidden things were permitted to the Jews, there was no need to *kasher* the utensils. This law governing the battles for *Eretz Yisrael* is deduced from the verse (*Devarim* 6:11), "And houses full of all good things, which you did not fill," on which *Chazal* state that all was permitted at that time, even sides of pig. If at the time the Jews captured the land of Sichon and Og it was still not *Eretz Yisrael*, one cannot say that sides of pig would be permitted to them, for the Torah introduces the verse just quoted by saying: "When Hashem your God brings you to the land which He swore to your fathers" (ibid. v. 10). Now, according to *Maharal*, they had not yet come to the land, for it only became part of *Eretz Yisrael* later. How then could they eat these forbidden things during the wars against Sichon and Og?

Kli Chemdah reconciles *Maharal's* view, using *pilpul*. Moshe was in doubt as to why the vessels taken from the non-Jews did not need *hag'alah*. Was it because the war against Sichon and Og was considered the conquest of *Eretz Yisrael*? If so, it meant the vow had been annulled. Or was it because the commandment of *hag'alah* was a special law, restricted only to the war against Midian? Thus, being in doubt, Moshe prayed in case the vow might have been annulled.

Abarbanel says that Moshe's doubt was an entirely different one. Moshe heard what Hashem told him: "Therefore you will not bring this congregation to the land" (*Bamidbar* 20:12). He thought Hashem meant that he would not be the one to bring Israel into the land; namely, that he would not be the leader, but he would be permitted to enter the land. Thus, he felt that once he handed the reins over to Yehoshua, Yehoshua would lead the people across the Jordan, and Moshe would be one of those crossing it, under Yehoshua's leadership.

A similar thought is to be found in *Mechilta*:

> Moshe said to Him: "Yehoshua will enter there and will divide up the land for them and will be their leader, and I will enter there as his assistant." Hashem said to him: "Is it then fitting that Yehoshua should be the one to command, while you sit by and watch? רַב לָךְ, is that fitting for you?"

Abarbanel explains the words רַב לָךְ as: "Are you willing to accept Yehoshua as your Rav?" Such a situation cannot be. Abarbanel also explains the phrase — one discussed by many commentators — "at that time" (in the first verse of our *parashah*) in light of the above. We will bring Abarbanel's interpretation later.

Ibn Ezra wants to explain that "at that time" refers back to the earlier verse, "I commanded Yehoshua" (*Devarim* 3:21). "At the time that I was commanded to appoint Yehoshua in my place," Moshe said, "I knew that the decision had been taken (that I would not enter the land), and I pleaded to Hashem."

Ramban explains that Moshe was referring to the time when he conquered Sichon and Og. It was then that Hashem told him (*Devarim* 32:49), "Go up on this Mount Avarim." At that time, Moshe pleaded for mercy, but Hashem did not accept his plea.

Abarbanel, though, disagrees with these interpretations, and asks: Why doesn't the Torah quote Moshe's plea at that time? Why would Moshe mention it only in the Book of *Devarim*? He therefore concludes that after Moshe had heard the decree that he would not bring the people into *Eretz Yisrael* (*Bamidbar* 20:12), it occurred to him at this time, that there was no decree against his entering *Eretz Yisrael*, but only on his being the leader. That was why, after he had said, "I commanded Yehoshua" (*Devarim* 3:21), which implied that he had handed over the leadership to Yehoshua, he felt he could ask to be permitted to cross over into *Eretz Yisrael*.

Meshech Chochmah expands on this idea. Aaron did not request to pass over into *Eretz Yisrael*, because he had not been the leader of the people, and in his case, Hashem had said that he "would not come" (*Bamidbar* 20:24) (as opposed to His statement that Moshe "would not bring" *Bnei Yisrael*) into the land. Moshe, who was the leader, thus thought that his punishment would consist of his loss of leadership, but that he would be permitted to make the crossing.

⋖§ "You Have Begun"

Many commentators have their own interpretations on the above words, and we mentioned that of Rabbenu Bachya above. *Ralbag* deduces from the words of Moshe's prayer a moral lesson for the proper way to behave. A person should not be vain about his wisdom and achievements, with the feeling that he has already attained a high level in these, but should always know that there is still much that he is lacking. Who was greater than Moshe? Yet, with all that Moshe had achieved, he felt that he had only begun: "You have *begun* to show Your servant Your greatness."

Avnei Shoham follows a similar line. Moshe received the Torah from Hashem Himself, and *Chazal* tell us that whatever any distinguished scholar would deduce in the future, throughout our history, was already told to Moshe at Sinai. In spite of this, when Moshe stood at the gateway to *Eretz Yisrael* and thought of what else he could yet accomplish in Torah and in the service of Hashem, he regarded his work as but the beginning, and he wanted to ascend to a higher level of service and knowledge of Hashem's greatness and exaltedness.

S'forno explains that Moshe felt that only if he entered *Eretz Yisrael* would his work be complete, in that if he entered the country and looked upon it with his benevolent eye, it would forever remain in the hands of the Jewish people. Moshe told Hashem, as it were:

> You changed the rules of nature in order to bring Israel to *Eretz Yisrael*. It is therefore important that steps be taken that they remain in the country, and are not exiled from it. That can only be accomplished if I enter the land, and through my influence. Therefore, "Let me please pass over and see the good land."

II.
"Do Not Add . . . and Do Not Detract"

he law regarding not adding to or detracting from the Torah is the source of innumerable explanations and *halachos*. We will discuss the above verse (*Devarim* 4:2) itself, as seen through the eyes of various commentators, and along the way we will discuss some of the laws stemming from it.

The basis for this law is that the Torah is the peak of perfection, and therefore any change by man can only diminish it. *Malbim* explains this in *HaTorah VeHaMitzvah*. Anything which is perfect cannot stand any addition or subtraction, just as no living creature can be called whole if it has any extra parts or is missing any parts. A creature which does not have the proper number of parts is considered to be impaired.

The Rebbe, R' Yehonasan Eyebeschutz, clarifies this further. The *mitzvos* have a curative property. Hashem wanted to purify and refine Israel, and that is why He gave us Torah and *mitzvos*. Just as medicines are not beneficial unless one follows the quantities dictated by the doctor, not taking too much nor too little, the same principle applies to the *mitzvos*, which only cure the soul if we follow precisely the prescription laid down in the Torah.

The Dubno Maggid compares the *mitzvos* to the physical framework of the body. The Torah is a combination of quality and quantity, where the totality adds up to the Torah and *mitzvos*, just as the body is a single structure made up of many parts, where — as we say in the *asher yatzar* blessing — if one part which should remain closed remains open, or one which should remain open is closed, the body cannot exist. *Chazal* in *Shekalim* said that, "Whoever says that Hashem is lax (in exacting punishment), may his bowels be lax." If a person says to his fellow, "Why do you need so many *mitzvos*?" the person can answer him, "Why do you need such long intestines?" We do not understand the composition of the body and its different organs, and it is all the more impossible for us to understand the nature of the Torah and *mitzvos*. We only know that the Torah is complete, and that whoever adds to it, subtracts. That is why we may not add or subtract from it.

ఆ§ What Does It Mean to Add to Mitzvos?

Rashi, quoting *Sifri*, states that "do not add" refers to the details of *mitzvos*, as, for example, placing five *parashiyos* of the Torah in one's *tefillin* instead of the four required, or taking five species on *Sukkos*, or having five *tzitzis* on one's garment, etc. The opposite of this is that we are not permitted to detract.

Ramban also quotes *Sifri*, and states that the rule not to add to the Torah would also include one who sleeps in the *sukkah* on the eighth day, or one who keeps only six days of *Sukkos* instead of seven.

Kli Chemdah uses close analysis (*pilpul*) to arrive at a dispute between *Rashi* and *Ramban* about sleeping in the *sukkah* on the eighth night, an item which *Rashi* does not mention among his examples of "adding to" the *mitzvos*. According to *Kli Chemdah*, *Rashi* holds, as *Da'as Zekeinim MiBa'alei HaTosafos*, that sleeping in the *sukkah* on the eighth night does not detract from the seven previous nights. *Ramban*, on the other hand, holds that one who sleeps in the *sukkah* on the eighth night invalidates the entire *mitzvah*, because the entire festival is one unit.

Ramban also notes that not only is one forbidden to add to the details of any *mitzvah* under the rule of not to add, but one is forbidden to invent any new *mitzvah*, such as Yerovam did, when he invented a new festival (*I Melachim* 12:32). The proof of this rule is that *Chazal* wonder about reading the *megillah* on *Purim*, and ask: "From where is this deduced?" Similarly, *Yerushalmi Megillah* (1:5) states that eighty-five elders, including prophets, were distressed at the desire of Mordechai and Esther to add the *mitzvah* of reading the *megillah*, and said:

> It states, "These are the *mitzvos*" (*Vayikra* 27:34); that no prophet has the right to innovate anything from now on. They then discussed the matter back and forth until Hashem enlightened their eyes and they found a hint at the *mitzvah* in the Torah.

Thus we see that a person who adds a *mitzvah* violates the prohibition of not to add to the Torah, even if it is a prophet who does so. It is true that *Chazal* added various matters, but they were primarily safeguards to ensure that the Torah is kept, such as extending the list of relatives one may not marry, etc. The concept that the Sages should create such safeguards is included in the Torah, and its source is the verse (*Vayikra* 18:30), "You shall keep My ordinances" (אֶת וּשְׁמַרְתֶּם

מִשְׁמַרְתִּי) — from which *Chazal* (in *Yevamos* 21) deduced, "make a safeguard (מִשְׁמֶרֶת) to My ordinances (מִשְׁמַרְתִּי)."

Kuzari's view appears to be different (Section III, Chapters 39-41). He lists a number of *mitzvos* that were instituted after the giving of the Torah. According to him, the command not to add or detract from the Torah only applies to,

> the multitude, who may not innovate of their own intellect or attempt to be wise of their own opinion, whereby they will establish for themselves Torah rules based on their analyses, as do the Karaites.

On the other hand, the sages and the judges and the prophets from "the place that Hashem will choose" (*Devarim* 12:5) are aided by the *Shechinah*, Divine Presence, and we are required to obey their words, as it states (*Devarim* 18:18-19):

> I will establish a prophet for them from among their brothers such as you (i.e., Moshe), and I will place My words in his mouth and he will speak to them whatever I command him. And the man who does not listen to My words that he speaks in My name, I will require it of him.

Kol Yehudah, on *Kuzari*, interprets *Kuzari* to mean that only "the multitude" are commanded not to add or subtract from the Torah, but not the *chachamim*.

If one examines *Kuzari's* words, it may be possible to deduce that he disagrees with *Ramban* as to whether the prohibition to add applies to a new *mitzvah*. *Ramban* himself, though, on *Devarim* 13:4, states:

> It appears that if one prophesies in the name of Hashem to order that a new *mitzvah* be observed, such as the reading of the *megillah*, that he is not guilty of a capital offense, but that others should not listen to him, as it states, "these are the *mitzvos*" — that no prophet is permitted to innovate anything from now on.

Thus we see that according to *Ramban* the law against adding to the Torah does not apply to a prophet.

Kli Chemdah points out this apparent contradiction between the two passages in *Ramban*, as shown above, and he leaves unanswered the question whether or not *Ramban's* view is that even adding a new *mitzvah* is forbidden or whether the only prohibition is to add a new festival, because the Torah states *"three regalim"* (*Sh'mos* 23:14), whereas the Torah never states how many *mitzvos* there are.

Ramban concludes his comments on this *parashah* by stating that takkanos (decrees) and gedarim ("fences" established to prevent one from violating a Torah law) are not included in the prohibition not to add to the Torah on condition that one knows that they were not given by Hashem, but were instituted by Chazal as "fences." In this, Ramban's view parallels that of Rambam in Hilchos Mamerim (2:9), where Rambam states that if a person claims that something forbidden by the Sages was really forbidden by the Torah — for example, if he claims that fowl is meat by Torah law — he has violated the law forbidding one to add to the Torah.

Ra'avad, though, argues with this, and says:

> Anything forbidden (by the Sages) as a fence and protection of the Torah is not included in the prohibition not to add (to the Torah), even if the Sages instituted it for all future generations and made it like a Torah law.

According to Ra'avad, the only time one can transgress the prohibition against adding to the Torah is in adding to a positive commandment like lulav, tefillin or tzitzis.

◆§ Whoever Adds, Detracts

It would appear that the prohibition against detracting from the Torah would be superfluous. If one is forbidden to add to it, one should obviously be forbidden to detract from it. Therefore there are commentators who explain that the meaning of the verse in the Torah is that one may not add to the Torah in order not to wind up detracting from it.

Meleches Machsheves explains that any time a person detracts from, or even adds to the Torah, it results in less observance of the Torah, as people will say that since the Torah can be changed, it is not anything of importance.

Torah Temimah brings proof that the word וְלֹא — "and you shall not" — detract from it (Devarim 4:2)) is used to mean "so that." This we see in the parashah dealing with the appointing of a king, where we are told (Devarim 17:16), "But he shall not multiply horses for himself and he will not (וְלֹא) return the people to Egypt." The meaning of the verse there is that the king should not have too many horses, so that he will not send the people down to Egypt. So too does the Torah state there, "Nor shall he multiply wives for himself and (וְלֹא — i.e., so that) his heart will not go astray" (ibid. v.17). Similarly, we find (ibid. 20:8), "Which man is there who fears and is faint of heart, let him go and return to his home, and (וְלֹא — i.e., so that) he will not let his brothers' heart melt as his." Here, too, one is not permitted to add *so that* he will not come to detract from the Torah.

The Dubno Maggid has a parable about this. This is analogous to a man who borrowed a wooden spoon from his friend and then returned two to him. The friend asked him where the second spoon had come from, and he answered that the first spoon had given birth to the second. The friend realized that he was dealing with a fool, so he happily took both spoons. The next time, the man borrowed a different utensil, and again returned two. This went on for some time — each time the person borrowed one item and returned two, claiming that the first had given birth to the second. One day, the man asked to borrow a silver candelabrum, and his friend was delighted to lend it, for he was sure he would get two back. This time, the man did not return anything. Finally, after waiting for some time, the friend came to ask for the return of his candelabrum. The man told him: "The candelabrum died." The lender screamed out: "Are you crazy? How can a candelabrum die?" The borrower laughed and answered, "If utensils can give birth, they can also die." The moral of this story is that the Torah is a gift from Hashem. If one is able to add to it, he is also able to detract from it. If a person believes the Torah is from Heaven, he will not dare to touch it, whether to add to or detract from it.

There is a basic difference between Divine religion and man-made religion, says *Divrei Shaul*. The latter is only for its particular time, and changes with the circumstances and conditions, whereas the former was given for all times, and is unchangeable, because He who wrote it saw into the future for all generations. It is here that we see the ignorance and heresy of the "reformers" who wish to "adjust" the Torah to the prevailing circumstances. If man can "rectify" the Torah, then there is no need to rectify or reform it, because if one has no faith in Torah having been given from Heaven, one can write one's own constitution in accordance with the needs of the time. That is the reason why, immediately after the law forbidding us to detract from the Torah, we are told that "all those who followed Baal Pe'or, Hashem your God destroyed before you."

According to *Alshech*, by this sequence the Torah wished to prove to what extent one is forbidden to rely on human intelligence regarding the Torah and *mitzvos*. Even those who thought that by worshiping Baal Pe'or they were discrediting that idol — for the worship of Baal Pe'or is a degrading ritual — were nevertheless destroyed for having violated the laws of the Torah, for in such matters we may not rely on our intellect.

S'forno explains the prohibition against detracting from the Torah as meaning that one may not detract from the *mitzvos* even if one thinks that he will not be affected by the thing that the *mitzvah* is meant to prevent. The classic example of this is King Shlomo, who said — in spite of the Torah prohibition against having too many horses — that he would take many horses and would nevertheless be sure not to return the people to Egypt, whereas that was exactly what he did in the end.

R' Ezriel Hildesheimer once told a certain reformer:

> "You may not detract from it to observe the *mitzvos* of Hashem" (joining together the two parts of *Devarim* 4:2) — do not detract from this *mitzvah* or that, with the excuse that by doing so you are strengthening the Jewish religion.

This *mitzvah* was said when Israel was getting ready to enter into *Eretz Yisrael*, as we see in, "You will come and inherit the land" (ibid. 4:1). The question one can ask is why this particular *mitzvah* is linked to coming to *Eretz Yisrael*. It appears, though, that in *Eretz Yisrael* there is a special reason to be afraid of adding to or detracting from the Torah. In *Eretz Yisrael*, they were to conduct a government based on the Torah, and there was the danger that frivolous people would come and say, "If we do not 'fix' the laws of the Torah and do not adjust it to the needs of the time, we will not be able to have the Torah control our lives." They were therefore told (ibid. v.4), "And you who cleave to Hashem your God, are all alive today" — our lives are dependent on the Torah, and the Torah does not depend on our lives. Whoever adds to it detracts, not only from the Torah, but from life itself, both that of the community and that of the individual.

Chazal brought an example of the prohibition against adding to the Torah even when it involves a blessing for Israel:

> How do we know that a *kohen* who goes up to the platform (to bless the people) should not say, "As the Torah gave me permission to bless Israel, I will add my own words"? We see this from the words, "you shall not add" (*Rosh HaShanah* 28).

One is not permitted to add for even the best of intentions, and it is all the more forbidden for a person to detract from the Torah.

HaKesav VeHaKabalah explains the reason for the difference in the language of the command not to add or detract in our *parashah* when compared to the same commandment in *Parashas Re'eh* (ibid. 13:1). Here, the commandment is in the plural, whereas in *Parashas Re'eh* it is in the singular. Here, where the plural is used, the warning is to the members of the Supreme *Beis Din* in Yerushalayim, even though it was the one which decided all *halachic* questions, and we are told that we may not deviate right or left from its decisions. As it had such strong powers, one might have thought that the *Beis Din* would have the power to say that a rabbinic decree was Torah law. The Torah therefore makes a point of saying that even that *Beis Din* did not have the power to declare anything to be Torah law (as *Rambam* says in *Hilchos Mamerim*).

R' Samson Raphael Hirsch looks at this from a different viewpoint, one which is particularly appropriate to our time. According to him, the Torah here addresses the totality of the people, telling them that they may not change the laws of the Torah. They may not add to, nor detract from it, but must set the Torah as it is as the law of the Jewish people. In *Parashas Re'eh*, on the other hand, the commandment applies to each individual, who may not add to or subtract from the *mitzvos* of the Torah, but must observe all of them, as commanded by Hashem.

Gra says that here the Torah orders us not to add to the 613 *mitzvos* of the Torah, whereas in *Parashas Re'eh* the Torah orders us not to add details to any one of the *mitzvos*.

Torah Temimah notes that this meaning is to be found in the text itself. In our *parashah*, the Torah writes (ibid. 4:1-2), "Hearken to the statutes and laws ... do not add." This implies that one may not add more laws. In *Parashas Re'eh*, on the other hand, the Torah states, "Everything which I command you ... you shall not add" (ibid. 13:1), which implies that the commandment is not to add details to the law itself.

Chizkuni holds that the law of not adding to or subtracting from the *mitzvos* is part of Moshe's *tochechah* — his rebuke — to Israel. "It was you who added to what I said," Moshe told the people.

> I told you, "Go up and possess," (ibid. 1:21) but you said, "We will send people before us" (ibid. v.22). It was that addition which caused your people to die in the wilderness. The opposite of this was also true. I told you, "Do not go up" (*Bamidbar* 14:42), but you detracted from what I had told you and went up to the mountain. As a result, "the Amelekite and Canaanite went down ... and smote them" (ibid. v.45). From now on, keep the *mitzvos* as they are, without adding to or subtracting from them.

Chizkuni continues that the law of not adding or detracting only applies to matters of Divine worship, for it was mentioned both times in that context. Here, the Torah mentions the case of Baal Pe'or (*Devarim* 4:3), whereas in *Parashas Re'eh* it refers to the prohibition mentioned previously, of those "who burn their sons and daughters in fire for their gods" (ibid. 12:31). Chizkuni used this to answer those heretics who asked, "How could the Sages have added so many *mitzvos*, when the

Torah forbade it as 'do not add'?" He answered by saying that that only applies to laws concerning Hashem and His service, as is clear from the passages just mentioned.

III.

How Is One to Fulfill the Mitzvah of Loving Hashem?

he *mitzvah* of loving Hashem requires man to use his emotions. The question then arises whether a person's emotions are subject to his will. Can a person control his emotions? Ibn Ezra raises this question in the name of R' Yehudah Halevi, regarding the *mitzvah* of not coveting (*Sh'mos* 20:14, *Devarim* 5:18). The same question applies to the *mitzvah* of loving Hashem, if we assume that the *mitzvah* is an emotional one.

Sefas Emes has a simple answer to this question. If the Torah commands it, that is clear proof that the power to love is embedded within man's soul, and one has only to convert the potential to actuality. Man must work hard until he is able to penetrate to the depths of this characteristic within his soul, so that he can use it for the aim for which it was created.

This idea is a fundamental one in *Chassidus*, and is to be found in the works of the Baal Shem Tov's disciples. According to *Chassidus*, all ideologies and visions are parts of the *"Ein Sof"* — the Infinite. As these characteristics are eternal and embedded deep within one's soul, all that is needed is to fan the spark and cause it to turn into a strong flame, which is linked to the fire Above.

A similar idea is expressed in the Testament of the Baal Shem Tov, which states that just as there are light and darkness in creation, man has various attributes and characteristics, either from the light or dark sides. Supernal love is from the light source, while earth-bound love is from the dark source. The light has the power to light up the darkness, and the same is true regarding man's attributes and characteristics. A person can use earth-bound love as a stage in his ascent, if he realizes and understands that the characteristic is itself rooted in holiness, and that its essence is from the sources of the *Ein Sof*, except that it fell into the *kelipos*, the negative forces of the universe, which convert the light to darkness.

Baal Shem Tov's close disciple, *Toldos Yaakov Yosef*, states in *Parashas Lech Lecha* that the ten *sefiros* above, the channels of Divine Creation, parallel the ten *sefiros* in man, the basic channels of personality. The *sefirah* of *yesod* in man, the urge to love, is linked to cleaving to the *Ein Sof*, and is part of the upper characteristic. Based on this, we can understand the words of *Sefas Emes* that the characteristic of love is embedded in man, and all he must do is refine it and raise it to its source.

The *Chassidic* works deal at length with the nature of the internal characteristics which man needs in order to raise up the characteristic of love from the depths of his soul, and to feel the pleasantness of the radiance of Hashem. The holy R' Chaim of Chernowitz, in his *Be'er Mayim Chaim*, gives an example of a man who made a pipe to carry water to his house from a pure source. In order for the person to be able to enjoy the water, the well from which it comes must be covered, so that mud and dirt don't fall into it. Similarly, the pipe carrying the water must be clean and rust-free. The same applies in drawing love from the source of love. Man must be a vessel who is fit to receive purity; he must be clean and free of any infestation or dirt. Then he is able to taste the extraordinary sweetness of the love of Hashem.

The Dubno Maggid gives a similar analogy. A certain villager brought a garment back to the tailor who had made it, and screamed that it was the wrong size. The tailor looked at the villager and burst out laughing. The villager had put the new garment on top of his old one. Of course it could not fit if there was an old, tattered suit underneath it. The same is true with man's characteristics. Love can only fill the space in a pure heart. If a person's heart is filled with dirt, he cannot taste what love is. This is what *Chazal* said in *Sifri*: "Do you not know how to love? It states, 'These words shall be . . . on your heart' " (*Devarim* 6:6). In other words, you must actually place these words on your heart, without any partition of uncleanliness or *tum'ah* (spiritual impurity) to fill your soul, and then you will feel the taste of love.

The great *Chassidic* masters had no problem understanding the meaning of love, for they were all consumed with love, cleaving totally to the *Ein Sof*. Those people who find it hard to understand the nature of love show thereby that they are lacking the basic conditions for this feeling. It is not that love is concealed from them, but the ways to it. These ways are Torah and faith. Without these, man cannot attain the love of Hashem. This is the answer to those who are surprised as to how the Torah commanded us to feel, when feeling is something over which man has no control.

Akeidah asks this same question, and does not give an answer. The answer to this question certainly cannot be found in the area of logic and study, but in the observance of the Torah and *mitzvos*.

⇜§ "Love Is Strong as Death"

Rambam in *Hilchos Teshuvah* says about the *mitzvah* of loving Hashem:

> The proper love is that one should love Hashem with the greatest love, the strongest, to the extent that his soul is bound up in the love of Hashem, and the person thinks of this constantly, as if he is sick with love, where his mind is not free of the love of a woman, and he thinks of her constantly, whether he sits or gets up, or when he is eating and drinking. More than this should be the love of Hashem in the hearts of those who love Him, who think of [their love] always, as He commanded us, "with all your heart and with all your soul" (*Devarim* 6:5). It is this that King Shlomo said, as an analogy: "For I am sick with love" (*Shir HaShirim* 2:5).

Reishis Chochmah, *Sha'ar Ahavas Hashem 1*, also says that the meaning of love is "the deep desire by the soul and its inclination by itself to the Creator, in order to cleave to His supreme light."

Ikarim (Part III, Chapters 36, 37), as well as many *rishonim* and *acharonim*, devote a great deal to explaining what it means to love Hashem. Most see this love as "clinging (*deveikus*) to Hashem," in that the person does not stop thinking of Hashem for even an instant, as we see in *Chinuch*:

> One who transgresses this, and devotes his thoughts to materialistic matters and the frivolities of this world not for the sake of Heaven, and only so as to enjoy them, or to achieve fame in this deceptive world, to aggrandize his name and not in order to do good to the good and to strengthen the hands of the just, has annulled (the fulfillment of) this positive *mitzvah*, and his punishment is great.

Rabbenu Bachya, though, makes a fine distinction between *deveikus* ("clinging") and *ahavah* ("love"). According to him, *deveikus* is a matter of a strong desire (*cheshek*), which is greater than *ahavah*, and that is the degree of "death by a kiss" of the righteous, where the person dies by clinging totally, as it were, to Hashem.

One who has a strong desire never has his mind wander from that which he desires. Even when he eats, he recognizes [that which he desires], and when he sleeps, he dreams of it. We were commanded to love Hashem with both our *yetzarim* — both our good and bad inclinations — and with our soul which desires, and with all our wealth. Man must love those [material] things which are essential to him since he is unable to live without them. Therefore He commanded that we should love them to the extent that they are indispensable; but we must love Hashem above all of them. That is the reason why it does not state וְחָשַׁקְתָּ — "and you shall desire" [Hashem], for if one would desire Him, one would separate his body from all these physical matters, and would not use them at all, even where this is essential, and there would be no place at all for the *mitzvos* of the Torah.

There is no reason why one must say that there is a difference between the way Rabbenu Bachya explains *ahavah* and the way the other commentators explain it. Other commentators are also not opposed to using material matters for the sake of Heaven. Rabbenu Bachya merely states clearly that Judaism permits a person to love those things which are essential for the existence of the world, but the love of Hashem must be greater than all other loves. One must not reject all the other loves, because the Torah depends on physical life, which is essential to one's needs.

The *halachic* works give a *practical* answer to the question of the nature of love of Hashem. According to these *sefarim*, the love of Hashem includes four types of actions: a) to learn Torah for its own sake, without the thought of being rewarded for it, as *Chazal* tell us in *Nedarim* 64 and in *Sifri*, "A person should not say, 'I will learn so that they will call me Rebbi,' but learn out of love." b) One should bless Hashem for the bad just as one blesses Him for the good. This is deduced by *Chazal* from the fact that the Torah says, "You shall love Hashem your God ... with all your measures" (מְאֹדֶךְ, *Devarim* 6:5), namely, regardless of whatever befalls you (בְּכָל מִדָּה וּמִדָּה שֶׁהוּא מוֹדֵד לָךְ). c) A Jew is required to forfeit his life if someone tries to force him to commit idolatry. *Chazal* in *Berachos* 54 deduce this from the words, "and with all your soul" (ibid.) — even if He takes your soul. *Rashi* in *Sanhedrin* 74 explains that the commandment "You shall love" (ibid.) means that "You shall not exchange Him for idolatry." d) We must make Hashem beloved among His creatures. According to *Chazal*, this means that "the name of Heaven should become beloved through you" (*Yoma* 86).

According to *Rambam*, this aspect includes the requirement to mention Hashem's name, to teach strangers and gentiles about His ways, "and just as when we love a person we tell his praises, we must call upon other people to love Him" (*Sefer HaMitzvos*).

All of these types of actions are derived from the commandment to love Hashem, but they do not diminish the plain meaning of the text, as *Rambam* states in *Hilchos Yesodei HaTorah* (2:1), "This great and revered God commands to love and fear Him, as it states (ibid.), 'You shall love Hashem your God.' " In later chapters, *Rambam* explains the ways to attain the love of Hashem.

ᥝᏏ Through Study and Through Deed

Rambam in *Hilchos Yesodei HaTorah* regards studying and contemplating Hashem's ways in nature, and the miraculous wisdom to be found in nature, as the most effective way to achieve love of Hashem. This is the way *Rambam* puts it:

> When a person contemplates His amazing deeds and creatures, and discerns in them His wisdom which cannot be measured and is infinite, he immediately praises, extols, and desires, with a great desire, to know the great and revered Name, as David said (*Tehillim* 42:3), "My soul thirsts for God, for the living God."

In Chapter 4 of *Hilchos Yesodei HaTorah*, *Rambam* says further:

> When a person contemplates about these ways, and recognizes all the creatures, from an angel and a celestial sphere to man, and so on, and recognizes the wisdom of Hashem with all creatures, he increases his love of Hashem, and his soul will thirst and his flesh will long to love Hashem.

Rambam states this more specifically in *Moreh Nevuchim* (3:28):

> You already know what comes from the power of the *mitzvah* to love Hashem with all your heart and with all your soul and with all your might, and we have already explained in *Mishneh Torah* that this *mitzvah* cannot be observed except through understanding all of nature, as it is, and His wisdom in it.

Thus, we see from all these quotations from *Rambam* that contemplating nature and the wisdom of Hashem in creation bring about the love of Hashem.

In *Sefer HaMitzvos* (*Mitzvos Aseh* 3), however, *Rambam* states that what one needs in order to be able to acquire love of Hashem is contemplation: "of His words, His *mitzvos* and His actions." He quotes the words of *Sifri*:

How does one love Hashem? It states, "These words which I command you today shall be on your hearts" (*Devarim* 6:6), that through it you will recognize Him Who spoke and created the world. What this means is that one who studies the Torah and performs *mitzvos* is led to the love of Hashem. Thus, if a person fulfills "These words which I command you today shall be on your hearts," he becomes worthy of the illumination of cleaving to Hashem and loving Him.

The above seems to be a contradiction to what *Rambam* says concerning the "contemplation" of nature which brings to love. *Kinas Sofrim* on *Sefer HaMitzvos* wishes to reconcile the two by stating that in *Hilchos Yesodei HaTorah*, *Rambam* is dealing with the general study of the act of creation, and that is why he does not mention delving deeply into Torah and *mitzvos* as a condition for loving Hashem. This answer, though, is a difficult one, given the clear statement by *Rambam* that the study of nature by itself and the contemplation of the wisdom of Hashem in Creation bring about love.

Also, in *Hilchos Teshuvah Rambam* says:

> One can only love Hashem through the knowledge with which one knows Him, and in accordance with the knowledge is the love. Therefore, a person must devote himself to comprehend the wisdom and understanding ... to the extent that the person can understand and grasp these.

Here, *Rambam* uses the term "knowledge," without explaining what this means. There is no doubt, though, that it includes at least contemplation of basic ideas, as those who are acquainted with *Rambam's* works are aware.

Ralbag includes both types of study and contemplation, both of the Torah and of basic concepts, as tools with which one can attain the trait of love of Hashem. He says we can attain this love,

> by devoting ourselves diligently to the *mitzvos* of the Torah, for they will lead us toward knowledge of God, and by the investigation of those wondrous actions of His which we can understand.

Rabbenu Bachya, though, mentions only contemplation "of the Torah and *mitzvos*." He even leaves out the phrase, "and His actions," mentioned in *Sefer HaMitzvos*. In his work, *Kad HaKemach*, too, in the section on Love, *Rabbenu Bachya* says:

> Man should contemplate the main paths of the *mitzvos*, and he

will achieve through them the understanding of Hashem, may He be exalted, and will enjoy that understanding with an ultimate enjoyment, until he makes the public righteous, and draws their hearts to His love, may He be blessed.

From our own experience, we know that appreciating nature and its extraordinary composition is not enough in itself to bring one to a recognition of Hashem and to love Him. There are many cultured nations in our time which are quite far from ethical virtue and from love of Hashem, even though they have already reached the moon and the planets.

Indeed, the *acharonim*, and even the German school of commentators of the previous generation, explain the commandment of "you shall love" as a commandment to elevate and sanctify our ways. None of them says that investigation and study of nature are the path to the love of Hashem.

HaKesav VeHaKabalah, commenting on this, says clearly:

We could have erred to believe that theoretical knowledge and natural rational investigation are what bring man to love Hashem. The Torah therefore explained that this is not so, and the truth is that the love of Hashem is only through studying Torah and the *mitzvos*. There have already been a number of great investigators of the heart and seekers of the truth who have proved beautifully, and with great proofs, that the love of Hashem and true service of Him do not depend on theoretical and rational investigation.

◄§ The Approach of Sa'adiah Gaon

Among those who list all 613 *mitzvos*, R' Sa'adiah Gaon is the only one who leaves out the love of Hashem in his listing. The reason for this omission is not known. R' Perla, in his commentary on R' Sa'adiah Gaon's 613 *mitzvos*, attempts to explain the reason for this omission as being due to the fact that R' Sa'adiah Gaon does not list both *mitzvos*, where there are a positive and a negative *mitzvah* on the same topic, but instead brings the one which is more comprehensive. This is unlike *Rambam*, who quotes both *mitzvos*. As an example of this, R' Perla quotes the commandment, "I shall be sanctified" (*Vayikra* 22:32), which R' Sa'adiah Gaon omits, because it is already included in the negative commandment of "You shall not desecrate My holy name" (ibid.). The latter is more comprehensive than "I shall be sanctified," as "I shall be sanctified" applies only in public, whereas the *mitzvah* of "you shall not desecrate My holy name" applies in private as well.

R' Perla adds on his own that R' Sa'adiah Gaon holds that the *mitzvah* of "You shall love" (*Devarim* 6:5) parallels the negative commandment of "You shall not desecrate," in that both require a Jew to be willing to give up his life if he is being forced to commit idolatry, and even if this is in private. Therefore, as R' Sa'adiah Gaon had already listed "You shall not desecrate" in the 613 *mitzvos*, he omitted the *mitzvah* to love Hashem.

R' Perla quotes also *Ran* in *Avodah Zarah* 27, regarding the statement by *Rif*, that the *halachah* is in accordance with R' Eliezer, who holds that a person must permit himself to be killed rather than commit idolatry, this being deduced from the words "and with all your soul" (ibid.). This is unlike the view of R' Yishmael, who rules even in regard to idolatry that a person should commit the sin rather than allowing himself to be killed, for it states in the Torah, "and [man] shall live by them" (*Vayikra* 18:5). *Ran* there explains the reason underlying the argument between the two *tannaim*. R' Eliezer holds that as there are two verses which contradict one another, as it were ("with all your soul" and "you shall live by them"), we apply the verse "you shall live by them" to all other *mitzvos*, while in regard to the verse "with all your soul," that applies to idolatry, teaching us that we cannot serve idolatry "even if he takes your soul from you." R' Yishmael, though, holds that the verse "with all your soul" is not meant to teach us that a person must be willing to offer up his life, but is meant to teach us how great should be a person's love for Hashem, to the extent that this love should completely encompass the person's soul and senses. This verse, though, does not require a person to do anything. As we rule in accordance with R' Eliezer, the *halachah* is that our love of Hashem must extend even to being willing to sacrifice our lives for Him if someone tries to force us to serve idolatry. In fact he even goes so far as to teach us that this applies even if the action is in private, and not only in public, as would be deduced from the expression, "I shall be sanctified." But since R' Sa'adiah Gaon has already listed the commandment, "You shall not desecrate My holy name" (*Vayikra* 22:32), which includes sacrificing one's life to avoid idol worship, he does not make special mention of the *mitzvah* to love Hashem, which implies the same obligation.

One can nevertheless question this interpretation of R' Perla. It is true that the verse of "You shall not desecrate" expresses an even greater obligation than the verse "I shall be sanctified," but that does not mean that it expresses a greater obligation than the verse, "You shall love," which by itself teaches us that we must be willing to sacrifice our lives and not serve idolatry, even in private. Why then, in listing the *mitzvos*, did R' Sa'adiah Gaon only list that of "You shall not desecrate" while omitting that of "You shall love?" This requires further study.

IV.
Knesses Yisrael's Mate

he *rishonim* attempt to analyze the differences between the *Aseres HaDibros* — the Ten Commandments — in *Sh'mos* and those in *Devarim* in regard to Shabbos, both in terms of the language used and in substance. In *Sh'mos* (20:8), we are told, "*Zachor* — remember the day of Shabbos," while in *Devarim* (5:12) it states, "*Shamor* — observe — the day of Shabbos." In *Sh'mos*, the Torah gives the reason for Shabbos as being a reminder of Hashem's creation of the world, while in *Devarim* we are told that it is a reminder of Hashem's taking us out of Egypt.

Ibn Ezra states that in *Devarim* (5:15), when the Torah tells us, "And remember that you were a slave in the land of Egypt," it is not meant to explain why we are to keep Shabbos, but is merely an explanation of the phrase in the previous verse, "in order that your manservant and female servant shall rest like you."

Ramban, though, proves that Ibn Ezra's interpretation is not correct, because when we make *kiddush* on Shabbos we mention that this is a remembrance of *yetzias Mitzrayim*, the Exodus, just as we mention that it is a remembrance of Hashem's creation of the world. This is a sign that Shabbos is based on both principles.

We must clarify the conceptual link between the two ideas, and why there are differences in the text in the *Aseres HaDibros*. *Chazal* tell us that the words "remember" and "observe" ("the day of Shabbos") were both uttered by Hashem at the same time. What is the meaning of these words of *Chazal*? If both words were said at the same time, what is the difference between the two?

Ramban in *Parashas Yisro* says that the commandment to "remember" Shabbos refers to the positive *mitzvos* of the day, whereas the commandment to "observe" it refers to the *lavim* — the negative commandments — of the day. According to *Ramban*, the positive commandments stem from the source of *rachamim* — mercy — and *ahavah* — love, because when a person does what his master orders him to do, he loves his master and is loved by him, and the master is merciful to him. The negative commandments, on the other hand, stem from the source of *yirah* — fear — and *din* — strict justice. Positive commandments are thus greater than negative commandments, just as *ahavah* is greater than *yirah*. When *Chazal* said that both words were uttered at the same time, they were referring to the two kinds of *mitzvos* included in Shabbos.

Meshech Chochmah in *Parashas VeZos HaBerachah* explains *Ramban's* words. While it is commonly known that it is worse to violate a negative *mitzvah* than a positive one, that is only true when the person goes against Hashem's word and wishes to rebel against Him. When a person keeps the *mitzvos*, on the other hand, the positive *mitzvos*, which come from the source of *ahavah*, take precedence over negative *mitzvos*. Thus we see that if a person has a garment with wool and places linen *tzitzis* in it, the *halachah* should allow him to wear the garment, because the positive *mitzvah* of *tzitzis* takes precedence over the prohibition against wearing *sha'atnez*, the forbidden combination of wool and linen. (*Chazal* nevertheless do not permit wearing such a garment, because if any threads tear off, the person is left with no kosher *tzitzis*, and is wearing *sha'atnez* — trans.)

R' Akiva Eiger and other *acharonim* express surprise at this interpretation of *Ramban*, because *Chazal* in *Yevamos* 7a ask, "Can a positive *mitzvah* take precedence over a negative *mitzvah*? Isn't a negative *mitzvah* more severe?" From this, we see that a negative *mitzvah* is more severe than a positive one. R' Chavel, in his commentary on *Ramban*, answers that *Ramban* too did not state that a positive *mitzvah* is more severe than a negative *mitzvah*. He only said that it is *greater*. Its greatness lies in its observance, because by observing it a person attaches himself to Hashem's mercy and love. Indeed, *Ramban* himself adds that the punishment for violating a negative *mitzvah* is greater. As this type of *mitzvah* comes from Hashem's attribute of strict justice, a person who violates it is more severely punished. In regard to positive *mitzvos*, on the other hand, the punishment is smaller because of the greatness of the *mitzvah*, which is derived from Hashem's mercy.

Mizrachi, though, has a different question on *Ramban*. *Ramban* says in *Parashas Yisro* that when *Chazal* tells us that both *zachor* ("remember") and *shamor* ("observe") were said with one utterance of Hashem, it means that the keeping of Shabbos entails both positive and negative *mitzvos*. If that is indeed so, then the *kiddush* that is made (we are told that *kiddush* fulfills the commandment to "remember") must be both a positive and a negative *mitzvah* (a positive *mitzvah* to say *kiddush* and a violation of a negative *mitzvah* if one does not do so), and we don't find the Talmud stating this anywhere.

Mizrachi also asks another question based on *Ramban's* interpretation that *shamor* implies a *lav* — a negative *mitzvah*. As we know, generally, when the Torah uses the passive form, *hishamer* (הִשָּׁמֶר, i.e., "guard yourself, beware"), it means a negative *mitzvah*. This implies, however, that if it uses the active form, *shamor* (שָׁמוֹר, i.e., "observe"), and it refers to a positive action, it indicates a positive *mitzvah*. Here the Torah refers to the *mitzvah* in positive terms: "Observe (*shamor*) the day of Shabbos *to sanctify it.*" Thus, even though *Ramban* explains the term "to sanctify it" as meaning not to desecrate it, nevertheless, as this is said in the positive form, it must be a positive *mitzvah*.

Furthermore, one cannot explain the term "to sanctify it" in regard to *shamor* differently from the way one explains the same term in regard to *zachor*. Just as with *zachor* the meaning is to take an action, the same must be true when this term is used with *shamor*.

Maharal, though, in *Gur Aryeh*, answers *Mizrachi's* questions. He quotes *Rashi* as saying in *Parashas Re'eh* that even when *hishamer* is used in reference to a positive *mitzvah*, it gives it the status of a negative *mitzvah*, except that one does not receive lashes for transgressing it.

Maharal, nevertheless, argues with *Ramban*. Why should we explain that the fact that the two words of *zachor* and *shamor* were uttered at the same time must refer to positive and negative *mitzvos*, when there are other instances of *Chazal* telling us that two words were said in the same utterance, without us interpreting these as referring to positive and negative *mitzvos*. Thus we see that *Chazal* said about not using Hashem's name — where in *Sh'mos* (20:7) and *Devarim* (5:11) it states "in vain" and in *Vayikra* (19:12) it says "with a lie" — that both "in vain" and "with a lie" were uttered at the same time, without deducing from this that one is a positive and the other a negative *mitzvah*.

Another question that *Maharal* asks is why *Ramban* does not explain that the two words were said in the same utterance because the first Commandments refer to the creation of the world and the second to *yetzias Mitzrayim*, the Exodus. Furthermore, *Chazal* rule that when a *mitzvah* appears earlier and in the Book of *Devarim*, the reference in *Devarim* is meant to add details to the previously mentioned *mitzvah*. If that is so, why did *Chazal* have to explain that the words *zachor* and *shamor* were said in the same utterance due to the contradiction between the two? Why couldn't they simply say that *shamor* adds a negative *mitzvah* to the positive *mitzvah* of *zachor*?

Maharal finally concludes that when *Chazal* state that the additional reference to a *mitzvah* in *Devarim* is only to be interpreted as adding further detail to the *mitzvah* itself, this is only so if there are *additional* words, but these do not indicate a change of the meaning. In the case of Shabbos, though, the changes are fundamental, because in *Sh'mos* the meaning of *zachor* is to remember Shabbos by saying something and by reciting *kiddush*, whereas *shamor* implies observing Shabbos by not doing any work. Such a fundamental difference cannot merely be an addition to what came before. The same applies when we are told not to bear witness "in vain" and "with a lie." As there are fundamental differences in the meanings of the two, *Chazal* were forced to say that both were said with a single utterance. By this means, all the contradictions are ironed out, for the single utterance includes all the possibilities.

Ikarim, too, attacks *Ramban's* interpretation, but from a different angle. If the *mitzvah* of *zachor* is a positive *mitzvah*, why does the Torah say in the same context, "you shall not perform any work" (*Sh'mos* 20:10)? As a result of this question, *Ikarim* gives his own original explanation. Shabbos does not come to teach us that there was a Prime Mover (i.e., Hashem) Who created the world, because even the gentile philosophers agree with that idea. Only total heretics deny that fact. Shabbos, rather, comes to teach us that after creating the world, Hashem still directs it on a constant basis, and that is something that the philosophers deny. The connection between *zachor* and *shamor* is that in the first passage (in *Sh'mos*) the Torah mentions only the existence of the Prime Mover, whereas the idea of Hashem continuing to direct the world is to be found in the second passage (in *Devarim*), where we are told of Hashem taking us out of Egypt. Both of these were said with the same utterance, namely that the *mitzvos* of Shabbos include both of these fundamental principles. Hashem created the world, and it is He Who still guides and controls it. This action of His is a continuous one, and this is in opposition to those who say that there is nothing new under the sun. *Yetzias Mitzrayim* was a new action by Hashem, after the world had been created by Him; it resulted from His continuing direction (*hashgachah*) of the world.

◆§ The Creation and Yetzias Mitzrayim Are the Same Thing

Ikarim's view that *yetzias Mitzrayim*, the Exodus, was the completion of the Creation, is almost identical to *Ramban's* view in our *parashah*, which, also, is based on the unity of the two principles, although there are slight differences between the two commentators. According to *Ramban*, not only was *yetzias Mitzrayim* a completion in terms of Hashem's creating the world and guiding it thereafter, but there is total identity between the two concepts, both really being one. In this, *Ramban* is consistent with his view on the first of the Ten Commandments, "I am Hashem your God Who took you out of the land of Egypt" (*Sh'mos* 20:2). On that verse, *Ramban* explains that *yetzias Mitzrayim*

> teaches that Hashem exists and that it is through His will that everything comes into existence. It also teaches that it is with His knowledge and providence that we left [Egypt]. It also teaches us of [Hashem's] power to change things, because according to the view that the world has existed forever, nothing can be changed of its nature. Furthermore, it teaches us of [Hashem's] omnipotence, that omnipotence indicating His unity, as it states (*Sh'mos* 9:14), "in order that you should know that there is none like Me in all the earth." The meaning of the expression of "Who took you out" is thus that [Israel] know and are witnesses to this fact.

It is in accordance with this view that *Ramban* explains the transition in our *parashah* from the creation of the world, as stated in the first *Dibros* (Ten Commandments), to *yetzias Mitzrayim* in the second. There is no substantive change between the two, but rather the second reverts back to the first. Both Shabbos and *yetzias Mitzrayim* teach us that Hashem created the world. If any person has doubts about the nature of Shabbos, which implies Hashem's creation, will and omnipotence, he should remember *yetzias Mitzrayim*, which will aid him in strengthening his faith. Shabbos thus serves as a reminder of *yetzias Mitzrayim*, and *yetzias Mitzrayim* serves as a reminder of Shabbos. *Yetzias Mitzrayim* teaches us that Hashem changes matter and does whatever He wishes, just as Hashem's creation of the world teaches us that fact. That is why in the second *Dibros*, too, the Torah states (*Devarim* 5:14), "The seventh day is a Shabbos to Hashem your God," namely that Shabbos is a sign of Hashem's power and ability to change the rules of nature, as shown in the creation of the world and in *yetzias Mitzrayim*.

Ramban also brings the view of *Rambam* in *Moreh Nevuchim* that *zachor* ("remember") refers to honoring Shabbos and enhancing it, regarding which we are told, "Hashem therefore blessed the day of Shabbos and sanctified it" (*Sh'mos* 20:11). As to *shamor* ("observe"), that teaches us to rest on Shabbos, because we were slaves in Egypt and were unable to rest. Hashem has commanded us to rest, so that we should remember His compassion in taking us out from slavery to rest.

Ramban criticizes *Rambam's* view. He asks: How can not working on Shabbos show that we left Egypt? While it is indeed an indication that Hashem created the world and rested on the seventh day, there is no reference to *yetzias Mitzrayim*. Those who see us resting will not remember *yetzias Mitzrayim* as a result.

Ritva answers *Ramban's* question. He states that there are *mitzvos* in the Torah which were at first symbolic of miraculous deeds. Later, this fact could not be seen in the acts themselves, but the traditions regarding the symbolic meaning were handed down from generation to generation. The generation which left Egypt knew the reason for resting on Shabbos, because in Egypt they were not able to rest for even an instant, and now they were free for a full day each week. This symbol has remained with us throughout the generations.

Other commentators on *Rambam* explain that what he meant, in saying that the first *Dibros* refer to honoring and enhancing Shabbos, was that the Torah wishes to explain why the seventh day of the week was chosen as the day of rest, and not another day, for any day of rest during the week would remind us of *yetzias Mitzrayim*. The Torah therefore explains that Hashem created the heavens and the earth in six days, and on the seventh day He rested. The second *Dibros*, on the other hand, explain why specifically *Israel* should keep Shabbos, and not the other nations of the world, for shouldn't the creation of the world and Hashem's resting afterwards be observed by everyone? The Torah therefore states that Shabbos is a reminder of *yetzias Mitzrayim*, and that is why only Israel is obligated to rest on that day.

HaKesav VeHaKabalah introduces a new element into the discussion. According to him, the two reasons of Hashem's creation of the world and *yetzias Mitzrayim* are not sufficient in explaining the *mitzvah* to keep Shabbos. The creation of the world was not the reason why we were commanded to rest on Shabbos, but only explains why that day is more holy than the other days. We are told specifically in *Bereishis* 2:3, "He sanctified it because He rested on it." The Torah speaks here about the holiness of the day, and not of resting on that day. In the first *Dibros*, the Torah does not state, "Hashem therefore commanded you to keep the Shabbos," but instead we are told (*Sh'mos* 20:11), "therefore Hashem blessed the day of Shabbos and sanctified it." Such holiness is not dependent on rest, but is an independent characteristic of the day. Nor is *yetzias Mitzrayim* the fundamental reason behind resting on Shabbos, because there are other *mitzvos* that also are meant as remembrances of *yetzias Mitzrayim*, and yet have nothing to do with resting. For example, when a person frees a Jewish slave, he is required to give him some basic provisions to be able to start over, and the Torah gives as the reason for this, "And remember that you were a servant in the land of Egypt and Hashem your God redeemed you" (*Devarim* 15:15). The same is true when the Torah gives *yetzias Mitzrayim* as the reason for observing the festival of Shavuos (ibid. 16:10-12), and not to pervert justice (ibid. 24:17-18).

Using this as his basis, *HaKesav VeHaKabalah* justifies Ibn Ezra's comment that the statement that we are to remember *yetzias Mitzrayim* is a reference to the *mitzvah* to allow our servants to rest on that day, and is not the reason why we should keep Shabbos. As to what the reason for keeping Shabbos really is, this is deduced from the verse, "you shall keep my Shabbosos, because it is a sign between Me and you." This sign teaches us that Hashem is always with us, and that we are His nation. We rest on the day that the creation rested, and by doing so we publicize Hashem's name in the world, and also show thereby our ties to Hashem, based on our eternal covenant with Him.

⋘ "Which Hashem Created to Do"

Abarbanel, in his commentary on the Torah, as well as in his commentary on *Moreh Nevuchim*, goes into great length in explaining *Rambam's* view that the first *Dibros* are a reference to honoring and enhancing Shabbos, as a reminder of Hashem's creation of the world, whereas the second *Dibros* are a *mitzvah* to refrain from doing any work, as a reminder of *yetzias Mitzrayim*.

Chazal said that both *zachor* ("remember", *Sh'mos* 20:8) and *shamor* ("observe", *Devarim* 5:12) were said with the same utterance, namely, that if we pay close attention to each one of the *Dibros* by itself, we will find both ideas reflected in each.

In the first *Dibros*, we are told (*Sh'mos* 20:9), "Six days you shall labor and do all your work," namely, that in Egypt you worked without any rest every day; now that you have left Egypt, "The seventh day is a Shabbos to Hashem your God, and you may not perform any work" (ibid. v. 10), such as you had to do in Egypt. That is why the Torah adds in the first *Dibros*, "and your manservant and maidservant . . . and your stranger who is in your gates" (ibid.), for this is to remind you that now you are a free man, and have your own servants.

In the second *Dibros*, the Torah states, "as He commanded you" (*Devarim* 5:12), and that is a hint back to the creation of the world which is mentioned in the first *Dibros*. When *Chazal* said that both expressions were said with the same utterance, they meant that the two resemble one another and are included together, with each having a reference to the other as well.

As to *Ramban's* question on *Rambam* as to how resting on Shabbos should be a reminder of *yetzias Mitzrayim*, as well as another question — how *resting* on Shabbos should be a reminder of Hashem's creation of the world, which was entirely a matter of Hashem's *action* (rather than of His rest afterwards) — Abarbanel gives a number of original answers. Resting and not doing work is a symbol of the creation of the world, in which Hashem created matter out of nothing. It was only that form of creation — of something from nothing — that ceased on the seventh day, but the formation of things one from another continued thereafter and has never stopped, as we see in the verse, "which Hashem created to do" (*Bereishis* 2:3), implying in the future as well. The world was only created *in potential* during the six days of creation, but in actuality Hashem renews the creation each day.

Abarbanel's comment on the reminder of *yetzias Mitzrayim* in not working on Shabbos is a very interesting one. Shabbos is not only a day of refraining from doing things, but is also a day of festivity and celebration. When the Torah states, "which Hashem created to do," it alludes to the *mitzvos* of Shabbos, these being, enjoying ourselves and rejoicing, which are tangible expressions. These actions remind us of *yetzias Mitzrayim*. They let everyone see that this day is different from the other days of the week, and this is a demonstration of our release from the house of bondage.

Various *acharonim* discuss the meaning of the expression "to do" in reference to Shabbos, each in accordance with his own view. R' Samson Raphael Hirsch states that Shabbos was created to be a tool in completing the aim of Hashem's creation. It is meant to complete man's education, spiritually and morally. Hashem's work in nature had been completed, but Hashem's work in history had just begun. Now a situation and a need arose to utilize the materially existent world as an educational tool to teach that Hashem controls mankind. *Chazal* said, "He rested from the work of His world. He did not rest from the work of the righteous and the wicked" (*Bereishis Rabbah* 11). Man's education to attain greater spiritual heights was delegated to Shabbos — "which Hashem created to do."

R' Isaac Breuer, in *Nachaliel*, expands on this idea. According to him, history begins with the act of creation. The six days of creation are already part of the historical time in which we are living. The fact remains, though, that the major aspect of history is our own deeds. These deeds are the direct continuation of Hashem's deeds of creation. After the six days of Hashem's actions, we have the six days of man's actions. Between the two sets of days lies Shabbos, whose purpose is to bind man's deeds to those of Hashem, Who created time and history.

HaKesav VeHaKabalah has a similar idea, while stressing the spirituality of Shabbos. According to him, the meaning of the word "Shabbos" is not only rest, but also study and investigation, as, for example, in the verse (*Yirmiyahu* 31:18), "After I contemplated (שׁוּבִי), I regretted," and (*Koheles* 9:11), "I contemplated (שַׁבְתִּי), and saw under the sun." Study is a way to go back and forth in the spiritual world. According to this, the word "Shabbos" implies a day devoted to study, "a Shabbos to Hashem" (*Sh'mos* 20:10).

Based on this, we can understand the words of *Chazal* in *Bereishis Rabbah*: "When Adam heard the power of *teshuvah*, repentance, he stood up and said, 'A psalm; a song for the day of Shabbos' " (*Tehillim* 92:1). This follows along with the idea that the word Shabbos (שַׁבָּת) means to return or repent (לָשׁוּב).

From this, we can deduce that the observance of Shabbos does not only consist of refraining from work, but also includes the requirement to improve and complete ourselves through Shabbos.

This will also explain a statement by *Chazal* in *Devarim Rabbah*, *Parashas VeZos HaBerachah*:

> Shabbos said to Hashem, "You have given a mate to each day of the week, but you have not given me a mate." Hashem said to it, "Knesses Yisrael (the Jewish people) will be your mate."

After Shabbos was set aside as a day of rest, it appeared that Shabbos indicated an absence of action. That was why Shabbos came with a complaint to Hashem. After all, each day involved creative work. Each day had the combination of man's power to work with the natural power of matter, through which the 39 categories of productive labor are formed. Shabbos, on the other hand, did not have a mate, and it appeared that its nature was one of nothingness, an absence of action. Hashem therefore told it that it too had a mate, that being Israel. Israel's spiritual creativity would be expressed on Shabbos, and that is a greater creativity than any on the other days of the week.

Eikev – עֵקֶב

I.

The Natural Treasures of Eretz Yisrael

he wealth of *Eretz Yisrael* is listed in three verses in this *parashah* (*Devarim* 8:7-9), in which the word *eretz* ("land") appears six times. In the first verse, it states, "a good *land*, a *land* of brooks of water, of fountains and depths that spring out of valleys and hills." The following verse goes on to say, "A *land* of wheat, and barley, and vines, and fig trees, and pomegranates; a *land* of olive oil, and (date) honey." Finally, we read, "A *land* in which you will eat bread without poverty, nothing shall be lacking in it, a *land* whose stones are iron, and from whose hills you will dig copper."

After all the above, the Torah uses the word *eretz* once more (ibid. v. 10), as a way to summarize everything, "You shall eat and be full, and you shall bless Hashem your God for the good *land* which He has given you."

Rabbenu Bachya states that the first six references to *eretz* refer to the six different climates in the world, all of which emerge and spread out from *Eretz Yisrael*, whereas the seventh reference to *eretz* refers to the climate of Yerushalayim, which is a combination of all the climates in the world, as in the verse (*Tehillim* 48:3), "Beautifully situated (נוֹף), the joy of the whole earth." According to Rabbenu Bachya, the word נוֹף refers to climate. Each climate is different from the others, depending on how far away the location is from the sun. A person who moves from one climate to another is harmed. Jerusalem, though, is composed of all climates, and that is why its climate is so marvelous. This is what we see in the verse, "You shall bless Hashem your God for the good land."

Abarbanel says that when the Torah lists those things for which *Eretz Yisrael* is praised, it mentions only the most vital and essential items. Thus, it does not mention apples and many other fruits, but rather stresses those things which are most suitable and worthwhile in man's diet, which are bread, wine, figs, dates, oil and honey. Galen, whom Abarbanel calls "the chief of the physicians," writes that a person must limit himself to these substances, which are the prime foods and which heal any disease. Other kinds of produce, on the other hand, cause putrefaction.

Abarbanel also explains that *Eretz Yisrael* is praiseworthy in that it does not require anything to be imported from outside the country: "nothing shall be lacking in it." Some countries have much grain, but are lacking money, and others have much money but little grain. The latter include — so says Abarbanel referring to his own time — such cities as Venice and Barcelona. The Torah tells us that *Eretz Yisrael* is lacking nothing. It has mines, and where there are mines there is everything.

Chasam Sofer sees in the fact that the Torah uses the word "land" twice in the second verse (*Devarim* 8:8), to divide up the different types of produce — "A *land* of wheat, and barley, and vines, and fig trees, and pomegranates; a *land* of olive oil, and (date) honey" — an allusion to the two times that *Eretz Yisrael* would be conquered: the first at the time of Yehoshua and the second when *Eretz Yisrael* will again be conquered in the Messianic Age. The conquest of the land in the Messianic Age is hinted at in the word "olive," as we see in the verse (*Zechariah* 14:4), "His feet will stand that day on the Mount of Olives," while the conquest of Yericho, the "city of the dates," by Yehoshua is hinted at in the word "honey." The reason why the Torah mentioned olives before honey (in effect, the second conquest before the first) is to stress the great importance of the Messianic conquest.

Gra, in his *Aderes Eliyahu*, regards the great detail of these verses as hinting at and stressing that in the holy *Eretz Yisrael* all four kinds of creation — mineral, plant, animal and man — are elevated in holiness by the land. "A land whose stones are iron" refers to the mineral. "You shall eat and be full, and you shall bless" is a reference to man. "A land in which you will eat bread without poverty" refers to the fact that you will eat bread with meat, and thus is a reference to the animal. Finally, "A land of wheat and barley" is a reference to plants. In the holy atmosphere of *Eretz Yisrael*, all are raised up higher and receive their necessary rectification (*tikun*).

The *rishonim* explain the verse, "a land of brooks of water, of fountains and depths that spring out of valleys and hills," to mean that those who live in the hills will not have to descend to the valleys to find water, while those who live in the valleys won't have to climb the hills for their water. Everyone will find his water in his own place.

Chizkuni holds that the blessing implied in this verse is that the individual will have to trust to Hashem's grace for his water. In *Eretz Yisrael* there are no rivers that water the fields. There are brooks and fountains which depend on rainfall, and the rainfall which supplies them is dependent on their listening to Hashem.

Ramban, though, sees a natural blessing in these brooks and fountains themselves. *Eretz Yisrael* is as a fruitful garden, which does not need rivers to water it, unlike Egypt. These brooks and fountains flow out of the valleys and mountains, and from them flow rivers. These fountains carry the moisture of the hills, either from the rainfall which the hills have absorbed, or from the mist. In addition, though, there are waters which come from the *tehom* — "the lower depths" — and these are known as *tehomos* — "depths."

Sifsei Kohen says that the Torah writes the words for "fountains" and "depths" as חָסֵר — lacking the letter *vav*. Thus the Torah writes the words as עֲיָנֹת וּתְהֹמֹת. This lack of the letter *vav* is an allusion to a single fountain and depth which supplied all the water of Yerushalayim, that being the Shilo'ach, and the Gichon which King Yechezkiyahu rechanneled (*II Divrei HaYamim* 32:30).

Chazal said that the whole *parashah* of the fruits is to be used to deduce the different *shiurim* — "minimal or maximal quantities" — that the *halachah* dictates. For example, wheat is used in relation to a measurement of time — the time needed to eat half a loaf of bread. Barley is used for a measure of ritual impurity (*tumah*), in that bone from a dead body, if it is the size of a barley grain, makes one *tamei*. The other items of produce mentioned in these verses are used for other *shiurim*.

Chasam Sofer, in his *Teshuvos, Orach Chaim* 181, notes that we are told that the fruits of *Eretz Yisrael* were tremendously large, as, for example, wheat grains the size of ox kidneys, and lentils the size of gold dinars. How then can one use such extraordinarily large crops as the basis for the various types of measurements? It is also not logical to assume that produce was specially brought into *Eretz Yisrael* from other countries to be used as a standard for measurement.

Chasam Sofer has an interesting answer. Just as the produce of *Eretz Yisrael* was different from the produce elsewhere in the world, so too were the people there different. They were larger and healthier than others. These people's measurement standards were based on their produce. Neither the people nor the produce were typical of the rest of the world.

➤§ A Land in Which You Will Eat Bread Without Poverty

The different commentators have numerous interpretations to stress the special value of *Eretz Yisrael* in supporting its rightful owners. *Kli Yakar* says:

> Our land is different from the land of Egypt, of which we are told (*Sh'mos* 1:11), "They built storage cities for Pharaoh, Pisom and Ra'amses," where they would store produce and wheat for bad years. (The word for "storage," מִסְכְּנוֹת, is almost identical with the word for "poverty," מִסְכֵּנוּת.) *Eretz Yisrael* doesn't need storage cities. It always has abundance, and there is no need to save from one year to another. Its crop is blessed every year, without a break.

Or HaChayim says that it is customary for the wealthy to feign poverty and spend little money and there are two reasons for this: a) They are afraid to appear to be too wealthy, because they fear that others may envy them or ask them for support. b) They are afraid that things may go badly, and their businesses may collapse. In *Eretz Yisrael*, though, there is no reason for these concerns. Society there was not divided into the rich and the poor. The land was divided up evenly. No person did better than another by trade or import, because this is a land in which "nothing shall be lacking" (*Devarim* 8:9). As an example of this, the Torah mentions two basic materials in manufacture and commerce, namely, iron and copper. In such a society of abundance, the rich man does not need to pretend he does not have any wealth. He is able to show his wealth, because all are the same.

Sifsei Kohen explains the verse as meaning that the bread of *Eretz Yisrael* is so tasty that there is no need to eat it with anything else.

Oznayim LaTorah goes further, and states:

It is known that doctors tell us to cut down on the eating of bread, as it is fattening, but that is not true of the bread of *Eretz Yisrael*. This bread has no ill effects on the body. One is able to eat it even without cutting down.

Sefas Emes adds that there is also a special spiritual dimension. Generally, when one consistently eats too much, he becomes engrossed in materialism, but that is not true for the bread of *Eretz Yisrael*. In eating this bread, there is no such cause for concern. One can eat without becoming engrossed in materialism.

Rabbenu Bachya interprets the verse as referring only to the spiritual dimension. The Torah is compared to bread, as we see in the verse, "Come, eat of my [the Torah's] bread" (*Mishlei* 9:5). The hearts of the people of *Eretz Yisrael* will be open as the gates to a large hall, and the gates of the Torah will be open before them, as *Chazal* tell us, "The gold of that land is good" (*Bereishis* 2:12) — there is no Torah like the Torah of *Eretz Yisrael*, and there is no wisdom like the wisdom of *Eretz Yisrael*. "A land in which you will eat bread without poverty" — you will not find any scarcity in the Torah of *Eretz Yisrael*. The very air of *Eretz Yisrael* makes one wise. "This is unlike the scholars outside *Eretz Yisrael*, who lack the preparations and the good air, and they certainly eat the bread of affliction, consuming their bread in poverty."

S'forno on this *parashah* gives five types of benefits and attributes of *Eretz Yisrael*, which do not exist in other countries. a) It is a land of brooks and fountains, and not of rivers and lakes. b) It is a land of wheat and barley, etc. — the place of the best food. c) It is a land of olive oil and (date) honey — all types of delicacies grow in it. d) "A land in which you will eat bread without poverty" — there will be no inflation or deflation. A scarcity of money is worse than a scarcity in food, as we see from *Chazal* in *Ta'anis*, "This only applies to a drought (i.e., scarcity) of crops, but in a case of a scarcity of money, one immediately sounds the alarm." In *Eretz Yisrael*, though, money was always available, and was not expensive. e) It is a land which contains iron — the stone is strong and is excellent for use as building material. The land contains everything: "nothing shall be lacking in it" — everything is available in abundance.

Or HaChayim HaKadosh has an interesting explanation of "nothing shall be lacking in it." There is no other country which is self-sufficient, for some countries which have abundant crops are missing other essentials. Thus, each country has to use whatever it has an overabundance of to pay to import those things it does not have. That means that these countries will simply break even, at best. Thus, when the Torah tells us that nothing is lacking in *Eretz Yisrael*, it means that whatever there is an abundance of will remain as profit, because there will be no need to spend the amount obtained from the surplus to import things not available in the country itself.

Melo HaOmer states that the greatest benefit of *Eretz Yisrael* consists of the fact that people in it will be content with what they have, and will find satisfaction in their work.

Maharam Shif used to explain the verse (*Mishlei* 30:8), "Give me neither poverty nor riches," to mean: Don't give me both of these together, that I should be wealthy and yet feel poor, not being satisfied with what I have. Shlomo asked Hashem in the same verse: "feed me with bread (i.e., food) fit for me," that I will be satisfied with my food, and will not be like those people who, when they have $100, wish to have $200. "Nothing shall be lacking in it" — the person will not feel there is something lacking in what he has. He will be happy and satisfied with what Hashem has given him.

Oznayim LaTorah explains the verse, "You shall eat and be full, and you shall bless," along the same lines. The word "full" refers to a person's being satisfied. In regard to Hashem, we are told that He (*Tehillim* 145:16) "satisfies the desire of every living thing." Hashem can sanctify man's desire, so that the person will feel satisfied with what he has. That was the blessing given to *Eretz Yisrael*, and even today those who are worthy are satisfied with whatever they have.

◄§ A Land Whose Stones Are Iron

Ramban explains the verse in its simple sense, namely that *Eretz Yisrael* is rich in mines. Wherever one digs for stone he will find iron. The Torah told Israel that in *Eretz Yisrael* they would find both iron and copper mines, because these two metals were vital for the inhabitants of the country. *Ramban* adds that "gold and silver resources are not a defect in a country."

Likutei Basar Likutei explains *Ramban* to mean that iron and copper are necessary for settling the country, unlike gold and silver, which are luxuries, and that is why the Torah does not mention the latter in the blessing of the land.

Targum Yerushalmi explains the verse, according to *Ramban's* interpretation of the *Targum*, to mean that the Torah praises *Eretz Yisrael* for having quarries of large granite rocks, from which they will be able to build houses, walls and guard towers, unlike the surrounding countries such as Egypt, which use clay bricks for construction, and which are, as a result, dangerous for their inhabitants.

Alshech has a beautiful explanation, which is in keeping with the reality of *Eretz Yisrael*. The Torah promises us that even where there are hard rocks and stony ground, a land "whose stones are iron," even there the Jews will be able to grow crops, "and you will eat and be satisfied and bless."

Chazal in the first chapter of *Ta'anis* learn from this verse the qualities of *talmidei chachamim* — "Torah scholars" — and they tell us, "do not refer to 'its stones' (אֲבָנֶיהָ) (are iron) but rather 'its builders' " (בּוֹנֶיהָ). *Talmidei chachamim* are very demanding, and their character is that of iron. Yehonasan Ben Uziel has a similar interpretation, when he renders the verse as, "This land, its scholars make decrees as hard as iron, and their disciples ask them questions as tough as copper."

Likutei Basar Likutei says that the simple meaning of the verse is that *talmidei chachamim* must be firm, must not show favoritism, and must be zealous for Hashem, without any egotistic intentions. *Chazal* hint at this when they state, "I never said anything and then turned back" — a *tzaddik* should not look behind him to see what people will say about his actions. The Torah promises us that that is the quality of the great *talmidei chachamim* of *Eretz Yisrael*.

Chasam Sofer has a beautiful *d'rush* interpretation of the verse. In *Ta'anis*, after *Chazal* say that a *talmid chacham* must be as firm as iron, Ravina said, "Even thus, a person must act gently, as it states (*Koheles* 11:10), 'Remove anger from your heart, and put away evil from your flesh.'" The question then arises, that if *Chazal* considered an iron character to be proper, why does Ravina say the opposite? The answer is to be found in *Chazal* in *Gittin* 6, where we are told:

> A person should not be too demanding in his home, because a
> certain great person was very demanding in his home, and who
> was that? R' Chanina ben Gamliel, and they gave him *eiver min
> ha'chai* (a limb torn from a live animal) to eat.

Rashi explains that a certain organ of an animal had gotten lost, and the servants were so in fear of their master that they cut the same organ from another animal. The *gemara* then asks, "Do you then think that they actually gave him to eat? [Even the animals of *tzaddikim* instinctively reject non-kosher food.] ... Rather, they tried to give him to eat." It is for this reason that Ravina opposes *talmidei chachamim* acting in too demanding a manner. In regard to *Eretz Yisrael*, though, the Torah promises us that even though its "builders" (*talmidei chachamim*) will be like iron and will be demanding, nevertheless, "you will eat and be full," and will not have to be afraid of being fed forbidden foods. Ravina lived outside *Eretz Yisrael*, and that was why he warned the *talmidei chachamim* against being too demanding.

⋙ You Will Eat and Be Full and Bless ... on the Land

According to *Ramban*, the simple meaning of the above verse (*Devarim* 8:10) is that you will eat and be full in your land, and will remember what it was like in Egypt just a short time ago; then you will bless and thank Hashem. In addition, *Ramban*, basing himself on *Chazal*, states that whenever one eats enough bread to be full, he must bless Hashem for the land, asking that Hashem should give us our inheritance and allow us to be satiated from its goodness. This obligation applies both to those in *Eretz Yisrael* and those outside it.

Zohar in *Parashas Terumah* asks that since *bircas hamazon* — "the grace after meals" — speaks about the blessing of the land, what does that have to do with those outside of *Eretz Yisrael? Zohar* explains at length that *Eretz Yisrael* is the center from which the entire world's sustenance is derived, and that is why, regardless of where a person is, he must thank Hashem for the good land, for it is through *Eretz Yisrael* that the rest of the world is sustained. It is interesting that *Mikra Meforash* by the *Gaon* of Kutna asks the same question and offers the same answer without mentioning the *Zohar*.

Baal HaTurim deduces from the fact that the words "you will eat and be full" are close to the phrase "lest you forget Hashem your God," that this is a hint that one must mention the day of death in *bircas hamazon*. This is the reason why *Chazal* ordained the fourth blessing of *bircas hamazon* in memory of those killed at Betar, in the major battle by the Jews against the Romans just after the fall of Jerusalem.

Meshech Chochmah has a beautiful explanation of the fact that *Chazal* instituted the fourth blessing of *bircas hamazon* — which speaks of Hashem as הַטּוֹב וְהַמֵּטִיב — "Who is good and does good" — in memory of those killed at Betar. *Bircas hamazon* was ordained as a blessing for the existence of the Jewish people under Hashem's *hashgachah pratis* — His direct intervention in our lives — as when Israel were in the desert, where their souls were refined and they learned Hashem's Torah, while eating the manna from heaven. The same *hashgachah pratis* was visible in *Eretz Yisrael*, where the *Beis HaMikdash* was situated, and Hashem's *Shechinah* dwelled. The blessing of הַטּוֹב וְהַמֵּטִיב was ordained because even when we are outside *Eretz Yisrael*, no one will be able to annihilate the Jewish people. Once the *Beis HaMikdash* was destroyed and Bar Kochba was killed, the Jews thought that the Jewish people had come to an end. After they saw that Hashem looked after them even in exile, in that He saw to it that the bodies of the people killed at Betar did not decay and that the surviving Jews were finally able to bury them, the Jews realized that Hashem is good and does good everywhere.

The reason why that blessing is recited over wine is so that we can increase our awareness of the miracle. Thus *Chazal* tell us on the verse (*Eichah* 1:3), "Yehudah has gone into exile out of poverty," that the rest of the nations of the world, who eat their own bread and drink their own wine, do not go into true exile, but Israel does go into true exile, not even drinking their own wine. In spite of this, they are saved by Hashem.

Finally, it is worth quoting what *Avnei Shoham* says on the blessing מֵעֵין שָׁלֹשׁ — "the blessing recited after cake, wine, and fruits for which *Eretz Yisrael* is praised in the Torah." In that blessing, it states, 'we will

bless You for it, in *kedushah* — "holiness" — and *taharah* — "purity."'
Avnei Shoham explains the concept of *taharah*. *Chazal* at the end of
Sotah tell us: "From the day that the *Beis HaMikdash* was destroyed,
the taste of fruit was taken away." The *gemara* there (p. 49) says: We
have learned: R' Shimon ben Elazar says, "*taharah* abolished taste and
smell." *Rashi* explains that when Israel lost its *taharah*, the taste and
fragrance of fruits were also lost, for when the Jews were pure and acted
in purity, Hashem also purified their fruits from any bad smells.
Afterwards, the *gemara* states, "Rav Huna found a juicy date. He said,
'My son (referring to the date), there is *taharah* in you.'" As *Rashi*
explains, that is why the date was so fragrant, and its fragrance had not
been taken away. From this, we see that the taste and fragrance of fruits
are derived from the *taharah* contained within the Jewish people. Thus,
in the blessing מֵעֵין שָׁלֹשׁ for fruit, there is a special stress on the words,
"we will bless You for it in *kedushah* and *taharah*," for when Israel
returns to its land and the *Beis HaMikdash* is rebuilt, flavor and
fragrance will return to the fruits once again, and the *taharah* and
kedushah of Israel will again be revealed.

II.
You Will Eat and Be Full and Bless

*C*hazal in *Berachos* 21a explain the verse "You will eat and be
full and bless"(*Devarim* 8:10) as a positive *mitzvah* of the
Torah, to bless Hashem after one's meal. R' Yehudah said,
"How do we know that *bircas hamazon* is ordained by the Torah? It is
deduced from 'You will eat and be full and bless.' " Thus the word, "you
will bless," is a special commandment, even though it is linked to the
preceding passage in the Torah.

Ramban brings examples of commandments in this form from "you
will make a fence for your roof"(ibid. 22:8), "you will take of all the first
fruits of the earth"(ibid. 26:2), and many similar positive *mitzvos*. The
link between this commandment and "the good land" refers to the
nature of the blessing. Whenever a person eats enough to be satisfied, he
must bless Hashem for the good land, although the *mitzvah* is not
dependent on being in *Eretz Yisrael*. *Chazal* in *Arachin* 4 said:

All are obligated in *zimun* (i.e., to recite *bircas hamazon* together if three or more ate together), even *kohanim*. Isn't that obvious? What this (statement) is needed for is where (the *kohanim*) eat *kodashim* — "sacred food," such as sacrifices. One might imagine that as this is eaten as an atonement (and not to become full, they should not have to recite *bircas hamazon*). The Torah therefore says, "You will eat," and this includes them as well.

Thus we see that the commandment to bless Hashem is only dependent on "you will eat."

From this, says *Torah Temimah*, we can conclude that the duty to recite *bircas hamazon* applies outside *Eretz Yisrael* as well, even though the Torah states, "for the good land." The major purpose of the blessing is to thank Hashem for eating and being satisfied, and thus there is no difference where one eats.

According to the *rishonim*, though, there is also another meaning of the verse. *Ramban*, Rabbenu Bachya, *S'forno* and others all mention this. The Torah tells us that when we remember the labor we performed in Egypt, and after we eat and are full in the land of our forefathers, we will automatically come to bless and thank Hashem for His mercies, and we will not forget this basic principle.

This interpretation is in no way in opposition to the interpretation of *Chazal*. Of course we must thank Hashem for His mercies, but as the Torah linked together "you will bless" to "you will eat and be full," there is also a duty to bless Hashem for the reason listed by the Torah in the previous verse, "a land where you will eat bread without poverty" — from which we deduce that whenever one eats bread made from grain, one must bless Hashem.

In any event, says Rabbenu Bachya, this is the only place in the Torah that, according to *Chazal*, we are told that one must recite a *berachah* (blessing) for something specific. That was why David said (*Tehillim* 145:1), "I will bless Your name," as well as (*Tehillim* 100:4), "Give thanks to Him, bless His name." The source for blessing Hashem is thus in our verse. In fact, the *berachos* before food are deduced by *Chazal* reasoning *a fortiori* (*kal vachomer*) from this present verse (*Devarim* 8:10).

In *Yerushalmi Berachos* 6:1, on the other hand, the *gemara* deduces the obligation to recite a *berachah* before eating from the blessing one must recite on the Torah, and in the case of the Torah there is a special deduction that this must precede the learning.

Chinuch explains why the Torah mentions only the *berachah* after eating, while in the case of learning Torah, it mentions only the *berachah* before learning. Food is linked to the animal part of man, and that feels satisfied only after eating. When it comes to learning Torah, on the other hand, which depends on man's mind and spirit, man's intellect knows the value of Torah study to his spirit. That was why the Torah obligated us to recite a *berachah* before learning Torah, as deduced in *Berachos* 21a from the verse (*Devarim* 32:3), "When I call on the name of Hashem, render greatness to our God."

⊰§ The Nature of the Berachah

Both *rishonim* and *acharonim* discuss the nature of the *berachos* in general. Does Hashem, Who owns the world and all in it, then need man to pronounce a *berachah*? Rabbenu Bachya says simply that the *berachos* are not needed by Hashem, but by man. When a person recites a *berachah* on something which he enjoys, he is testifying to Hashem's providence, *hashgachah*, in that Hashem by His good Will gives His creatures food so that they can live. Hashem wants man to recognize His good, and by doing so man is exalted over all His other creatures. In addition, says Rabbenu Bachya, the act of saying a *berachah* also serves another purpose, in that when a person recites a *berachah*, Hashem increases the abundance in the world. Thus *Chazal* tell us, "If someone enjoys anything of this world without a *berachah*, it is as if he is stealing from Hashem and from *Knesses Yisrael*, the Congregation of Israel." A person who eats without a *berachah* steals from Hashem, in that he denies Hashem's *hashgachah*, for the *berachah* is the acknowledgement of that *hashgachah*.

Yalkut Yitzchak, quoting *Oros HaMitzvah*, explains the connection between the *berachah* and the acknowledgement of Hashem's *hashgachah*. The Torah itself, in our *parashah*, gives the reason for *bircas hamazon*, when it tells us, "Lest you eat and be full ... and your heart will be haughty, and you will forget Hashem your God"(*Devarim* 8:12,14). The Torah understands how man's mind works, in that being full makes a person forget his Creator, Who gives food to everyone and makes all full. As man must plow, sow, reap, stack, thresh, winnow, clean, grind, sift, knead and bake until he finally has bread to eat, there is reason to fear that he may begin to believe that whatever he has, comes about through his own efforts. In order to remove such thoughts from man's mind, we were commanded to bless Hashem, and to proclaim, to all, our faith in Him, as we see with David, who proclaimed, "For all is from You, and what we have given You [came] from Your hand" (*I Divrei HaYamim* 29:14).

R' Samson Raphael Hirsch also explains the need for *berachos* as a means to elevate man's spirituality. After enjoying a meal, we have acquired the renewed power and strength to understand matters, and we must recognize that this power is a gift from Hashem, and that whatever power we have acquired must be used to serve Hashem.

Chinuch sees the content of the *berachah* as a tool for bringing upon us Hashem's goodness, as also mentioned earlier in the name of Rabbenu Bachya. An aspect of Hashem's great perfection is that He seeks the good for His creatures and wishes to bring upon them as many blessings as possible. When we remember that all good comes from Hashem, we are worthy of having Hashem bring more blessings upon us. We thank Hashem for everything which He has done for us, and hope that all people will appreciate that the source of all blessings is Hashem, and that they will all acknowledge Him. Through our blessing Hashem, His blessing will descend upon the world, and His desire to benefit the world will be carried out to completion.

The Dubno Maggid, following along these lines, explains the words of *Chazal* in *Berachos* 35:

> R' Chanina said: "If someone enjoys anything of this world without a *berachah*, it is as if he is stealing from Hashem and from *Knesses Yisrael* ... He is 'a comrade of a destructive man' (*Mishlei* 28:24) ..." What did he mean by "a comrade of a destructive man"? A comrade of Yerovam ben Nevat, who corrupted Israel before their Father in Heaven.

One can ask what the connection could be between Yerovam ben Nevat and a person who doesn't say a *berachah*. However, as we mentioned, the purpose of *berachos* is to bring about plenty in the world and to extend blessings to the world. We can therefore understand the law that if a person ate a number of different items and mixed up their *berachos*, he has not fulfilled his obligation. Each type of food has a special "pipe line," through which its blessing comes to the world. That is why it is so important to be sure to ascertain the correct *berachah* on each food and thereby to assure that the blessing of that food will come down to earth. One who eats without saying a *berachah* brings about a loss of that particular type of food, and thus diminishes the blessing and bounty to the public. It is in this that the person resembles Yerovam ben Nevat. Yerovam ben Nevat, we are told, not only sinned, but caused others to sin; in other words, not only did he sin, but caused others to lose by his actions, just as a person who eats without a *berachah*.

This idea of increased abundance as a result of man's actions below is not only found in the kabbalistic works. The kabbalists see added awareness of Hashem's holiness through Israel's *berachos*. This idea is brought in their name by Rabbenu Bachya, but the idea of added abundance as a result of the *berachah* is found in both *rishonim* and *acharonim*, and is considered to be a basic fundamental aspect of the *berachos*.

Meshech Chochmah gives as the reason why *berachos* are necessary the fact that when a person eats or drinks, he may rebel against Hashem, as in the verse (*Devarim* 32:15), "and Yeshurun became fat and rebelled." To prevent this phenomenon, we were commanded to mention Hashem and to recite a *berachah* when we eat or drink. This explanation is almost the same as those brought above, that the purpose of the *berachah* is to proclaim that it is not our efforts which have given us whatever we have, and that whatever we have is from Hashem. *Meshech Chochmah*, on the other hand, goes further and states that the very act of eating leads one to a kind of intoxication and to forgetting Hashem, and that is why there is a need to mention Him.

Meshech Chochmah uses this approach to explain the words of *Chazal* in *Arachin* 4, that we cited above, that one might imagine that the *kohanim* who eat sacrifices should be exempt from saying *bircas hamazon* as the primary purpose of their eating is atonement, which, in itself, is a religious matter, and one should not therefore need any other further religious reminder. The *gemara* then concludes that this is not so. Eating, regardless of what its purpose is, is enjoyable to one's body, and the person is thus liable to rebel and forget about Hashem.

⊸§ How Shall I Not Favor Israel?

Chazal regard the quantities over which one recites a *berachah* as a show of favoritism by the Jewish people toward Hashem, and therefore Hashem shows favoritism to them. *Chazal* tell us in *Berachos* 20:

> Hashem said to the angels, "How can I not show favoritism to Israel, for I wrote in the Torah, 'You will eat and be full, and bless,' and they are so scrupulous about themselves even to the extent of the size of an olive or of an egg."[That is, they recite *bircas hamazon* not only if they ate to satiety, but even after eating an amount of bread equivalent to an olive or an egg.]

At first glance, it seems strange to say that Israel are scrupulous over quantities the size of an olive or an egg. Aren't such measurements themselves dictated by the Torah, and isn't this what it refers to when it states, "you shall be full"(*Devarim* 8:10)? R' Eliyahu of Greiditz in *Hagahos HaShas* explains that we see in *Midrash Tanchuma*, *Parashas Naso*, that even a person who has bread only the size of an olive is not included among those of whom Yeshayahu said (*Yeshayahu* 8:21), "when they are hungry, they shall curse their king and their god, and look upward." Not only do Israel not complain if all they have to eat is the size of an olive, but they even bless Hashem after eating that amount, as if they became full from that bite, in terms of "Whatever Hashem does is for the good." That is the greatness of Israel, for which they are worthy of being shown favoritism.

Torah Temimah has a similar explanation. *Chazal* explain the verse in *Parashas Bechukosai*, "you will eat your bread and be full"(*Vayikra* 26:5), to mean that even though a person will eat little, he will be full, because the food will be blessed inside him. It follows that a person who recites *bircas hamazon* over food the size of an olive or an egg has faith in Hashem, trusting that the food will be blessed inside him.

Torah Temimah also explains the statement, "they are so scrupulous about themselves even to the extent of the size of an olive . . ." as to mean that the Jews are scrupulous only in regard to *themselves*, and not about others. Thus, in regard to *ma'aser ani* — "the tithe for the poor" — where the Torah says (*Devarim* 26:12), "they will eat in your gates and be full," one might imagine that all the poor must be given is the amount considered to be "full" in regard to *bircas hamazon*, namely, the size of an olive. In the case of the poor, though, a different measurement is used for the definition of "full," as stated in the Mishnah (*Pe'ah* 8), namely, not less than half a *kav* of wheat and half a *kav* of barley. [A *kav* is equivalent to twenty-four eggs or forty-eight olives.] Thus we see that Israel interpret the word "full" differently in regard to themselves than they do in regard to others. For themselves, "full" means a single olive, but for the poor, "full" means a whole *kav* (half a *kav* of wheat and half a *kav* of barley). It is this generosity which draws down a corresponding generosity from on high.

As to why the *gemara* says "to the extent of the size of an olive and of an egg," the reason that both are mentioned is that this is a dispute between R' Meir and R' Yehudah in *Berachos* 45 regarding the minimum amount of bread that requires *bircas hamazon*. Thus *Chazal* quote both views. *Maharatz Chajes*, though, asks whether this refers to a *chumra* — "an added stringency" — that Israel adopted for themselves; for requiring the reciting of *bircas hamazon* after eating bread the size of an olive is a greater *chumra* than requiring it after eating bread the size of an egg. If that is so, *Chazal* should have reversed the order and said "to the extent of the size of an egg and of an olive." *Maharatz Chajes* answers that *Chazal* are referring here to two separate *halachic* measurements. The measurement of the size of an olive refers to the *berachah* after drinking wine, where there is doubt whether the person should recite the *berachah* if he did not drink wine at least equivalent to the size of an olive. People therefore make sure to drink at least the size of an olive of wine, to be sure that they are obligated to recite the *berachah*. As to the size of an egg, that refers to *bircas hamazon*, for, as there is a view that one does not recite *bircas hamazon* on less than the size of an egg, people make sure to eat at least that quantity, to be sure that they are required to recite *bircas hamazon*.

◆§ The Contents of Bircas Hamazon

Chazal in *Berachos* 48 and in *Yerushalmi Berachos* 7:1 state:

R' Nachman said, "Moshe decreed for Israel the blessing of הַזָּן (the first blessing of *bircas hamazon*, "Blessed are You, Hashem, Who feeds the whole world . . .") when the manna came down to them. Yehoshua decreed the blessing of הָאָרֶץ ("the land" — the second blessing) when they entered the land. David and Shlomo decreed בּוֹנֵה יְרוּשָׁלַיִם ("Who builds Yerushalayim" — the third blessing) . . . The blessing of הַטּוֹב וְהַמֵּטִיב ("Who is good and does good" — the last blessing) was decreed for those killed at Betar."

Meshech Chochmah asks how it can be that *Chazal* would institute a blessing for all time to commemorate a single incident, the miraculous burial of Betar's slain, and why it is that the blessing on wine is said on the fourth blessing. He answers that *bircas hamazon* was decreed to reflect the building up of our nation as it is with *hashgachah pratis*, Divine Providence from Hashem, through manna and food, Tzion and Yerushalayim. The last blessing, of הַטּוֹב וְהַמֵּטִיב, was instituted to show that the nation exists under Divine Providence in exile as well, and that whoever tries to crush it will fail. This was after the destruction of the *Beis HaMikdash*, when people thought that everyone had been killed and everything destroyed. After people saw, though, that the dead bodies did not decay after seven years, and finally received proper burial, and that there is *hashgachah pratis*, they instituted the blessing of הַטּוֹב וְהַמֵּטִיב.

R' Kook expands on this idea. The thread running through the entire Torah is the relationship between the community and the individual, and how the individuals find contentment within the community. As eating brings man down to the base feelings of his individual senses and pleasures, Hashem prepared, in advance, a ladder which rests on the earth, but whose top reaches the heavens, so that we can ascend from the lowliness of the individual to the heights of the community.

The building of the community, though, must begin with individuals. First of all, there is need for the bodily survival of the individual. This is followed by the bodily survival of the community. After both of these, we must begin with the molding of the form of our nation as regards its own specific existence and character, and afterwards of its more general nature, in relationship to the different nations which were created in the image of Hashem. During our long exile, the main struggle had to be to maintain our own individual character as a nation, which will, in the course of time, extend its beliefs to all of mankind. But we are guaranteed that the individual form of our nation will be maintained, even when we are considered by all to be dead, for the spirit of Hashem will revive us. From that base, we will emerge from potential to realization at the end of days, to call upon the name of Hashem in the hearing of all mankind.

Moshe thus decreed the blessing of הַזָּן when the manna fell for the bodily existence of the individuals. It is true that the manna was miraculous, but the point is that the first aim must be the individual bodily existence of each person, without which there is no one with which to build the nation. Afterwards, we ascended from this, when we entered *Eretz Yisrael* and were able to establish the physical existence of the nation as a whole. It was for this that Yehoshua decreed the blessing of הָאָרֶץ. Later, David and Shlomo decreed the blessing on Yerusha-layim, when the time had come to mold the spiritual form of the nation as a whole. This blessing requests Hashem's mercy "upon Israel Your nation and on Yerushalayim Your city," namely, that Israel would be unified spiritually through Yerushalayim into a single nation. Shlomo decreed the reference to הַבַּיִת הַגָּדוֹל וְהַקָּדוֹשׁ — "the great and Holy house" — with its supreme spiritual mission, as he said when the *Beis HaMikdash* was founded, "So that all the nations of the world will know that Hashem is God and there is no other" (*I Melachim* 8:60).

That is the meaning of the Jewish table: that we should not become depressed by our exile, for Hashem is הַטּוֹב וְהַמֵּטִיב "He Who is good and does good," as in the case of Betar. The fact that the bodies of those who died at Betar were buried symbolizes for us that a seed of life was hidden away for the future, from which we would continue to live. The bodies did not decay, leaving a gap in the soul of the nation; rather, they will rise at the end of days to receive their reward.

III.

Only to Fear Hashem

iras shamayim, fear of heaven, is a positive *mitzvah*, such as loving Hashem (*ahavah*). *Chazal* in *Sotah* said that *yirah* is in the place of *ahavah*, and *ahavah* is in the place of *yirah*. Both *mitzvos* stem from a single source, and combine together, just as *Rambam* included both together in *Hilchos Yesodei HaTorah*, and even described the way to achieve them — through studying the greatness of Hashem and His wonders.

The works of *mussar* (Torah ethics and character building) examine the differences between these two concepts, which are listed as two separate *mitzvos* of the 613. In *halachic* terms, there are special *halachos* which are derived from each, but in *hashkafah* (philosophical) terms, the differences between the two are subtle and profound. (We have already quoted *Ramban's* words above, that the positive *mitzvos* of the Torah are derived from *ahavah*, while the negative *mitzvos* are derived from *yirah*.)

There is also a dispute as to which of the two comes first, especially when this refers to *yirah* of Hashem's majesty (*yiras harommemus*), which is a supreme attribute.

The Torah tells us that *yirah* is something easy to achieve, and states (*Devarim* 10:12), "And now, Israel, what does Hashem your God require of you, but to fear Hashem your God." *Chazal* in *Berachos* 33b and in other places express astonishment at this statement, and ask: "Is *yiras shamayim* then a minor matter?" They answer: "Indeed, for Moshe it is a minor matter." This statement by *Chazal* is discussed by both *rishonim* and *acharonim*, for Moshe always spoke to the Jewish people in terms that they would understand and absorb. If this was indeed a difficult matter for the people as a whole, why does the Torah present it in a way which was only appropriate for Moshe?

In truth, this astonishment is somewhat uncalled for. According to *Chazal's* explanation, Moshe served as an example to all of Israel, to show them that what they considered to be difficult was basically easy. *Yirah* consists of recognizing the yoke of Hashem's kingdom and feeling its existence, as in the verse (*Tehillim* 16:8), "I have set Hashem always before me." Moshe achieved this, not because of inspiration from

Hashem, for, as *Chazal* tell us, "everything is in the hands of *shamayim* — "heaven" — except for *yiras shamayim*." Moshe achieved this by his own free will, and this is something that any person can achieve. If people then think that this is a far-off goal, Moshe came to teach us, based on his own personal experience, that it is in man's power, if the person has enough faith.

What still needs explaining is why Moshe chose to tell us that a person can, through great *emunah*, achieve this attribute of *yirah*, rather than, for example, *ahavah*. The greatest commentators have discussed this question in giving their views of how one must serve Hashem.

Some commentators invert the words of the verses, so that, instead of reading them as (*Devarim* 10:12-13), "And now, Israel, what does Hashem your God require of you, but only (כִּי אִם) to fear Hashem your God ... for your good," they understand them to mean, "And now, Israel, what does Hashem your God require of you? To fear Hashem your God ... but only (כִּי אִם) for your good." By moving the words כִּי אִם to the end of the second verse, they understand the Torah to mean that the reason one must fear Hashem is so that it will be for the person's own good. What the Torah is telling us here is that Hashem does not need us to serve Him for His benefit, but for our benefit. Earlier the Torah mentions other incidents in which the nation's sins and transgressions are described. Afterwards, it continues by telling us that Hashem wants nothing from us; all He wants is to help us and to improve our ways through the Torah and *mitzvos*, through *yirah* and *ahavah*, and through clinging to the holiness (*kedushah*) of Judaism.

≥§ For the Perfect

Rambam in *Moreh Nevuchim* 2:39 explains the verse on *yirah* in the simple sense of the words. The Torah was given to people whose souls are perfect and whose hearts are noble, who have the ability to absorb and understand it easily. One cannot evaluate the Torah in accordance with the way it is regarded by wicked and violent people, who are harmed by the Torah's rules. Nor is the Torah to be measured according to people who lust for all kinds of forbidden things, and who, as a result of the Torah laws, must restrain their lusts. By the same token, the Torah cannot be measured according to people who have no *yirah* for Hashem, to whom the *mitzvos* are a burden. All of these classes of people see the Torah as making life difficult for them, not because the Torah itself is difficult, but because of their own *yetzer hara*, "evil inclination." For people who are pure and upright, on the other hand, the Torah is easy to observe, and such people find it easy to attain *yiras shamayim*. That is why the Torah said, "And now, Israel, what does Hashem your God require of you, but to fear Hashem your God."

In another place in *Moreh Nevuchim* (3:29), *Rambam* follows his well-known approach and explains that what the Torah meant to do was to teach the Jewish people to understand the aims and goals of Judaism, these being the moral and spiritual elevation of every person, that being the reason for all of the *mitzvos*. "What does Hashem your God require of you" is an explanation for all the *mitzvos* that the Torah commands us, which are meant to separate us from idolatrous practices and foreign beliefs.

Kuzari (2:47), too — according to *Otzar Nechmad's* explanation — says the same thing, and establishes this commandment as the fundamental basis for coming close to Hashem and as the root of Judaism, as opposed, for example, to the place that the sacrifices played in the people's comprehension.

Abarbanel and *Akeidah* have a different view. Both say the same thing, but the way they explain it and their thought processes make it appear as if they hold different views. According to them, when the Torah talks here of *yirah*, it refers to Hashem's continuous *hashgachah*, namely, that man knows that there is a superior force which controls him, and, as a result of this knowledge, the person refrains from doing evil. This *yirah* is not the fear of Hashem's grandeur, as Rabbenu Nissim explained it, because *yirah* of that kind is not a minor matter, and not even for Moshe. It is certainly not *yirah* (fear) of punishment, which is a defective type of *yirah*.

Rambam, on the other hand, in *Sefer HaMitzvos* does see the *mitzvah* of *yirah* as including the fear of punishment, and he states:

> He commanded us to believe in the fear of Him and to fear Him, and that we should not be as the heretics who go as their hearts carry them and by chance, but we must fear His punishment at all times.

According to Abarbanel, *yirah* means gratitude for what Hashem does for us, through which a person will not do anything to anger Hashem or to violate His *mitzvos*. In reality, *yirah* is *ahavah* — "love" — which is also based on gratitude to Hashem. *Ahavah*, though, means *deveikus* — "clinging to Hashem" — while *yirah* means refraining from sin, out of awareness of Hashem's *hashgachah* — "His personal supervision" of the world, and the abundance of His goodness.

Chazal tell us that one who serves Hashem out of *ahavah* is greater than one who serves Him out of *yirah*, but at the least, Hashem demands that we refrain from sinning, and if (*Tehillim* 111:10), "the fear of Hashem is the beginning of wisdom," then "all who do [His *mitzvos*] have a good understanding" (ibid.). This *yirah* is not fear of punishment, and that is why there is such a great reward for it and why *Tanach* and *Chazal* praised it so highly.

Akeidah follows a different path in dealing with the verse, but he too reaches the conclusion that *yirah* and awareness of *hashgachah*, Hashem's involvement in earthly events, are identical. What the Torah wishes to do is to remove from our hearts any false beliefs, as if the world is run by chance. According to the latter view, there is no reason to have *yirah* or fear, but one's sentiments should rather be despair and depression, for what purpose does fear have when one cannot do anything to change matters? Thus, the Torah teaches us to have *yirah* of Hashem and to fear His actions, and wherever there are both awe and fear, there is also contemplation, and there is the belief that man is able to be saved from evil by doing what is good in Hashem's eyes. Thus, the essence of *yirah* is recognizing Hashem's *hashgachah* and that one has free will. Elisha bar Avuyah (known in the *gemara* as *Acher*) heard a *bas-kol* — "a Divine voice" — which proclaimed, "Return O you wayward children, except for *Acher*." He believed that there was no longer a cure for his wrongdoing, but Judaism proclaims (*Tehillim* 130:3-4), "If You, God, guard the memory of sins, Hashem, who shall stand? Rather, forgiveness is Yours, so that You will be feared." *Yirah* spurs one on to do *teshuvah*, and changes one's expected fate by one's own actions. This is the concept which the Torah wishes to instill in man when it commands *yirah*.

It is worth mentioning another view regarding *yirah*, which affects the understanding of our *parashah*, and moves us from the theoretical to the practical. R' Yosef Albo, in *Ikarim* 3:31, says that if the *mitzvah* of *yirah* is one of the 613 *mitzvos*, it is a general one, which stems from the observance of the other *mitzvos*. Avraham achieved *yirah* after he observed all the *mitzvos*, as it states (*Bereishis* 22:12), "Now I know that you fear Hashem." One must keep the *mitzvos*, and by doing so one achieves *yirah*. *Yirah* is an elevated stage to attain. Hashem tells Israel:

> I should indeed have asked of you (*Devarim* 10:12) "to fear Hashem your God, to walk in all His ways, to love Him, and to serve Hashem your God with all your heart and soul." However, as I know that you are weak by nature, I ask you only — כִּי אִם — "to observe the *mitzvos* of Hashem and His statutes that I am commanding you this day, that it should be good with you."

In other words, by observing the *mitzvos*, we will eventually be able to attain the highest levels of *yirah* and *ahavah*, and total good for our souls. *Yirah* and *ahavah* are thus arrived at through observing the *mitzvos*, and are also comprehensive *mitzvos* which include all the others.

⇜§ For Moshe It Is a Minor Matter

The *acharonim* devote a great deal of effort to discussing the above words of *Chazal* on our verse. The Dubno Maggid says, quoting *Gra*, that a vessel which is filled with *yirah* overflows its rim and pours *yirah* on everything about it. Thus, *Chazal* said, on the verse, 'You shall fear Hashem your God' (*Devarim* 6:13, 10:20), "This includes *talmidei chachamim* (Torah scholars)," because the abundant *yirah* of *talmidei chachamim* affects the entire environment about them, and saturates it with *yiras shamayim*. Thus, when *Chazal* tell us that "for Moshe it was a minor matter," that was because Moshe's generation, which lived near him and saw his *yirah*, was affected by his *yirah*, and did not need to work hard to attain *yirah* on its own. For Moshe's generation, it was indeed a minor matter.

Kli Yakar has a similar explanation. *Maharal*, though, in *Nesivos Olam* 1, relates the word "minor" to *yirah* itself. If a person does not have *yiras shamayim*, that represents a flaw in his character, but *yirah* is not an added attribute for the person that has it. It is not a separate attribute of man, but an integral part of him, where a person must fear the Master of all, and must realize how insignificant he himself is. That was why Moshe, for whom *yirah* was an integral character trait, was able to say, "what does Hashem your God require of you, but to fear Hashem your God?" (ibid. 10:12). For the person who has *yirah*, it is all very natural, but for people that lack that character trait, that deficiency is stupendous. Thus the word "minor" in regard to *yirah* by Moshe, and the question "Is *yiras shamayim* then a minor matter?" are two sides of the same coin. A person who has *yirah* has not accomplished anything beyond his natural being, while one who is missing it is missing everything.

Netziv, in *Ha'amek Davar*, has an interesting and penetrating interpretation. This interpretation explains the four levels which the Torah specifies, which are difficult to attribute to one and the same man. According to *Netziv*, the Torah refers to four strata of society, each of which requires different attention. a) Those who are involved in taking care of the public's needs. b) Those who study Torah. c) The majority of people, who devote their time to earning a living. d) Women, slaves and children. Those in the first category are exempt from any obligation of *deveikus* — "clinging to Hashem" — for, as *Chazal* tell us, "Hachnasas orchim — "taking in guests" — is greater than receiving the *Shechinah* — "Divine Presence." The people in this category are nevertheless required to have *yiras shamayim*, so that whatever they do will be done honestly, without flattery or favoritism. To them, the Torah says, "What does Hashem your God require of you, but to fear Hashem your God?"

The Torah scholars are required to have both *deveikus* and *ahavah* — "love" — and the Torah says to them, "to walk in all His ways and to love Him, and to serve Hashem your God with all your heart and all your soul (ibid.)."

Those people who spend their lives earning their living are commanded to observe the *mitzvos*, and to them the Torah says, "to observe Hashem's *mitzvos*" (ibid. v.13).

As to women, slaves and children, they are exempt from many of the *mitzvos* that men are required to observe, but are required to observe the laws of society and proper behavior, and to instill Torah in their children and to obey their husbands or owners or parents. To them the Torah says, "that I command you this day, that it should be good with you" (ibid. v.13) — namely, the good of society.

As *Netziv* explains it, the *gemara* is astonished, and asks in regard to the *mitzvah* of those involved in serving the public: Is *yirah* then a minor matter? On this, the *gemara* answers: As far as Moshe, who was both a leader and a *talmid chacham*, was concerned, *yirah* was a minor matter, because leaders such as Moshe are commanded regarding both *ahavah* and *deveikus*, and it is no great matter for them if they also conduct the community matters honestly.

◆§ The World Is Filled with Yirah

The great Chassidic rabbis explain the verse, "And now, Israel, what does Hashem your God require of you, but to have *yirah* of Hashem your God," as good advice to a person in order to free himself from the fear that envelops the world, by linking himself to the original Divine *yirah*.

The world is full of fear, says *Toldos* in the name of the Baal Shem Tov. Mice are afraid of cats, cats fear dogs, dogs fear man, and so on. Fear is an integral part of Creation, and the purpose of fear is so that man should attain, through it, *yirah* of Hashem, and should accept the yoke of the *mitzvos*. This *yirah* appears in different garbs in Creation, but the person who is able to see what lies behind these garbs finds the original point of *yirah*, the one which frees man of all other fears — which are only garbs of *yiras shamayim*.

Chazal said, "Be עָרוּם — "cunning (or naked)" — in *yirah*"; namely, that one should strip the *yirah* of its garbs and should recognize the underlying, original *yirah*. This is what the Torah means when it tells us, "And now, Israel, what does Hashem your God require of you, but to fear Hashem your God." Every person has the duty to free himself of all other fears, and to fear only the great majesty of Hashem. By realizing this, a person frees himself of all the nightmares of fear and comes to recognize the underlying purpose of *yirah*. Moshe achieved this outstanding quality so that it became a "minor matter" to him. He reached the peak of understanding and recognized the essence of *yirah*, which includes within it all the fears of the world.

On the verse (*Devarim* 20:8), "Every man that is fearful and faint hearted, let him go and return unto his house," *Chazal* tell us that this refers to those men that are fearful of the sins which they have committed. *Toldos*, in another place, explains that the very fact that the person is afraid is an indication that he is full of sin, and has not been worthy of attaining true *yirah*, for that annuls all fears.

There is a verse (*Koheles* 3:14), "Hashem did it, so that people should fear Him." On this, *Chazal* tell us in *Berachos* 59: "Thunder was created so as to straighten out the crookedness of the heart." R' Nachum of Chernobyl, quoting his holy rebbi, explains this. The aim of fear in this world is to achieve *yiras shamayim*, as in the above verse. Thus, thunder and other such things which produce fear and alarm were created for the aim of "straightening out the crookedness of the heart."

Fear exists in the world. Through it, man can purify and elevate himself, and find the purpose of Creation. The Chassidic works devote considerable space to explaining the efficacy of fear in achieving knowledge of Hashem. *Keser Shem Tov* says this is analogous to a minister who sits before his king and who has none of the fears that other people have, because his only fear is of his king.

Chazal said a *tzaddik*, when compared to Hashem, is like a candle compared to a torch. A person's human emotions are annulled when he attains an exalted spiritual feeling, just as a candle is of no significance in bright daylight. That is why we are told (*Tehillim* 111:10), "The fear of Hashem is the beginning of wisdom." If one has *yirah*, he has everything else as well, for then the person and his feelings all cling to their root, and there is no other fear present.

In itself, *yirah* is easy, because it is part of man's makeup, but recognizing it is very difficult, because man must attain it through his own efforts, without help from Heaven. Thus, *Chazal* tell us, "all is in the hands of Heaven except fear of Heaven." This quality, says *Toldos*, is the only one of all the qualities that Hashem does not "clothe Himself" in. *Yirah* of Hashem lies outside Hashem, and that is why this quality is so precious and great.

Re'eh – ראה

I.

You Will Dispossess Them and Dwell in Their Land

Hundreds of books and thousands of articles have been written about the *mitzvah* of *Yishuv Eretz Yisrael* — "living in *Eretz Yisrael*" — and there is no attempt here to contribute anything new. Instead, this is an attempt to set down that which was said and written, so that we can understand clearly the *mitzvah* and its content, even though this is also discussed in *Parashas Mas'ei*.

In *Sifri*, on *Devarim* 12:29 below, we are given the basis for the *mitzvah* of *Yishuv Eretz Yisrael* as one of the *mitzvos* of the Torah. *Sifri* states there:

> Once R' Yehudah ben Beseira and R' Masia ben Charash and R' Chanina the nephew of R' Yehoshua and R' Yehonasan were leaving *Eretz Yisrael*. When they arrived at Paltum, they remembered *Eretz Yisrael*. They cast their eyes upwards, shed tears, tore their clothes, and recited the verse, "You will dwell in their land." They then returned to their own homes. They said, "Living in *Eretz Yisrael* is equivalent to all the *mitzvos* in the Torah."
>
> Once R' Eliezer ben Shamua and R' Yochanan HaSandlar were going to Netzivin to learn Torah with R' Yehudah ben Beseira, and they arrived at Sidon. They remembered *Eretz Yisrael*. They cast their eyes upwards, shed tears, tore their clothes, and recited the verse, "You will dispossess them and dwell in their land." They then returned to their own homes. They said, "Living in *Eretz Yisrael* is equivalent to all the *mitzvos* in the Torah."

These words, that the *mitzvah* of living in *Eretz Yisrael* is equivalent to all the *mitzvos* in the Torah, are the basis for *Ramban's* and *Charedim's* listing of the conquest of *Eretz Yisrael* as one of the 613 *mitzvos* of the Torah. *Ramban in Parashas Mas'ei*, on the verse (*Bamidbar* 33:53), "You shall possess the land, and dwell therein; for I have given you the land to possess," says that it is a positive *mitzvah* to live in *Eretz Yisrael* and take possession of it, and this *mitzvah* applies in all generations and circumstances. All the statements by *Chazal* on the importance of *Yishuv Eretz Yisrael* and all the laws based on this *mitzvah*, such as the law that one can force one's spouse to move to *Eretz Yisrael*, etc., are derived from the *mitzvah* of *Yishuv Eretz Yisrael*. *Ramban* thus states that the *mitzvah* to take possession of *Eretz Yisrael* is one of the 613 *mitzvos*. (Also see what we wrote above in *Parashas Mas'ei*.)

Ramban has two proofs that this is an obligatory *mitzvah*: a) Regarding the spies' refusal to go up to *Eretz Yisrael*, we read, "You rebelled against the word of Hashem"(*Devarim* 1:26, 9:23) and "you would not listen" (ibid. 9:23). b) *Chazal* referred to the war to conquer *Eretz Yisrael* as a *milchemes mitzvah* — a "mitzvah war." *Ramban* proves that this *mitzvah* applies to all generations, for this is the *mitzvah* which *Chazal* referred to as the *mitzvah* of *Yishuv Eretz Yisrael*.

Charedim, too, in the section on the positive *mitzvos* dependent on *Eretz Yisrael*, Mitzvah 15, gives this as a positive *mitzvah*, and quotes what *Chazal* said about it: that it is equivalent to all the *mitzvos* in the Torah.

Ran, too, at the end of *Kesubos*, quotes *Ra'avad* that women, too, are obligated in the *mitzvah* of *Yishuv Eretz Yisrael*, and even non-Jewish slaves (who have the same obligations in *mitzvos* as women) can force their masters to move to *Eretz Yisrael*. The same law about forcing a person to move to *Eretz Yisrael* is quoted by the other *poskim*.

In this, we find a basic dispute as to whether the *mitzvah* is to live in *Eretz Yisrael* or whether it is to move to *Eretz Yisrael*. *Rivash*, in his *Teshuvos* 101, rules that when *Chazal* permitted one to acquire property in *Eretz Yisrael* on Shabbos through telling a non-Jew to do the work of writing the deed (normally one may not tell a non-Jew to perform work for oneself on Shabbos), this is permitted only for the *mitzvah* of living in *Eretz Yisrael*, but not in order to permit one to move to *Eretz Yisrael*, because the move is only a preparation for the *mitzvah*.

Tashbatz 1:21, on the other hand, holds that the move is also a *mitzvah* and not only a preparation for a *mitzvah*. Many *rishonim* and *acharonim* discuss the difference between the two views. We have brought only a summary of their views, whose source is *Ramban*, and which are ultimately based on *Sifri* quoted above.

◦§ The Opposing View

The source for the opposing view is *Tosafos* at the end of *Kesubos*, referring to the question of a man who wants to move to *Eretz Yisrael* but whose wife refuses to do so. *Tosafos* there brings the view of R' Chaim:

> Today it is not a *mitzvah* to live in *Eretz Yisrael*, because there are a number of positive and negative *mitzvos* that are dependent on the land, and we are unable to be meticulous and to observe them.

Based on this *Tosafos*, *Megillas Esther* answers the question of *Ramban* as to why *Rambam* does not list *Yishuv Eretz Yisrael* in the 613 *mitzvos*. According to *Megillas Esther*, not only is there no *mitzvah* to conquer *Eretz Yisrael* in our time, but, in fact, at the end of *Kesubos* (p. 111), *Chazal* said that one of the three oaths that Hashem made Israel take when they went into exile was שֶׁלֹּא נַעֲלֶה בַּחוֹמָה — "not to storm the fortress" (by making *aliyah* to *Eretz Yisrael en masse*). Thus, according to him, the *mitzvah* of conquering *Eretz Yisrael* and living in it applies only when we have the upper hand, i.e., after the redemption from exile. Not only that, but *Chazal* also said in *Kesubos*, basing themselves on *Yirmiyahu*, "Whoever moves from Babylon to *Eretz Yisrael* violates a positive *mitzvah*." If, then, the *mitzvah* of living in *Eretz Yisrael* applied to all generations, how could Yirmiyahu come and annul the words of Moshe? *Megillas Esther* also rejects the proof brought from *Sifri*, and says the *Tannaim* quoted in *Sifri* cried because this *mitzvah* does not apply to our times, for if it was in effect, why would they cry? All they would have to do is keep the *mitzvah*.

The words of *Megillas Esther*, based as they are on R' Chaim in *Tosafos*, find almost no echo among either the *rishonim* or *acharonim*, who do not question the opinion of *Ramban*, even though many of them set certain conditions and limitations to this *mitzvah*.

Maharit, in *Yoreh De'ah* 28, rejects the view of R' Chaim in *Tosafos*, and writes that a student must have made an error in writing the view down. This view of the statement by R' Chaim in *Tosafos* was shared by almost all *rishonim*, until the idea of returning to Zion was reawakened at the end of the last century, and a dispute broke out anew. There were many who opposed the idea, who attempted to prove that the *mitzvah* of *Yishuv Eretz Yisrael* does not apply in our times. The holy *geonim*, the Munkatcher and Satmar Rebbes, followed this view. The Satmar Rebbe even put out a book, great in both size and quality, entitled *VaYoel Moshe* to prove that this *mitzvah* does not apply today.

In this work, he collected the views of those who state so directly or by implication.

Those who reject the idea of *Yishuv Eretz Yisrael* applying in our time based themselves on the *gemara* about the "three oaths" of Hashem when the Jews went into exile. On this, there are innumerable debates, for after all the United Nations did authorize the partition of *Eretz Yisrael*, and one is thus not forced to say the Jewish state represents a "revolt" against the other nations. On the other hand, doubts can arise in those areas which were not allocated to the Jewish state, but which Israel conquered in the War of Independence and thereafter. According to some, this territory was captured under the *mitzvah* of conquering the land, whereas according to others it is a revolt against the nations of the world.

Again, there are those who hold that the "three oaths" were annulled by the other nations of the world, for one of the three was "that they should not enslave Israel beyond measure," and that oath has certainly been disregarded. These people feel that since the nations disregarded their oath, Israel's oath also no longer applies, and there is therefore no prohibition against "revolting against the nations."

As opposed to this, those who reject the conquest of territories hold that the oaths are independent of one another. R' Shmuel Zvi Herman, of the United States, proves that if the oath of one side was annulled, that of the other is also annulled. On the verse (*Shoftim* 13:5), "he will begin (יָחֵל) to deliver Israel," *Chazal* tell us in *Sotah* 9, R' Chama bar R' Chanina said, "the oath of Avimelech had been annulled" (הוּחָל). On this, *Rashi* comments, "because they had violated the oath first." Thus we see that the oath of one side is dependent upon the oath of the other.

R' Yisrael Zalushinski, though, has commented that the two cases cannot be compared. In the case of Avimelech, there was an oath between the two sides who came to an agreement between them, whereas with the "three oaths," the oaths were imposed on both sides from above by Hashem.

There are also numerous disputes about the "three oaths," especially as they are not mentioned in either *Rambam* or the other *poskim* (except for *Megillas Esther*, as noted), and they are never mentioned as *halachah* in any source.

On this, too, R' Shmuel Zvi Herman has an interesting comment. In *Kesubos* 110, there are two statements by R' Elazar: R' Elazar says (on the verse — *Shir HaShirim* 2:7), "by the roes, and by the hinds of the field," that Hashem said to Israel, "If you observe this oath, it will be well, and if not, I will make your flesh free for all as that of the roes." This statement of R' Elazar is not mentioned anywhere in *Rambam*. On the other hand, the second statement of R' Elazar (on *Kesubos* 112) is mentioned. In it, we are told: When R' Elazar came to *Eretz Yisrael*, he said, "I have escaped one penalty . . . (that of — *Yechezkel* 13:9), 'they shall not enter into the land of Israel.'" This is brought in *Rambam, Hilchos Melachim* 5:12. *Rambam* also brings the words of R' Elazar that "whoever lives in *Eretz Yisrael* remains without sin." It is interesting that *Rambam* brings those quotations of R' Elazar that are in favor of moving to *Eretz Yisrael*, while leaving out his words on the "three oaths."

Avnei Nezer, at the end of *Yoreh De'ah*, has a number of *teshuvos* regarding living in *Eretz Yisrael*. He holds that *Ramban's* view is the *halachah*, and one cannot diverge from it. As to the statement by *Megillas Esther*, that the *tannaim* wept only because they were unable to fulfill the *mitzvah* of *Yishuv Eretz Yisrael*, *Avnei Nezer* states that this is proof that *Megillas Esther* never saw *Sifri* in the original, for there it states clearly, "they returned to their homes."

Avnei Nezer states further that *Megillas Esther* must also have not noticed *Rambam's* words in *Hilchos Avadim*, that even in our days, if a slave fled to *Eretz Yisrael*, his master can be forced to move to *Eretz Yisrael*. As to why *Rambam* did not mention *Yishuv Eretz Yisrael* in his listing of the *mitzvos*, the reason is the same as the reason why *Rambam* did not mention the making of the ark (*aron*) and the *kapores* — "the lid of the *aron*" — in the 613 *mitzvos*. The reason for the latter was that the purpose of the *Beis HaMikdash* was to have a place to put the *aron*, and *Rambam* had already listed the building of the *Beis HaMikdash* in the *mitzvos*. By the same logic, one can say that *Rambam* had already mentioned the *mitzvah* of destroying the nations living in the land (*Devarim* 20:17), the purpose of which was to clear the land for the Jewish people, and that was why there was no need for a special mention of a *mitzvah* of living in *Eretz Yisrael*. *Ramban*, on the other hand, who listed the making of the *aron* and the *kapores* among his 613 *mitzvos*, also listed the *mitzvah* of *Yishuv Eretz Yisrael*.

Avnei Nezer's view, though, that *Rambam* includes the *mitzvah* of living in *Eretz Yisrael* in that of the *mitzvah* to destroy the Seven Nations at the time of Yehoshua, is rejected by *Ramban* in *Sefer HaMitzvos*, where the latter writes:

> Do not err by thinking that this *mitzvah* (of living in *Eretz Yisrael*) is (included in) that of the war against the Seven Nations, in which we were commanded to utterly destroy them, as it is written, "You shall surely destroy them (ibid.)." This is not so, for we were commanded to kill those nations when they fought

against us. If, though, they wished to make peace, we would leave them alive under the well-known conditions. But we would not leave the land in their hands nor in the hands of anyone else in any of the generations.

There are some who say, and they, of course, are among those who say that there is a *mitzvah* to live in *Eretz Yisrael* nowadays, that *Rambam* did not list this *mitzvah* among the 613 as it is the *basis* for the *mitzvos*, and in his *Sefer HaMitzvos*, Principle Four, Rambam wrote that it is not proper to list the *mitzvos* that *include* the entire Torah, as, for example, the *mitzvah* of "you shall be holy" (*Vayikra* 19:2) — as this is the basis of all *mitzvos*.

There are many interpretations and explanations of this whole topic, and we have just touched the tip of the iceberg.

As mentioned, the holy *gaon*, the Satmar Rav, *zatzal*, devoted a book, great in size and quality, to the clarification of this subject and his opinion of it.

✑§ Rambam's View

Those who hold that *Rambam's* view is different from that of *Ramban*, as the former does not mention *Yishuv Eretz Yisrael* among the 613 *mitzvos*, are contradicted in innumerable places. For example, *Rambam* rules in *Hilchos Avadim* 8:9 that if a slave wishes to move to *Eretz Yisrael*, his master is forced to move with him, or else must sell the slave to someone who will move to *Eretz Yisrael* with him. (This law would apply only if there is a *mitzvah* to live in *Eretz Yisrael*, for then the slave can insist on his right to live in *Eretz Yisrael* and observe the *mitzvah*. Had there not been such a *mitzvah*, the slave would not have been able to force his master to move to *Eretz Yisrael* — trans.)

By the same token, *Rambam* ruled that if a master and slave are living in *Eretz Yisrael* and the master wishes to leave the country, he cannot take the slave out with him, unless he consents voluntarily to leave with his master. This law, writes *Rambam*, applies at all times, even when *Eretz Yisrael* is ruled by non-Jews. Similarly, in that same chapter, *halachah* 10, *Rambam* writes that if the slave fled from his master to *Eretz Yisrael*, the *beis din* frees him. In the *gemara*, *Kesubos* 110, the reason given for this is because of the *mitzvah* of *Yishuv Eretz Yisrael*.

Rambam in *Hilchos Melachim* 12 brings many *halachos* regarding the obligation to live in *Eretz Yisrael*, and even in a city where everyone else is not Jewish. In *Hilchos Akum* 9, *Rambam* rules that one may go to non-Jewish fairs to buy from them houses, fields, vineyards, cattle, and slaves, and one even uses their court system where needed (something Jews are normally forbidden to do) because it is considered as if he is saving these things from their hands. *Rashi* in *Arachin* 47 says that all of these are because of *Yishuv Eretz Yisrael*. (My brother-in-law, R' Yitzchak Levi, noted that *Kesef Mishneh* brings another reason for this, while *Rashi* also brings a second reason.)

Rambam also rules in *Hilchos Shabbos* 6:11 that one is permitted to tell a non-Jew on Shabbos to write a property deed that day, for, while telling a non-Jew to do work on Shabbos is normally forbidden *m'd'rabbanan* — "by rabbinic law" — *Chazal* did not make that decree where *Yishuv Eretz Yisrael* is involved. Similarly, there are countless other places where *Rambam* gives *Yishuv Eretz Yisrael* as the reason for various *halachos*.

There are those, though, who claim that nowhere in *Shulchan Aruch* are there *halachos* because of *Yishuv Eretz Yisrael*. It would seem that they have evidently overlooked *Yoreh De'ah* 267:4- 5, where *Shulchan Aruch* also brings the laws regarding the slave we mentioned above in regard to *Rambam*. By the same token, we find in *Even HaEzer* 75:3-4 that a spouse can force the other spouse to move to *Eretz Yisrael*. Again, in *Choshen Mishpat* 409:1, *Shulchan Aruch* rules that one may not raise the small species of farm animals (goats, sheep, etc.) in *Eretz Yisrael*, because they normally graze in other people's fields. (In *Bava Kama* 79, *Rashi* says this is because of *Yishuv Eretz Yisrael*.) It is true that *Shulchan Aruch* adds: "Nowadays, that Jews do not have fields in *Eretz Yisrael*, the laws revert to what they were," but the implication of this is that if a time will come when the Jews will again have fields in *Eretz Yisrael*, the laws will come into effect once again.

The most specific reference by *Shulchan Aruch* to this whole topic is in *Orach Chaim*, *Hilchos Shabbos* 248:4, that since going to *Eretz Yisrael* is a *mitzvah*, if a caravan comes through one's city on its way to *Eretz Yisrael*, the person is permitted to make up to accompany the caravan, provided that they rest each Shabbos, and one may set out with them even on Friday. Then, if they are in the desert and they refuse to rest, the person may accompany them even on Shabbos, because it is *piku'ach nefesh*. *Magen Avraham* there brings two views: a) that this is referring to a person who joins the caravan because he wishes to settle in *Eretz Yisrael*; b) that this is even referring to a person who is just traveling there for a visit, because walking four cubits in *Eretz Yisrael* is a *mitzvah*.

On the verse, "You will possess the land and dwell in it" (*Bamidbar* 33:53), *Rashi* and *Or HaChayim* both explain the words as a promise that if Israel drives these people out of the land, it will be able to dwell in the land in tranquility. There are some who see the fact that *Rashi* makes no mention here of the *mitzvah* of *Yishuv Eretz Yisrael* as a proof that he does not hold it to apply in our time. This is incorrect, for there are numerous other places in the *gemara* where *Rashi* gives as the reason for various laws, "*Yishuv Eretz Yisrael.*" Similarly, at the beginning of *Parashas Ki Savo*, *Or HaChayim* states:

> Living in the land is a *mitzvah* in its own right, as we find that *Chazal* greatly emphasized the *mitzvah* of *Yishuv Eretz Yisrael*.

Similarly, *Or HaChayim HaKadosh* concludes his commentary on *Parashas Nitzavim* by saying:

> Living in the land is a *mitzvah* that encompasses the entire Torah. One can see this from the fact that *Chazal* said that whoever walks four cubits in it has a portion in the World to Come, which is eternal life.

Thus we see that *Or HaChayim* holds that the *mitzvah* of *Yishuv Eretz Yisrael* applies to our times as well.

One can thus conclude that, according to most *poskim*, *Yishuv Eretz Yisrael* is a comprehensive *mitzvah*, and one should then investigate whether *piku'ach nefesh*, danger to life, is a valid reason for not observing it. The question of whether *piku'ach nefesh* takes precedence is found in regard to another *mitzvah*. *Chinuch*, *Mitzvah* 425, regarding the *mitzvah* of destroying the Seven Nations, notes that this *mitzvah* applies, provided one can perform it "without endangering oneself in the process." On this, *Minchas Chinuch* comments:

> This requires further study, for while it is true that all (other) *mitzvos* are deferred in the face of danger to life, nevertheless in this *mitzvah* — as the Torah does not rely on miracles, as explained in *Ramban* — it is normal that in war both sides suffer casualties. Yet we see the Torah decreed that we fight them, even though there is danger. That being so, in this case the *mitzvah* supersedes the danger.

The same applies in regard to the *mitzvah* of conquering *Eretz Yisrael*, and the question needs further clarification.

Chazon Ish, in his letter, 1:175, writes: "The *mitzvah* of *Yishuv Eretz Yisrael* was accepted by *Rambam*, *Ramban* and the other *poskim*, and it is well known how much the *Chafetz Chaim* wished to move to *Eretz Yisrael*."

The previous Gerer Rebbe, too, writes (as printed in his collected letters): "It is indeed my view that the *mitzvah* of *Yishuv Eretz Yisrael*, that we were commanded in our holy Torah, is not dependent on any time, but only on one's ability and the possibilities."

II.
If You Say: "I Will Eat Meat"

arious Torah commentators, including *Ramban* and others, explain the above verse (*Devarim* 12:20) according to the view of R' Yishmael in *Chullin* 16, that the Torah here permits the eating of *besar taavah* — "regular meat" (as opposed to meat of the sacrifices, which was the only meat permitted to the Jews in the desert). R' Akiva, on the other hand, holds that even before the Torah stated the above, the Jews were permitted to eat regular meat, and, in fact, until then they were permitted to kill the cattle by any method they wanted. According to R' Akiva, the Torah in this verse forbade the killing of cattle for food by any means except kosher slaughtering.

The Torah makes the permission to eat regular meat conditional on "the expansion of borders" of *Eretz Yisrael*, when it states (ibid.), "when Hashem your God will expand your borders as He spoke to you."

Ramban says that this expansion is not the same one mentioned in connection with the addition of three more cities of refuge — עָרֵי מִקְלָט — where, too, the Torah uses similar wording (ibid. 19:8-9): "when Hashem your God will expand your borders ... you will add for yourself three more cities." The latter refers to the conquest of the Ten Nations, as promised to Avraham. Here, though, the Torah stresses, "as He spoke to you," referring only to the conquest of the Seven Nations when the Jews entered *Eretz Yisrael*. Immediately after the land was conquered and divided, they were permitted to eat regular meat. Based on this, *Ramban* explains that the verse (ibid. 12:21), "If the place where Hashem your God has chosen to put His name is far from you," is an explanation why regular meat is to be permitted after Hashem expands the borders. After the expansion, the *mishkan* (Tabernacle) — where the sacrifices are offered — will be far away from people's homes, unlike when they were all camped around it in the desert. That is why regular meat would then be permitted in every place. The only exception would then be the *mishkan* or (later) the *Beis HaMikdash*, where one would not be permitted to slaughter regular meat, as in the inference of *Chazal*: "You are permitted to slaughter when you are far away, but not when you are close [i.e., in the *Beis HaMikdash*]."

According to *Rashi*, there are two meanings of the Torah concepts of "expanding" the borders (ibid. v. 20) and "being far away" (ibid. v. 21). The first does not refer to the expansion of the borders of *Eretz Yisrael*. Rather, the Torah wished to teach us *derech eretz* — "proper conduct" — that a person should not desire to eat meat unless he is comfortably off (i.e., where his "borders have been expanded"). This is the view of R' Elazar ben Azaryah in *Chullin* 84, who permits only a person who has fifty *manehs* (a considerable reserve of capital) to eat meat. Thus, when the Torah at first speaks of expansion, it refers to the expansion of the individual's wealth, and not the expansion of the nation's border. Afterwards, the Torah writes about the *mishkan* being far away, to teach us that regular meat is permitted as the *mishkan* is too far away for people to get to it easily, and they can no longer subsist solely on the meat of *shelamim* — "peace offerings."

Mizrachi adds, in his commentary on *Rashi*, that this interpretation is not in keeping with that of R' Akiva and R' Yishmael above, for according to them the words "if the place ... is far from you" (ibid. v. 21) are needed to teach us that one is forbidden to slaughter regular meat in the *azarah* — "the *Beis HaMikdash* courtyard" — as explained in *Sifri* on this verse: "You are permitted to slaughter when you are far away, but not when you are close."

Mizrachi's interpretation, though, appears difficult, for if that is the explanation, from where do we deduce that regular meat was permitted only after they entered *Eretz Yisrael*? After all, both these verses are needed for other purposes. The only way to answer this question is to say that, in spite of these deductions from the verses, this *halachah* must be contained in the plain meaning of the verses themselves.

Maharal in *Gur Aryeh* says that the law that one is permitted to slaughter regular meat only outside the *Beis HaMikdash* is not deduced directly from the words "if the place ... is far from you," but from the way the words are phrased. In order to permit regular meat to be eaten after entering *Eretz Yisrael*, the Torah could have said, "When you cross the Jordan." Why then did it state "if the place ... is far from you"? We are thus forced to say that this is to teach us that one is permitted regular meat only when one is far away from the *Beis HaMikdash*, but not when one is in it.

Or HaChayim has an interesting view, that one is forbidden to slaughter regular meat (*besar taavah*) in the entrance to the *azarah* — "Temple courtyard" — and the Torah permitted it only further away, as defined by *halachah*. *Chazal* debate in *Pesachim* 93 the meaning of "far away." There are those who say from the outer threshold of the *azarah* and on is considered to be "far away." But even according to this opinion, within the entrance to the *azarah* is considered to be close, and one may not slaughter non-sacred meat (*chullin*) there.

R' Reuven Margolios, in his commentary on *Or HaChayim*, states that *Or HaChayim's* view is surprising, for the discussion in *Kiddushin* 57 revolves only about slaughtering *chullin* in the *azarah* itself, and there is no one that forbids slaughtering *chullin* in the entrance. He therefore explains that the prohibition in the entrance to the *azarah*, according to *Or HaChayim*, is not the prohibition of slaughtering non-sacred meat (*chullin*) in the *azarah*, but of slaughtering regular meat (*besar taavah*). According to him, when the Torah talks about a place being far away (ibid. v.21), it means really far away and not the close-up place of the entrance to the *azarah*.

Or HaChayim's view is still surprising, as he is the only commentator who holds this way. It is also surprising that *Or HaChayim* quotes three views of what "far away" means, while the *gemara* only gives two, one from Modi'in and beyond, and one from the *azarah's* outer threshold and beyond, but there is no view that defines "far away" as everywhere outside Yerushalayim. Yet, according to *Or HaChayim*, regular meat appears to be forbidden, according to one opinion in *Chazal*, throughout all of Yerushalayim.

Or HaChayim also explains the meaning of the verse in the Torah permitting the eating of regular meat, where it states, "you will say," (ibid. v. 20) and, "because your soul desires to eat meat" (ibid.). According to him, here the Torah clearly emphasizes the permitting of such meat, as opposed to what happened at *Kivros HaTaavah*, (*Bamidbar* ch. 11) where the Jews were punished for asking for meat. In the latter case, the Jews had said, "Who will give us meat to eat?" (ibid. v. 4), and that is why the Torah here states, "You will say" (*Devarim* 12:20). After the land is conquered and divided up, one may say that he desires to eat meat, whereas in *Kivros HaTaavah* the Jews were punished for even desiring to eat meat.

R' Samson Raphael Hirsch holds that there is no comparison to *Kivros HaTaavah*. There is a difference in the meaning of the words *avah* (אָוָה) and *taavah* (תַּאֲוָה). The word *taavah* means desiring something which is forbidden, while *avah* is a desire for something permitted. Here, the Torah speaks of a permissible desire, and therefore "in all the desire (אַוָּה) of your heart you may eat meat," whereas at *Kivros HaTaavah* the people lusted for something forbidden.

HaKesav VeHaKabalah has a different interpretation. According to him, תַּאֲוָה means a desire which comes of itself, whereas מִתְאַוֶּה refers to a person who willfully brings about a desire. When the Torah speaks of אַוָּה in the verse, "in all the desire (אַוַּת) of your heart you may eat meat" (ibid.), it refers to natural desire. The same is true in the verse, "you shall pay the money for whatever your soul desires (תְּאַוֶּה)." Therefore, as this desire comes of itself, the Torah mentions the word נֶפֶשׁ — "soul" — in connection with the word "desire."

This is unlike the verse (II Shmuel 23:15), "And David longed (וַיִּתְאַוֶּה), and said, 'Oh that one would give me drink of the water of the well of Beis Lechem, which is by the gate!' " There, David was not thirsty, and there was other water available, but David wished to test the spirits of his warriors. The proof of this is that when they brought him the water, he did not drink it. It states here, (Devarim 12:20), "If your soul desires (תְאַוֶּה נַפְשְׁךָ) to eat meat." From this, Chazal deduce that the Torah wished to teach us proper conduct, that a person should not eat meat unless the desire to do so comes of itself. Otherwise, the Torah would have used the word תִּתְאַוֶּה rather than תְּאַוֶּה.

◈§ A Mitzvah to Eat Meat

R' Sa'adiah Gaon gives, in his list of the 613 mitzvos, the verse "when Hashem your God expands your borders" (ibid. 12:20), as a positive mitzvah. He interprets this verse to mean that it is a positive mitzvah to eat meat after Hashem expands Israel's borders. R' Sa'adiah Gaon is the only one among those listing the 613 mitzvos who includes this as one of them.

R' Yerucham Perla, in his monumental work on R' Sa'adiah Gaon's Sefer HaMitzvos, takes great pains in trying to understand what R' Sa'adiah Gaon means here. At first, he wishes to say that R' Sa'adiah Gaon refers only to the rule that "this is to teach us proper conduct, that one should not eat meat unless one has an appetite for it."

From the words of Rambam in Hilchos De'os 10, it appears that such a prohibition is only m'd'rabbanan — "by rabbinic decree" — but R' Sa'adiah Gaon evidently seems to believe that it is m'd'oraisa — "by Torah law." Thus, it is a positive mitzvah of the Torah for a person to act with proper conduct, and that he should take care of his belongings and not squander them, e.g., he should not eat meat unless he can afford it.

In the end, though, R' Perla concludes that according to this interpretation, this would be a לָאו הַבָּא מִכְּלָל עֲשֵׂה — "a negative mitzvah derived from a positive one" — and R' Sa'adiah Gaon does not normally list such mitzvos with the positive mitzvos, but rather with the negative ones.

It is therefore reasonable to assume that R' Sa'adiah Gaon holds that it is a positive *mitzvah* to eat meat when Hashem expands one's borders, i.e., gives one the means to afford it. In this, the Torah does not mean only meat, but also everything like it. We see this in the *Yerushalmi* at the end of *Kiddushin*:

> R' Chezkiyah and R' Kohen in the name of Rav say, "In the future, each man will have to give an accounting for that which his eye saw and he did not eat." R' Elazar was concerned regarding this statement, and saved up money to eat every single item one time a year.

It is true that *Tashbatz* explains the words of *Yerushalmi* as referring to an attempt by R' Elazar to recite as many *berachos* as possible, but *Yefei To'ar* explains it differently. According to him, the soul is tormented when it longs for something, and thus the person is sinning against his soul. In this, *Yefei To'ar* refers to what *Chazal* tell us in the first chapter of *Nedarim* and other places, on the verse (*Bamidbar* 6:11), "he (the *Kohen*) shall atone for him (the *nazir*), for he sinned against the soul." Against which soul did he sin? Rather, this refers to the fact that the *nazir* afflicted himself (by refraining) from wine.

It is true that this is no proof to R' Sa'adiah Gaon, for from this we see only that a person who vows to completely refrain from wine, such as a *nazir*, or fasts, is considered to be a sinner, but a person who doesn't drink wine and does not satisfy all his desires is not referred to anywhere as a sinner.

In any event, it appears that R' Sa'adiah Gaon relies on the words of the *Yerushalmi*, that in the future a person will have to give an accounting of that which he saw and didn't eat, because by doing so he transgressed a positive *mitzvah*.

The question that can then be asked is why the Torah had to make a point of specifying that a *nazir* is considered a sinner, for, after all, according to this view, any person who refrains from eating or drinking something is a sinner. The answer is that a person who simply does not drink wine is not referred to as one who "sins against his soul," although he has violated a positive *mitzvah* of the Torah, whereas a person who forbids himself by a vow to drink wine, as is the case of the *nazir*, is considered to be one who "sins against his soul." This is a new and interesting view. The words of R' Sa'adiah Gaon clearly indicate this, and are not to be interpreted in any other way.

Avnei Shoham uses this to explain a verse stated in regard to Shlomo (*I Melachim* 5:2-4):

> Shlomo's supplies for one day were thirty measures of fine flour,

and sixty measures of flour; ten fat oxen, and twenty oxen out of the pastures, and a hundred sheep, beside harts, and bucks, and deer, and fatted fowl. For he had dominion over all the region on this side of the [Euphrates] River.

One could then ask: What is the purpose of the last line quoted above, that Shlomo "had dominion over all the region on this side of the River"? According to R' Sa'adiah Gaon, though, the verses are explained simply, for as Shlomo had dominion over so large a region, in keeping with the verse, "when Hashem expands your borders," he therefore brought much meat to the table, thereby fulfilling a positive *mitzvah*.

◆§ Why Was Man Permitted to Eat Meat?

Abarbanel on our *parashah* brings the different views as to why Adam was forbidden to eat meat, why Noach and his sons were subsequently permitted to do so, and why the Torah permits Jews to eat the meat of certain species of animals, but not of others.

According to *Ramban*, immediately after Creation, no species was permitted to eat another. All animals had to survive by eating herbs and grasses, while man, because of his superiority, was also permitted to eat fruits and vegetables. After Hashem brought the flood and all of life was wiped out because of man's sins, the animal species remained alive only through Noach and his ark. As the animals were saved by man, Hashem gave Noach and his descendants permission to slaughter animals and eat their flesh in order for man to survive. As far as Israel are concerned, some animals were forbidden, as Hashem knows the damage they cause to man, either physically or spiritually. The reason why animals may be eaten is nevertheless the fact that the animals were saved by Noach.

Ikarim (3:15) has another view. According to him, eating meat is harmful and is also cruel. That was why Hashem forbade Adam to eat meat. Afterwards, Cain and Hevel followed in their father's footsteps, making their living from farming. Cain thought that man is no better than any other creature, and therefore he did not bring Hashem an offering of animals. Instead he brought of the produce of his land. Hevel, though, knew that man is superior to animals, and rules them. Therefore, even though they were not permitted to eat meat at the time because of the damage done by such an act, men were still able to offer animals as sacrifices to Hashem. Hashem endorsed Hevel's view. Afterwards, people's views became confused and they followed those of

Cain that man is not superior to the animals, so that they sank into all types of loathsome and despicable acts.

After the people were destroyed off the face of the earth, and in order to ensure that Cain's view would not prevail again, Hashem accepted Noach's sacrifice gladly. Thus, Hashem demonstrated man's superiority over the animals. In order to make absolutely sure that Cain's view would not triumph again, Hashem then permitted man to eat the flesh of animals, thus clearly indicating man's superiority. Once the Torah was given to Israel, there was no longer any question of Cain's viewpoint coming to the fore, and therefore Hashem forbade Israel to eat the flesh of certain animals, for this flesh is harmful to man, instilling in him bad qualities. Even when Hashem did permit certain types of meat, it was only against man's *yetzer hara*. Thus *Chazal* (*Chullin* ch. 6) tell us that man should not eat meat except when he has the appetite.

A third view holds that meat was forbidden to Adam because Hashem foresaw that he would sin and the subsequent generations would sink to a bestial level. They were not privileged to eat the animals they resembled, just as an *am ha'aretz* (person ignorant of Torah) is forbidden to eat meat. But since Noach and his sons were *tzaddikim*, they were permitted to eat meat. The same applied to the Jewish people at Sinai. Nonetheless, certain animals were forbidden because eating them is harmful.

A fourth view is that of Abarbanel himself, who, in a number of places, tends toward vegetarianism, as we see here in regard to his view on the eating of meat. According to him, Adam was forbidden to eat meat because he was at so high a spiritual level. After man fell, mankind, from Noach on, was permitted to eat meat. Eating meat results in cruelty and a desire for materialism. Ideally, then, man was created to subsist only on plants. After Hashem saw that even though men were not eating meat, the generation had still become corrupt, He permitted the people to eat meat, as a doctor who gives up on a patient as beyond all hope, and permits him to eat anything. When the Torah was given, though, mankind was not on the high level of Adam when he was first created, but neither were they at the low level of Noach and his children, and therefore Hashem permitted the Jews only the best of meat, in order to reinforce their intellect and to be subservient to Hashem's rule, while forbidding them to eat those foods which would achieve the opposite purpose. The purpose of Creation, though, was to have man subsist on vegetation. Adam and the subsequent generations were strong. In later generations, though, people became weaker "for he is flesh as well, and his days [have been reduced to] a hundred and twenty years" (*Bereishis* 6:3) and therefore Hashem controlled only the type of meat they ate, and the manner of eating, rather than forbidding all meat.

⌑ Only Be Strong not to Eat the Blood

At the same time that Hashem permitted the Jews to eat regular meat, He gave another warning against consuming the blood. According to *Rashi*, the fact that the Torah stresses this is an indication that the people were very much involved in and habituated to violating this prohibition. *Rashi*, though, does not indicate the link between this prohibition and the permission granted to eat regular meat.

R' David Zvi Hoffmann explains this all simply. The Torah notes, in regard to keeping this *mitzvah*, that "it will be good for you" (*Devarim* 12:25), as it customarily does with all *mitzvos* which show an element of mercy and humanity, such as honoring one's parents and sending away the mother bird before taking the young. The prohibition against consuming blood is also included in this. Before the Flood, people were forbidden to eat the flesh of any creature. Only after the Flood was this permitted. At the same time that Hashem granted this permission, He said (*Bereishis* 9:4), "But do not eat flesh with its life-force, its blood," in order to stress the importance of mercy. It is true that, according to *Chazal*, this verse forbids only *ever min he-chai* — "the cutting off of a limb from a still-living animal" — and blood from a living animal, but in this too we see the stress on the idea of mercy. At Sinai we were again warned that we are forbidden to spill the blood of an animal unless the animal is offered as a sacrifice. In *Vayikra* 17:4, it is considered to be bloodshed. When the Torah permitted the eating of regular meat, it again forbade the consuming of meat with its blood, because of the cruelty involved. It is just because the Torah permitted eating regular meat that it had to reiterate and stress the prohibition against consuming blood.

Ramban holds that the reason the Torah came to reinforce the prohibition here is because the people had been accustomed to offering their sacrifices to the *se'irim* — "a form of idolatry which includes the use of blood" — as explained in *Moreh Nevuchim*. *Ramban* adds: "That is not the major reason for the prohibition of blood, because the Torah gives its reason: 'for the life-force of all flesh is its blood' " (ibid. v. 14). (This also answers a question posed by Abarbanel. Abarbanel asks how *Ramban* can agree with *Moreh Nevuchim* here, after *Ramban*, in *Parashas Acharei Mos* attempts to disprove this very statement of *Moreh Nevuchim*. The truth is that here too, *Ramban* stresses that this is not the main reason, and in *Parashas Acharei Mos* too he says that *Rambam's* reason is good in itself.) Those who sacrificed to the *se'irim* were habituated to eating the blood, and would use it to foretell the future. That is why this *parashah* is juxtaposed with the *parashah* of the false prophet — the Torah is coming to warn us that if a person hears those who forecast the future by eating blood, even if what they forecast comes true, he may not believe the person who did the forecasting.

III.
The Difference between a True and a False Prophet

The *parashah* that deals with false prophets has a number of surprising aspects that are dealt with by the commentators. First of all, the Torah refers to a person who tries to lure others into serving idolatry as a "prophet," and states (*Devarim* 13:2), "If there arises among you a prophet, or a dreamer of dreams." Even after the Torah mentions that the individual has tried to entice people to serve idolatry, it still refers to him by the same term. What is no less surprising is the fact that this false prophet has the power, as the Torah tells us, of performing signs and wonders. He gives a sign as to what will occur in the future, and it comes to pass. How is this possible with a person who has come to deny Hashem as God and wants to have people serve idolatry?

The Torah answers this question by telling us (ibid. v. 4), "for Hashem your God is testing you, to know whether you love Hashem your God with all your heart and all your soul."

The type of test involved still needs to be explained. Can a person who is detestable and an idol worshiper, who preaches idolatry and incites people to perform abominations, have the ability to show signs that are meant as a test? What is the basis for this test, and what does it come for?

Ramban, Rabbenu Bachya, and R' Sa'adiah Gaon state that the Torah refers to this person as a "prophet" based on the fact that this is how he refers to himself. The term is used here in a mocking tone.

Ramban has an interesting view. The person involved is one who has been shown to have the ability to see what will happen in the future. According to *Ramban*, there are such people in the world. He calls him כָּהִין — what we would call a "medium" in our times. Such a person is labeled a "prophet" because of his ability to see into the future and foretell things that others cannot see. Basing himself on this ability, the person exploits his power and influence over simple people in order to spread heretical views and to claim to them that he is a true prophet.

According to *Ramban*, the nature of the "test" mentioned here by the Torah is unique. It is not a question of testing Israel's faith, but of exhibiting their faith and bringing it out from potential to actuality. The power of faith lies embedded in the hearts of all Jews, but it is through such tests that it is revealed to the world in all its glory. It is through the test that the Jews are given an opportunity, through the supernatural qualities of the false prophet, to prove their loyalty to Hashem, and to bring into the open the spiritual power contained within their very essence.

This view of *Ramban's* is repeated numerous times in his various works. It comes to answer the question raised by many of those who study the Torah: Why are tests needed? After all, Hashem knows everything that everyone does and will do in the future. According to *Ramban*, then, the test is not meant to prove anything to Hashem, but to give increased reward to the Jewish people for passing it. They receive reward for passing the test in concrete form. In the case of a false "prophet," the test consists of the Jews maintaining their belief in Hashem, in spite of the "prophet's" signs and wonders, which are supposed to show them differently.

It is interesting that one of the most original commentators on the Torah in recent generations, R' David Zvi Hoffmann, accepts this statement of *Ramban* as axiomatic. In mentioning *Ramban's* statement that there are certain mediums that can foretell the future, R' Hoffmann states that one should not doubt this, as *Ramban* testified to it. The Torah raises the possibility that a person with these qualities may exploit them for an anti-Torah purpose. According to R' Hoffmann, the test consists of the fact that there are people who can foretell the future and can lead people astray by their actions.

Abarbanel is more of a rationalist in this. He does not accept the view that some people have supernatural powers, with which they can undermine Hashem's wishes. He therefore has an original view on the topic. The Torah, here, is "exaggerating," as it were, in order to educate man. Moshe taught Israel that even if it were possible for a person to stop the sun in the heavens, in order to lead people astray, even then Israel would be required to remain firm in their beliefs, and not stray from the truth which they received at Sinai, for that is greater than any signs and wonders. But that does not mean that such a possibility exists. All that the Torah tells us is that even if it did exist, one would be forbidden to be impressed by it, and to diverge even a hairsbreadth from one's faith.

Abarbanel also adds, as proof to his view that we are not speaking here of actual signs and wonders, that the Torah says, "he will *give you* a sign or wonder" (ibid. v. 2), rather than stating, "he will *make for you*." Had the Torah been referring to signs which were supernatural, it would have used "he will make." The word "he will give" (וְנָתַן) means giving a sign or wonder within nature itself, and not outside of it, by a "prophet" who wishes to deceive the people.

According to Abarbanel, as stated by him in numerous places, it is possible to predict the future by astrology or witchcraft. But he says that these signs are natural, and they do not represent changes in nature. A person who foresees events in advance is not, as *Ramban* would have it, a person with supernatural powers, but one who is sufficiently trained in reading the stars. It is true that R' Yose HaGelili says in *Sanhedrin* 90 in regard to a false prophet: "Even if he makes the sun stop for you in the middle of the sky," but that statement, according to Abarbanel, is an exaggeration, and not a real possibility. Nevertheless, even if such a thing would occur, Israel would not be permitted to lose their faith.

⊷§ The Dispute Between R' Yose HaGelili and R' Akiva

The dispute between R' Yose HaGelili and R' Akiva in the *gemara* parallels the dispute between the commentators. Their words contain the different views mentioned by later authorities. This is the way the dispute is mentioned in *Sanhedrin* 90:

> We have learned: R' Yose HaGelili says, "The Torah understood the mind of idolatry. Therefore the Torah gave [the false prophet] dominion, so that even if he stops the sun in the middle of the sky, do not listen to him." (*Rashi* explains: "Even if you see that prophet wielding power and doing as he wishes, as it states, *Devarim* 13:2, 'he will give you a sign or wonder.' ")

Later, the *gemara* goes on:

> We have learned: R' Akiva said, "Heaven forbid that Hashem should have the sun stop for those who transgress His will, but this is as Chananiah ben Azur, who was at first a true prophet, and in the end a false prophet." (*Rashi*: "When the Torah states, 'he will

give you a sign,' that refers to the time when he is still a true prophet, that he will give you a sign about another prophecy, and in the end when he becomes wicked, he will tell you to serve idolatry, and tell you, 'Rely on me, for I have been authenticated by the signs and wonders that I gave you before.' ")

One who delves deeply into these words of *Chazal* will see that they contain the different views of the commentators on the Torah. R' Yose holds that the forces of *tum'ah* can also show signs and wonders. His words could possibly be reconciled with the opinion of Abarbanel, who holds that the Torah is only talking hypothetically. R' Yose says: "even if he stops the sun in the middle of the sky," namely, that the Torah understood exactly how far the idolaters will go — that they will stop at nothing in order to have people err. That is why the Torah exaggerates and states that one should not listen to such people, even if they have the sun stand still for them. But that does not mean that they can make the sun stand still. R' Akiva, on the other hand, says, "Heaven forbid that Hashem should have the sun stop for those who transgress His will." It appears that he understood R' Yose HaGelili to have said that false prophets are indeed able to carry out signs such as having the sun stand still, but he himself rejects that possibility. That is why he interprets this to mean a person who performed signs as a true prophet, but later became a false prophet, where he used the information he had gained earlier in order to deceive people.

Many commentators finds this explanation surprising. Abarbanel asks: How is it possible that a true prophet will become so corrupt as to now preach idolatry? This question can be answered easily. Theoretically and practically, we know that each person has free will, and one cannot trust himself until the day of his death. What is difficult, according to this interpretation, is to understand what type of a test Israel is involved in here. After all, what the prophet prophesied has to come true, because at the time he made the prophecy he was still a true prophet!

Ibn Ezra says that the test consisted of the fact that Hashem did not kill the prophet before he became corrupted, and before he used his knowledge for evil purposes. But this type of a test is really a daily occurrence. Hashem does not punish the evildoers in this world. R' Yochanan, the *kohen gadol*, served righteously in that function for eighty years, and then became corrupted, and yet Hashem did not kill him. Why is the false prophet different from all other wicked people in the world? Should the rules of nature be changed for a person such as this?

It is interesting that *Rambam*, in *Moreh Nevuchim* 3:24, and *Ramban*, Ibn Ezra, *Ralbag* and others, follow in the path of R' Yose HaGelili, that the reference here is to a person who was always a false prophet. Their only argument is in explaining the phenomenon involved whereby a person such as this can show signs and wonders.

Ibn Ezra proposes that this false prophet heard the truth of what will happen from a true prophet, and he then used the information which he had received from that person in order to lead other people astray. Later commentators, though, have tended to interpret the verses literally as they stand.

Recanti expresses surprise at *Ramban*, who was forced to explain the "prophet" along natural lines, as opposed to the way he normally explains matters. He asks: After all, the magicians in Egypt also performed signs and wonders, so why should this be impossible for the forces of *tum'ah* in later generations? According to *Recanti* and other kabbalists, the forces of *tum'ah* — "impurity" — are able to perform wonders, just as the forces of *kedushah* — "holiness" — are able to, and Hashem created both of these forces in parallel fashion. Thus, it is indeed a great test for ordinary people.

It is very interesting that *Rashbam*, who is normally known as one of the leading commentators of *p'shat* — "the plain meaning" — explains these signs and wonders as witchcraft, which are meant to test Israel's faith.

R' David Zvi Hoffmann brings proof of the truth of *Rashbam's* commentary from the warning in *Devarim* 18:9-15 not to seek to foretell the future through witchcraft, as the other nations do, but only to rely on the true prophets that Hashem will send us. The Torah does not deny the power of the people who practice witchcraft to do signs and wonders, but only defines them as "abominations" (ibid. v. 9), as opposed to the powers of *kedushah* which are to be found among the Jewish people.

R' David Zvi Hoffmann also mentions the statement of *Chazal* that the founder of Christianity "used witchcraft, instigated and perverted Israel."

R' Meyuchas ben R' Eliyahu, in his commentary on *Devarim*, says on the *parashah* of the false prophet, that "it was clear to Him that Jesus the Nazarene would arise, and that was why He gave this warning in advance."

Oznayim LaTorah notes how the righteous converts to Judaism in Czarist Russia used this *parashah* to overcome the priests that the Russian government sent to dispute with them on matters of faith and to try to get them to convert back to Christianity. The priests began to tell them of all the signs and wonders performed by the Nazarene, and asked them if that was not enough reason to believe in his "prophecy." One of the elders answered them that the Nazarene's "prophecy" was based, according to what he himself stated, on the Torah, and in the Torah it states quite clearly (*Devarim* 13:2-4):

> If there arise among you a prophet, or a dreamer of dreams, and gives you a sign or a wonder; and the sign or the wonder of which he spoke to you comes to pass, where he said, "Let us go after other gods, which you have not known, and let us serve them;" you shall not hearken unto the words of that prophet or that dreamer of dreams; for Hashem your God is testing you.

Recent commentators have also accepted this assumption as a basic principle. R' Eliyahu Dessler (Part 3, p.277) brings the view of R' Tzadok HaKohen of Lublin that the fact that prophecy was abolished at the time of the second *Beis HaMikdash* was only as the by-product, as it were, of another action: As *avodah zarah* was abolished in those days, the counterpart in *kedushah*, the prophecy of the true prophet, was also abolished. *Anshei Knesses HaGedolah* — "the Men of the Great Assembly" — decided to abolish *avodah zarah*, even though they knew that the direct result would be that prophecy also would be suspended.

In another place, R' Dessler (Part 1 p. 238) quotes R' Yerucham that the false prophets were not plain liars and swindlers, but were actually able to tell the future by the powers of the *sitra achra* (negative spiritual forces). Had they only been swindlers and cheats, the Torah would not have referred to them as "prophets."

As mentioned, this dispute, whether the *sitra achra* has power or not, is the dispute between R' Yose HaGelili and R' Akiva. *Rashbam* and the others who agree with him follow along in the footsteps of R' Yose HaGelili, while other commentators follow the view of R' Akiva. It is interesting that *Rashbam*, who is renowned for using *p'shat*, goes into kabbalah here, while *Ramban*, the father of the kabbalistic interpretation of the Torah, uses *p'shat* here.

ܗܥ Faith Above All

The *parashah* of the false prophet comes to teach us that faith in Hashem is the supreme value in man's life. The Jew does not have to prove his faith through signs or wonders. On the contrary, the signs and wonders need to be confirmed and proven by faith. Seeing and hearing are not criteria for determining the truth, for after Israel saw the miracles at the Sea, the Torah tells us that they reached the level of "and they believed" (*Sh'mos* 14:31).

Rambam, in *Hilchos Yesodei HaTorah* 8:2, explains at length the connection of this idea and the law of the false prophet. He says that signs and wonders do not determine whether a person is a prophet or not, because such signs can be done through witchcraft as well. If we, nevertheless, believe in the mission of a prophet, it is not because of his signs, but because that was what the Torah ordered us to do. The prophet is not confirmed by the sign he performs, but by the fact that the Torah said he is to be confirmed if he performs such signs. This is similar to the law that the Torah established, whereby any matter is to be determined by the testimony of two witnesses. Here, too, two witnesses are not conclusive proof that a person is telling the truth, but they confirm the facts because the Torah decided this should be so. Thus, if a prophet comes to deny the authenticity of the Torah by showing signs and wonders, one does not listen to him, "because the prophecy of Moshe Rabbenu was not based on signs, so that we should evaluate one group of signs against another, but with our own eyes we saw and with our own ears we heard."

We find an explanation of *Rambam's* words in *Ikarim* 1:18, where he writes that there are signs to authenticate the messenger which indicate that this person is worthy of prophecy, whereas there are (other) signs that authenticate the mission. This is analogous to a pharmacist who compounds different substances for medical purposes. There is one type of pharmacist who chooses the substances in front of everyone, explaining and proving the properties of each substance, and who makes the people understand the reason behind the medicine which he has prepared. Such a pharmacist is to be trusted in terms of what he does and what his mission is. But what happens when the pharmacist does not authenticate his actions in the medicine which he compounds, but passes through fire without being burned, and on the basis of that wonder he demands general trust in his medicine? Generally, people are willing to transfer trust from one area to another and to trust a person who performs wonders such as these, even though all the person has proven is that he can do wonders, but has not proven that his medicine is of value. The same is true for prophecy. The mission of Moshe was proven to be true, not only because of the signs and wonders, but it was because our eyes, and not those of others, saw that Hashem spoke from the midst of the fire, and that He gave the Torah to Israel through him. This confirmation is the confirmation of the mission, and not only the confirmation of the messenger. The mission is not confirmed by the confirmation of the power of the messenger to do wonders, for that is only the confirmation of the messenger. That is the reason why prophets need signs, but not *talmidei chachamim* and *poskim*. This is

stated clearly in *Yerushalmi Berachos* 1:4: " 'He will give you a sign' —
You may demand a sign from a prophet, but you may not demand a
sign in the Torah, as it states, 'all that they will instruct you.' "

The power and glory of faith are so great that one is even forbidden
to argue with a false prophet and to ask him for a sign. When such a
person states that even a single *mitzvah* of the Torah is to be abolished,
that is enough to reject him out-of-hand. According to *Rambam*, the
meaning of the negative *mitzvah*, "You shall not listen" (*Devarim* 13:4),
is that one is forbidden to enter into a debate with such a person, and is
certainly not permitted to ask him for confirmation. As opposed to this,
Ramban holds that the prohibition is only to believe the words so as to
be willing to act on them.

Chinuch follows in *Rambam's* path and explains the reason why one
is forbidden to even debate with a false prophet, because "the error that
people constantly have, and their intellect is not healthy enough to
understand the real truth in these matters." The Torah was afraid that
possibly, because of the false claims and long discussions, a person will
be enticed into following the false prophet. Even if a person will not be
enticed, he may nevertheless begin to have certain doubts in his heart,
even if only for a few moments. The Torah wanted to ensure that not
even for a moment in our lives will we have any doubts in this crucial
matter. Based on the above, one should think carefully whether it is
permitted to hold intellectual discussions on religious matters with
heretics, for there is the reason to fear that in our case, too, a doubt might
register, even if only for a few moments.

IV.
The Torah's Social Regime

The Torah's approach to the social system is expressed clearly in
our *parashah*. While property is indeed private, there are
limitations on how one may use it. The Torah refers to a
person who considers his money as belonging to him alone, to do with
as he sees fit, as בְּלִיַּעַל — "a wicked or worthless person."

One is forbidden to withhold loans to the poor even shortly before
the *shemittah* (Sabbatical) year, though he knows that *shemittah* will
cause the debt to be canceled. If a person does refrain from lending
money, he violates two laws, phrased in the Torah as (*Devarim* 15:9)

פֶּן ... הִשָּׁמֶר — *"Beware lest* there be a wicked (בְּלִיַּעַל) thought in your heart, saying, 'The seventh year, the year of release, is at hand;' and your eye be evil against your poor brother." This law is in clear opposition to the "freedom" of a capitalistic society. It indicates that there is a Divine dictate regarding the individual's money and property.

In his commentary on the Torah, the *Chafetz Chaim* notes this. He quotes the words of *Chazal* in *Kesubos* 68:

> Whoever averts his eyes from *tzedakah* (charity) is like an idolater, for it states here (i.e., in reference to *tzedakah*), "Beware lest there be a wicked (בְּלִיַּעַל) thought in your heart," and it states there (i.e., in reference to idolatry), "Wicked (בְּלִיַּעַל) people went out of you, and corrupted the members of their city" (*Devarim* 13:14).

That is the extent to which the Torah condemns a person who, under a liberal regime, would be considered to be an upright member of society.

According to *Or HaChayim*, the Torah also gives reasons for this approach. We are told (ibid. 15:4), that "there will be no poor among you" — namely, that if there are poor people among you, it is because of you, in that the other man's portion is in your hands. Whatever he is lacking, you have in excess.

Or HaChayim explains this along the same lines in *Parashas Mishpatim* as well (*Sh'mos* 22:24): "When you lend money to My people, to the poor among you" — you are required to lend to your fellow, because his portion is in your hands.

The Dubno Maggid gives a parable to explain this: A certain person prepared ten portions for ten people. One of the men was a glutton, and snatched two portions. Those at the dinner pointed out to the host that one person had not received a portion. The host answered: "I set aside a portion for each person, but one of you has taken two portions, thus depriving another man of his. You have the extra portion, and return it to the one missing a portion." The same is true for the poor of Israel. "There will be no poor among you." "It was not I," says Hashem, "that caused the poor to exist in the land. It was not My error, because all received an equal portion in the land, but you took away the poor man's portion, and it is your duty to return it. When it states that (*Devarim* 15:11), 'the poor shall not cease in the land,' it is because of your actions."

R' Amiel, in his *Derashos El Ami, Parashas Shekalim*, uses this in explaining the Torah's view on the social regime that should exist. The Torah does not oppose private property, but it places limitations on the use of that property, so as to prevent a person from exploiting his property for evil purposes. The Torah requires the land to be divided up equally. Furthermore, it instituted the *shemittah* (Sabbatical year) and *yovel* (Jubilee year) for the cancellation of debts and the return of property to its original owner. The Torah also forbade the taking of interest, which is, in effect, a prohibition against having one's money earn more money. The Torah also imposed innumerable obligations on a person who has the means, including *ma'aser ani* (the tithe given to the poor in the 3rd and 6th years of the *shemittah* cycle), *leket* (not picking up a single stalk or two stalks of wheat dropped while harvesting, but leaving it for the poor), *shichechah* (not returning for any bales of wheat forgotten in the field, but leaving them for the poor), and *pe'ah* (leaving a corner of one's field unharvested, so that the poor can harvest it), etc. A person who observes the Torah and keeps these laws cannot live by exploitation or by using his money for evil purposes.

Now, when the Torah states that the poor will never cease in the land, it means that there will always be different classes of people, and that private property should not be abolished totally. Nevertheless, when the Torah states further that "there will be no poor among you," it wishes to teach us that we must not be the ones that cause a poor class to develop or exist. We must guard ourselves against harming the rights of others, and must do what we can, to ensure that a true Torah regime is established, by observing the social laws of the Torah.

Chizkuni takes this idea further. By observing *shemittah* and *yovel*, we will be instrumental in ensuring that "there will be no poor among you." The poor who sell themselves or their daughters as slaves go free in *yovel*. Their debts are canceled in the *shemittah* year and their property returns to them in *yovel*, so that there will simply not be any poor in the land if these laws are observed.

Sifri may possibly have this same thought in mind when it reconciles the two apparently contradictory verses about "there will be no poor among you," and "the poor shall not cease in the land." On this, *Sifri* comments: "The first refers to where people do the will of the Omnipresent, and the second where they do not do the will of the Omnipresent." The keeping of the *mitzvos* and doing the will of the Omnipresent must lead to a state where there will be no poor in the land. What the Torah wishes to do is to curtail the harmful effects of property ownership and to maintain equality among all segments of the population. If one person nevertheless has more than another, he is commanded about *tzedakah*, which means doing *tzedek*, or justice, so that equality will return.

The Dubno Maggid says that the warning in the Torah, "Beware lest there be a wicked thought in your heart"(*Devarim* 15:9), is meant to uproot the fraudulent belief that it is only natural that there are different classes in society. That is simply wrong. It is not naturally so. We must rectify this condition, and must gave back to the poor his portion which we have in our hands, because Hashem supports him through us. Hashem loves the poor and wants them to be happy, and it is our duty to fulfill the social *mitzvos* of the Torah, so as to restore the balance as it should be.

◆§ You Shall not Harden Your Heart, nor Shut Your Hand

The different commentators interpret this *parashah* in accordance with the social values involved in the *mitzvah* of *tzedakah* (charity), each commentator in his own way.

The soul of the Jew is a generous one, says R' Samson Raphael Hirsch. By the same token, the Jew's hand is open to all those who are in distress. By its nature, the Jew's soul is filled with compassion and pity, but the *yetzer hara* (evil inclination) sometimes gets in the way. The Torah warned us not to harden our hearts against our innate desire to do good and not to shut our hands against our natural inclination. Allow the natural tendency of your heart to develop, without trying to suppress the tendency. Then you will see how great is the generosity in your heart to do what is good and proper.

Alshech sees these verses (*Devarim* 15:7-8) as a moral lesson for man, which comes to explain the logic of the *mitzvah* of *tzedakah*: "You shall not harden your heart, nor shut your hand from your brother who is poor; rather, you shall surely open your hand to him." Whatever you do now, when you die you will have to open your hands. At that time, none of your gold and silver will go with you. All that will accompany you will be your good deeds. Why, then, do you refrain from opening your hands when you have the ability to do so?

Some of the *darshanim* give a parable to explain this. What does this resemble? It is like the grasp of a monkey. Monkeys love coconuts. Those who want to hunt monkeys place a coconut in a bottle whose base is wide but whose stem is narrow. The monkey places its paw in the neck of the bottle to reach the coconut. Now that it has the coconut in its grasp, the monkey refuses to let go, even though it is unable to pull the nut through the narrow stem. Finally, the hunter arrives and grabs the monkey, at which time it is forced to release its grip on the coconut. Had the monkey been intelligent enough to open its hand before the hunter arrived, it would never have been captured. The same is true for a person who is miserly and who keeps his hands tightly clenched his whole life. In the end, he is forced to open his hands on the day of his death.

Meleches Machsheves explains the Torah's warning as being aimed at those who do not give charity, claiming that they have relatives who are poor. "You shall not shut your hand" using the excuse of "your brother who is poor" (the continuation of the same verse), but rather, "you shall surely open your hand" to every person. It is true that one's relatives take precedence over other people, but giving to one's relatives does not give one the excuse not to help other people.

One of the *rishonim*, *Bechor Shor*, explains the Torah's warning as forbidding one to say: "God has punished this poor person, and one is therefore forbidden to pity him and to give him charity." The latter was the statement made by the wicked Turnus Rufus, as quoted in *Bava Basra* 10.

R' Shmelki of Nikolsburg explains the text after this (*Devarim* 15:9), "and [lest] your eye be evil against your poor brother," along the same lines. Do not see the "evil" of your poor brother, and use that as your excuse for not helping him. If you do that, he "will cry unto Hashem against you, and it will be a sin unto you"(ibid.). Hashem will search for the sins that you have committed, just as you search for the sins of others.

Yalkut HaGershuni develops this idea further. The people of S'dom also ignored the suffering of the poor, claiming that "their sin is very grievous" (*Bereishis* 18:20) — that the poor were sinners and did not deserve to be supported. As a result, "Hashem said, 'I will go down and see if indeed they have done as their cry which has come to Me' " (ibid. v. 21) — I will go and see if they themselves are not involved in the very same sins which they accuse the others of, and if that is the case, "I will bring destruction upon them" (ibid.). These words of *Yalkut HaGershuni* are *d'rush*, but they are very true in regard to the excuses that people with means use not to give *tzedakah*.

Oznayim LaTorah says that the Torah specifically warned us against such excuses when it tells us, "You shall surely give him" (*Devarim* 15:10) — upon which *Chazal* comment, "even a hundred times." A person should grow accustomed to giving *tzedakah* by giving time after time, and then giving will become second nature with him, and he will not attempt to avoid giving by using various excuses.

⋖§ "The Shemittah Year Approaches"

The commentators attempt to explain the excuse given by the rich man when he claims, "the seventh year . . . is approaching" (ibid. v. 9). According to *Chazal*, the meaning of the verse is that the rich man does not want to lend money to the poor man because he knows that the *shemittah* year cancels all debts. But the commentators do not limit themselves to this interpretation, for, according to them, this verse is not referring to a loan, but to a gift, as the verse concludes, "Your eye will be evil against your poor brother, and you will give him nothing." (See below the words of *HaKesav VeHaKabalah*.)

Abarbanel therefore explains that this refers to the giving of *ma'aser ani* (the tithe of the poor) to the poor in the sixth year of the *shemittah* cycle. The rich man may claim, "Why should I give it to the poor? After all, in one more year (i.e., in the *shemittah* year) everything will become ownerless, and he will be able to take whatever he wants for himself." That will compensate him also for what I don't give him now. It is that approach that the Torah forbids.

Chasam Sofer has a similar interpretation. Misers have a habit, when approached for a donation, to say, "Soon it will be Chanukah (or Purim), and then I will give a large amount. Why should I donate right now?" By the same token, as the *shemittah* year approaches, the rich may try to avoid giving *tzedakah*, claiming that in a short time it will be *shemittah*, everything will become ownerless, and the poor will be able to take what they want. All that the poor have to do is to be patient until then.

HaKesav VeHaKabalah also explains our verse along these lines, but in regard to a loan. *HaKesav VeHaKabalah* notes the words of *Chazal* that the verse refers to a loan, with the Torah stressing that one should loan to the poor even though *shemittah* cancels outstanding loans. This, though, presents a difficulty. The previous verse (*Devarim* 15:8), to which our present one refers back, states וְהַעֲבֵט תַּעֲבִיטֶנּוּ — "you shall surely lend him," and this choice of words indicates that this is a loan against a pledge item (עֲבוֹט) left by the borrower. Now, the *halachah* is that a loan against a pledge is not canceled by *shemittah*, so why should the Torah need to stress the need to lend money to the poor in the sixth year? As a result of this question, *HaKesav VeHaKabalah* interprets our verse to refer to a poor man who comes to ask for a loan, whether it is to be backed by a pledge or not, and the rich man refuses the loan, telling him, "Why bother taking a loan? In a little while it will be *shemittah*, and then everything will be ownerless, and you will be able to take whatever you want freely." The Torah therefore teaches us that this too is forbidden, because the poor man may wish to work hard to repay his loan, rather than to resort to taking from others.

Ohel Yaakov, by the Dubno Maggid, explains this simply. The Torah came to warn us to give *tzedakah* not only when we are doing well financially, but also when we are not doing well, just as with the law that we are obligated to give *tzedakah* even in the *shemittah* year.

By the same token, we see that David said in *Tehillim* (41:2), "Blessed is he that considers the poor in time of trouble: Hashem will deliver him." When the *shemittah* year draws close, a person begins to worry about himself, thinking that he is in a "time of trouble," but even then he is not exempt from being concerned about how the poor will survive.

Bechor Shor has a beautiful explanation. The Torah's warning refers back to what was stated above (*Devarim* 15:8), "you shall surely lend him," which, as indicated above, refers to a loan guaranteed by a pledged item. You are required to return the pledge to the poor person, even though *shemittah* is drawing near, and a loan not covered by a pledge is canceled by the *shemittah* year. (My brother-in-law R' Yitzchak Levi, נ״י, points out that this *halachah* is mentioned by *Rambam*, *Hilchos Malveh Veloveh* 3:5.) Beware lest you do not return the pledge, in order to assure yourself of repayment of the loan.

This is analogous to a ship that is caught in a fierce storm, says *Sha'ar Bas Rabim*, where the passengers are forced to throw their possessions overboard in order to lighten the load. Some people throw the *tallis* and *tefillin* overboard first. The same is true in our case. As the *shemittah* year draws closer, many major problems arise. The first thing that some of the rich people want to do is to free themselves of their obligations to give *tzedakah*. By doing so, they don't solve any of their own problems, but they have compounded the poor man's problems.

According to *Kli Yakar*, the major purpose of the *mitzvah* of *shemittah* is to undermine a person's confidence in his possessions. Hashem did not want a person to feel that his land belongs to him and his descendants forever, so that everyone will appreciate that the earth belongs to Hashem. Through this *mitzvah*, everyone realizes that the stability of his ownership is undermined. This way, people realize that, while they may be wealthy today, tomorrow they may be poor and the poor man may be rich. By giving to the poor when you are wealthy, as it were, you are ensuring that if you become poor the rich will give to you.

⊰§ You Shall Surely Open Your Hand to Him

When the Torah repeats the words (*Devarim* 15:8), פָּתֹחַ תִּפְתַּח (usually translated as "surely open"), it comes to stress, says *Sifsei Kohen*, that when you give *tzedakah* (charity), you are opening a gate not only for others, but even, and primarily, for yourself. King Shlomo defined miserliness when he said (*Koheles* 6:1-2):

There is evil under the sun, which I saw, and it is common among people. A man to whom God has given riches, wealth, and honor, so that he lacks nothing for his soul of all that he desires, yet God does not give him power to eat of it, but a stranger eats it: This is vanity, and it is an evil disease.

The Torah therefore stresses that when one opens his hands to the poor, he is at the same time opening the gates to his own soul and will be cured of the evil of not being in control of his own possessions.

After the Torah states, "you shall not harden your heart" (*Devarim* 15:7), it continues with what the phrasing implies is the reason for this: "For you shall surely open" (ibid. v. 8). *Or HaChayim* asks what type of reason this is. He answers that this may possibly be a reference to the verse (*Mishlei* 11:24), "There is he that scatters, and yet more is added." If a person does not harden his heart but instead opens his hand, there will be the double opening of פָתחַ תִּפְתַּח, and the Heavens will open the gates of plenty to him.

Meshech Chochmah sees this phrase as a hint to a certain *halachah*. *Chazal* in *Bava Basra* 9 say: "One examines (to see if a person is poor) before (contributing toward his) clothing, but one does not examine before (contributing toward his) food expenses." This is hinted at in the Torah here, where it states, "you shall surely open your hand to him," whereas in regard to clothing, you may investigate to see if he has anything in his home and then, "you shall surely lend him" (ibid.).

R' Yosef Shaul Nathanson also deduces a *halachah* from this *parashah*. One does not give all poor people the same amount, but the more important should be given a larger donation, even to the extent of giving an important person a horse to ride on. When the fist is clenched, all one's fingers are the same length, but when the hand is open one can see differences in the lengths of the fingers. When the Torah states, "you shall not shut your hand" (ibid. v. 7), it means that your donations should not be given along the lines of the clenched fist, with all the fingers the same length, but, "you shall surely open your hand" — give each poor person according to his worth and his importance.

Above, we reconciled the contradiction between "there will be no poor among you" (ibid. v. 4) and "the poor shall not cease in the land" (ibid. v. 11) using a conceptual approach. There are, however, commentators who reconcile the two using *p'shat* — "the literal meaning of the text." Ibn Ezra says that if all or most of the Jewish people obey the laws of the Torah, then Hashem promises that "there will be no poor among you," but as Hashem knows that there will be generations in which the people will not do so and "the poor shall not cease in the land," he therefore commands us to give *tzedakah*.

Ramban disagrees with this interpretation, and says that one cannot assume that the Torah would prophesy that Israel would not keep the *mitzvos*, and that is the reason why there will be poor people. According to *Ramban*, what the Torah means is that the reality of the situation is that there will always be poor people. It is true that Hashem promises that if the Jews obey the Torah there will not be any poor people, but over the course of time there will be poor people as a result of our evil deeds, and it is because of this that we are commanded to give *tzedakah*. *Ramban* does not differ with Ibn Ezra about the meaning of the verses, but merely opposes Ibn Ezra's statement that Hashem prophesied in advance that the people will sin.

S'forno holds that the promise that there would be no poor people was indeed fulfilled at the time of Yehoshua and the elders that lived after Yehoshua (*Yehoshua* 24:31). At that time, after the land was divided up equally among the different families, and as the Jews kept the *mitzvos*, there were no poor among the Jewish people.

◆§ Why Is This Mitzvah Connected with Eretz Yisrael?

The Torah mentions the *mitzvah* of *tzedakah* in regard to *Eretz Yisrael*, as we see in the verse (*Devarim* 15:7), "If there is among you a poor man of one of your brothers within any of your cities in your land which Hashem your God gives you," and (ibid. v. 11), "You shall open your hand wide unto your brother, to your poor, and to your needy, in your land." This emphasis on "in your land" requires an explanation, for obviously this *mitzvah* is not meant only for those living in *Eretz Yisrael*.

Sifri deduces from this that the poor of *Eretz Yisrael* take precedence over the poor of other countries.

Torah Temimah raises a question as to when the poor of *Eretz Yisrael* take precedence. Obviously, for people living in *Eretz Yisrael* the poor of *Eretz Yisrael* come first, because the *halachah* is that "the poor of your city take precedence." The question arises regarding people living outside *Eretz Yisrael*: Do we say that the poor of one's city take precedence, or do the poor of *Eretz Yisrael* take precedence even over the poor of one's own city? *Torah Temimah* concludes that the order is as follows: a) the poor of one's own city; b) the poor of *Eretz Yisrael*; c) the poor of other cities outside *Eretz Yisrael*.

It is somewhat surprising that *Torah Temimah* discusses the case before coming to this conclusion, because this is stated clearly in *Shach*, *Yoreh De'ah* 251 quoting *Bach*, that the poor of one's own city take precedence, even over the poor of *Eretz Yisrael*.

Chasam Sofer in his *teshuvos*, *Yoreh De'ah* 233, states that even in *Eretz Yisrael* the poor of Jerusalem take precedence over the poor of other cities in the country.

Meshech Chochmah concludes that the *halachah* is that the poor of Judea and Galilee take precedence over the poor in Transjordan, as the Torah states, "that Hashem your God is giving you" (ibid. v. 7), and *Sifri* deduces from a similar verse that the fruit of Transjordan is exempt from *bikkurim* — "first fruits."

Rabbenu Bachya, though, states that the Torah mentions here "in your land" (ibid.) to teach us that the major aspect of *tzedakah* is in *Eretz Yisrael*, and the same is true for the other *mitzvos*, as mentioned at the beginning of the *parashah* (*Devarim* 12:1), "These are the statutes and judgments, which you shall observe to do in the land." All the *mitzvos* are for the Jewish people living in their land, and, as *Chazal* tell us, are obligatory outside *Eretz Yisrael* in order for us not to forget how to observe them when we do return to the country. Thus, *Chazal* tell us on the verse, "you shall place them on your heart" (ibid. 11:18), that "even after you are exiled, be distinguished by your performance of the *mitzvos* — put on *tefillin*, place a *mezuzah* — so that they will not be new to you when you return to the land."

HaKesav VeHaKabalah says that "in your land" teaches us that even in *Eretz Yisrael* one is required to give *tzedakah*, and all the more so in the other lands. One might think that since in *Eretz Yisrael* we have *shemittah* and the canceling of all debts every seventh year, one might be exempt from *tzedakah*. The Torah therefore came to tell us that, in spite of this, even in *Eretz Yisrael* we are required to give *tzedakah*.

Shoftim – שפטים

I.

Even if They Tell You Right Is Left

Rashi, on *Devarim* 17:11, quotes *Chazal* that the obligation to listen to the *beis din*, the Torah court, extends even to "when they tell you right is left, and left is right." The meaning of this is that even when a person is totally sure that the *beis din* has made a mistake in ruling the *halachah*, he is still required to listen to its ruling. This appears astonishing: How can the Torah place the power of the *beis din* even above the power of the Torah itself? There are thus commentators, such as Abarbanel and others, who say that this law only applies where "it appears" to the person that the *beis din* has erred, but not where it is absolutely certain, without any chance of a doubt, that the *beis din* erred. *Sifri* too states, "it appears to him" that the right is the left, and the left is the right. The term "it appears" implies that while the observer thinks something is true, reality is not so.

Rashi was the one who deleted the words, "it appears." There are commentators on *Rashi*, though, who explain *Rashi*, also, to mean that this law only applies when it appears to a person that the *beis din* has erred. However, *Ramban*, *Ran*, and others take Rashi's words at face value — that one must obey the *beis din* even when it has certainly erred.

The commentators, who state that this law applies only where "it appears" to the person that the *beis din* erred, have their source in *Yerushalmi Horiyos* 1:1:

> One might imagine that if they tell you that the right is left and the left is right, that you should obey them. (The Torah) therefore states, "right and left" — [one need obey them only] when they tell you that the right is the right and the left is the left.

Ramban explains how we can have a *halachah* which appears to place the *beis din* (*Sanhedrin*) above the Torah itself. He says:

> Do not say, "How can I eat this *cheilev* (forbidden food) or execute this innocent person?" Rather say, "Thus the Master of the *mitzvah* commands me about the *mitzvos*, that just as I should obey all His *mitzvos*, so should I obey the rulings of those who stand before Him in the place He has chosen." As to the meaning of their opinion, He gave us the Torah to be accepted as [the Sages] explain it to us, even when they err. This is as in the case of R' Gamliel and R' Yehoshua regarding *Yom Kippur*, which, according to R' Yehoshua's calculations fell on a certain day, and yet, in spite of this, he appeared with his staff and his traveling bag, and presented himself to R' Gamliel (on the day that R' Yehoshua felt was *Yom Kippur*) in accordance with [R' Gamliel's] command (*Rosh HaShanah* 25).

Ramban explains this remarkable law as follows:

> The Torah was given to us in written form, and it is common knowledge that people do not agree about every possible situation which arises. Arguments would thus increase, and the Torah would become a number of Torahs.

Thus the Torah delegated the final decision to the *beis din*. As to why one must obey the *beis din* even when one is absolutely positive that its ruling was incorrect, it seems that *Ramban* relies on the verse (*Tehillim* 119:126), "There is a time to do the will of Hashem, even when they have made void Your Torah." Sometimes the Torah permits an individual to act in a certain way, based on the ruling of the *beis din*, even where the person is absolutely certain the *beis din* is wrong, just to ensure that the people do not become divided into numerous sects and groups.

Based on this reasoning, *Ramban* states, in his comments on *Sefer HaMitzvos*, that where a *beis din* ruled that something is permitted, where a person is totally convinced that the *beis din* was wrong, that person is permitted to act more stringently for himself and act in accordance with what he feels the *halachah* should be. If, however, the *Sanhedrin* discussed the topic, heard the view of those who wished to forbid this particular item, and nevertheless rejected this view, "the person must accept their view" and in such a case he may not act more stringently than the *Sanhedrin*'s ruling, even for himself.

Torah Temimah, though, has certain hesitations as to the meaning of *Ramban*, and wishes to interpret his words not in accordance with the simple meaning. According to the way *Torah Temimah* interprets *Ramban*, a person is required to follow the *beis din* only where it "appears" to him that the *beis din* erred, but not when he is positive that it has erred. *HaKesav VeHaKabalah* also follows along these lines.

It appears, though, that that is not what *Ramban* meant. *Ramban's* words are also quoted in Rabbenu Nissim, and he adds that even if following the *beis din* can result in clear damage to body and soul, such damage sometimes occurs in nature as well, in exceptional cases. The Torah is not concerned about exceptional cases, and preferred to have the principle in effect at all times, for in the majority of cases it is beneficial and brings benefits to the nation. We thus see that Rabbenu Nissim understands *Ramban* to mean that one always must accept the ruling of the *beis din*, even if this can result in errors on rare occasions.

Chinuch, too, states clearly: "Even if they erred and we are aware that they erred, we cannot disagree with them, but must act in accordance with their error. It is better to suffer one error and to have all follow [the *beis din's*] proper guidance constantly, and not have each do what he feels is right, for then the Torah will be destroyed."

Eileh HaMitzvos, by R' Moshe Chagiz, explains this law more clearly:

> It is better to make a mistake in accordance with the ruling of a *talmid chacham* (Torah Sage) than to make a mistake on one's own. A mistake in accordance with a *talmid chacham* will happen once and to one individual, but a mistake that a person makes himself will occur numerous times and to many people. If the decision of the Torah is left to each person in accordance with his own opinion, and he explains it according to his logic, disputes will multiply in Israel, and the Torah will, Heaven forbid, become thousands of Torahs, based on the number of opinions there are in the world. This is what the Torah meant when it warned us categorically to obey the *talmidei chachamim* who understand the tradition handed down from generation to generation. Even if they erred on one matter, one may not disagree with them.

Many *acharonim* follow in the same path, namely, that even if a person is certain that the *beis din* erred, he is required, by Torah law, to obey the *beis din's* decision. In such cases the Torah allowed itself to become subservient to the decision of the *beis din*.

Taz, in *Divrei David*, reconciles the contradiction between *Yerushalmi* which we brought above (that one only must listen to the *beis din* when it says that the right is the right and the left is the left), and *Rashi's* statement that "even if they tell you right is left," implying that one must listen to the *beis din* even when one is totally convinced that it is in error. *Taz* states that *Yerushalmi* is referring to a case where a person is able to evade having to carry out the decision of the *beis din* by passively not doing anything. In such a case, the person need not heed the ruling of the *beis din*. However, if the person cannot evade the issue, he must listen to the *beis din* absolutely. *Taz* bases himself on a statement by *Chazal* that if a person comes from a place where the people do not work on *Tishah B'Av* to a place where they do work on that day, if he is able to avoid working by claiming that he has no work that needs to be done, he may avoid working on that day. If, however, it would be clear to all that he is deliberately refraining from work on *Tishah B'Av*, he must act as everyone else acts. This is all the more true where the *beis din* has issued a decision which a specific person is convinced is incorrect.

Taz goes on to say that this law is the way it is because the commandment,"you shall not diverge left or right from the thing they tell you" (*Devarim* 17:11), is a law of the Torah just as the other laws of the Torah, and one cannot reject one law because of another; one is thus required to listen to the *chachamim* in any event. In addition to the Torah base for this principle, it also benefits the public because it serves to prevent the Torah from being made into many Torahs.

◆§ Every Rule Has an Exception

Ran asks: According to those who believe that every *mitzvah* in the Torah is beneficial to the body and every sin is harmful to it, how will the damage to the body by following an incorrect ruling by the *beis din* be rectified? *Ran* answers the question by stating that it is true that by doing a sin the body is harmed, but that harm is balanced by the good to the body caused by keeping the Torah's commandment to listen to the *beis din*. *Ran* also adds that the imaginative powers of the soul have an effect on the body. Thus, when a person listens to the *beis din*, and realizes that in so doing he is obeying a Torah commandment, "you shall not diverge (לֹא תָסוּר)," this influences and inoculates his body so as to prevent it from being harmed by any possible damage which would otherwise come to the body by doing a sin under the incorrect ruling of the *beis din*.

Abarbanel rejects this view in its entirety, and states that the laws of the Torah have nothing to do with psychosomatic effects on the human body.

Ran, though, has another explanation as well. The exception to a rule does not undermine the rule, but, on the contrary, strengthens the rule. In general, the body's powers are strengthened by performing the *mitzvos*, but there are cases which are exceptions, such as the present case. That, however, does not undermine the rule itself, just as the natural rule that food strengthens the body is not undermined by the fact that sometimes food is harmful to the body. It may indeed be true that by listening to the *beis din* and thereby committing a sin the body is harmed, but this is merely the exception that proves the rule: Generally the *mitzvos* of the Torah are meant to aid the health of the body, at least according to those who explain all the *mitzvos* of the Torah along the lines of nature.

This also explains why in reference to this law, the Torah (ibid. v. 8) writes כִּי יִפָּלֵא, which normally is translated to mean "if one is in doubt" about a *halachah*, one should go to the *beis din*. This case, though, is a פֶּלֶא — "astounding" — it is an exception to the rule. A person who transgresses the law (by following the *beis din's* ruling) is causing damage to himself, but the alternative, of the damage to the body of all Israel by having more than a single Torah, outweighs the damage to any individual.

Abarbanel uses a similar explanation of the Torah prohibition ("You shall not diverge" — *Devarim* 17:11) against disobeying the ruling of the *talmidei chachamim*, the Sages. The Torah is a just and true law for both the individual and the community. Sometimes, though, there is a contradiction between justice to the community and justice to the individual. In such a case, justice for the community must take precedence over justice for the individual, and it is the justice for the community which is decisive. There are, for example, *halachic* principles in the Torah, such as הַמּוֹצִיא מֵחֲבֵרוֹ עָלָיו הָרְאָיָה — a person who has a monetary claim against another must bring proof to his claim; or the presumption (חֲזָקָה) that no borrower will repay a debt before its due date; or other such principles. These rules do not indicate the absolute truth. It is possible, for example, that the person who has no proof of his monetary claim is nevertheless in the right, but as he has no proof, he will lose his case. In the second example, where a promissory note is found that carries a due date in the future, the note is returned to the lender, as the presumption is that no borrower pays back a loan before its due date. Now, it is possible that a specific person may have repaid his loan before the due date, but nevertheless the *beis din* will not return the promissory note to the borrower. The same is true for various other cases. The Torah determines the *halachah* based on the overwhelming majority of cases. It is nevertheless possible that in a specific case that comes before the *Sanhedrin* the person may be absolutely correct, even though according to the general principles he is not considered to be such. In such a case, the Torah gives the *beis din* the right to rule in accordance with the way it sees the case, in accordance with absolute justice, and not in accordance with the general principles. Similarly, there may be cases where, because of the needs of the hour (e.g., an emergency situation), the *beis din* may issue a ruling which goes against the general rules. It is to such cases that the Sages refer when we are told, "even if they tell you that right is left." This "left" is really "right," because it is in accordance with absolute justice, even though it is not in keeping with the generally accepted principles of *halachah*.

A *zaken mamreh* — literally "rebellious elder" — is a member of the *beis din* who refuses to accept its verdict when it diverges from the general principles of *halachah*. The Torah, though, has given the *Sanhedrin* permission to ignore the general rules when there is a specific need in a specific case, or where it is convinced that there is a deviation from the absolute truth, based on the way it understands the matter.

According to the foregoing, a *zaken mamreh* is a person who has a Karaite mentality, although not in the normal Karaite form. He accepts the binding authority of the rules of *Torah she'be'al peh* — the Oral Law — but he denies the right of the Sages to deviate from these rules, even where they are convinced that this is an exceptional case, where the plaintiff is correct, even though this runs counter to the general rules in the majority of cases. The Torah permitted the *Sanhedrin* to ignore these general principles where they are convinced that justice is in opposition to these rules.

This right, says *Nachalas Yaakov Yehoshua*, is only given to a *beis din* which is steeped in Torah and *yirah* (fear of Heaven), all of whose actions are for the sake of Heaven, but not to a *beis din* composed of *Tzadokim* (Sadducees — who believed only in the written Torah) and those like them, whose whole aim is to introduce changes into our religion in order to "bring it in line with the times," and against the *halachah* itself.

According to *Nachalas Yaakov Yehoshua*, this is exactly the meaning of *Yerushalmi Horiyos*:

> One might imagine that if they tell you that the right is left and the left is right, that you should obey them. (The Torah) therefore states, "right or left" (*Devarim* 17:11) — [only] when they tell you that the right is the right and the left is the left.

The words "when they tell you that the right is the right" in the above passage come to teach us that only a *beis din* which has proven itself in the past to always say that the right is the right is to be trusted even when it says that the right is the left. Thus there is no dispute between *Yerushalmi* and *Sifri* brought above. *Yerushalmi*, too, agrees that a *beis din* which is known for its Torah and *yirah* is accepted regardless of what it decides, and it must be obeyed. *Yerushalmi*, though, adds that such a *beis din* must be commonly accepted as having *yirah* and issuing its rulings in accordance with *halachah*. Now, when it states that the right is left, not in order to "bring the Torah in line with the times," but in order to reinforce the Torah, the *beis din* is to be accepted and obeyed.

This is also stated in *Sifri* in a different form:

> "You shall not diverge from the thing they tell you" (ibid.) — that refers to negative commandments; "which they teach you" (ibid.) — that refers to positive commandments. "Left or right" (ibid.) — even though they show that the right is left.

Thus we see that *Sifri* states that only if a *beis din* has been known consistently for ruling the *halachah* correctly ("the thing they tell you"; "which they teach you") can it be accepted when it diverges from what would normally appear to be the *halachah*. Thus the views of *Yerushalmi* and *Sifri* are in agreement.

⊷§ Both These and Those Are the Words of the Living God

Kli Yakar on our *parashah* has an interesting explanation of "even if they tell you that right is left and left is right." *Chazal* tell us: "If you should say, 'as this group holds the person innocent and the other holds him guilty, how can I study the Torah?' It therefore states (*Koheles* 12:11), 'The words of the Sages . . . were given by a single Shepherd.' " How does the verse quoted by *Chazal* answer the question? The truth, though, is that there is no absolute logic to either side of a disagreement among Torah sages. There are logical reasons to rule something *tamei* (ritually impure) or to rule it *tahor* (ritually pure), and in the final analysis the true decision is made by considering where the preponderance of proof is, while ignoring the minority of contrary proofs. There are cases, though, where עֵת לַעֲשׂוֹת — "There is a time to do the will of Hashem, even when they have made void Your Torah" (*Tehillim* 119:126) — and the decision is radically different. That is why *Chazal* in *Sanhedrin* stated that a person cannot be appointed to the *Sanhedrin* unless he can deduce 150 reasons to declare a *sheretz* (a dead rodent, which the Torah states clearly is *tamei*) *tahor*. Why do we need these 150 reasons? Because there are occasions when one must use them, and must base the *halachah* on them, under special circumstances. Thus, when the majority of the *Sanhedrin* rules that right is left, their decision is combined with the minority of reasons to declare that way, and thus their decision becomes a Torah ruling.

Chazal said, "Bend your ear to listen to the words of those who declare *tahor* and those who declare *tamei*." One should also listen to the opposing opinions on every issue, for one sometimes learns something from the opposing opinion, which, too, is not totally without any foundation.

This is the meaning of *Chazal* when they stated: "If you should say, 'as this group holds the person innocent and the other holds him guilty, how can I study the Torah?' It therefore states (*Koheles* 12:11), 'The words of the Sages ... were given by a single Shepherd.' " The Torah includes two logical sides to the argument, which are in opposition to one another. The decisions rendered are in most cases in accordance with the stronger and more numerous proofs, but one should not utterly reject the opposing viewpoint, which is sometimes a basic source for the *halachic* decision. That is why one should not regard the *Sanhedrin* as having erred in *halachah* when it declares right to be left. The left, too, is part of the *halachic* process, even though we do not rule in accordance with it. If, however, the *beis din* did decide the *halachah* in accordance with the left, it has a basis for ruling as it did.

Finally, it is worth bringing here the view of *Meshech Chochmah*, in his comments on לֹא תָסוּר — "You shall not diverge from the thing they tell you" (*Devarim* 17:11). To better understand what follows, it is important to be aware of the following rule: *Chazal* tell us that if a person has doubt about a certain item, if the question regards a Torah law (e.g., whether a certain fat is *cheilev*; where the Torah specifically forbade the eating of *cheilev*), one is required to take the more stringent course (לְהַחֲמִיר). If, on the other hand, the doubt relates to a rabbinic law (e.g., where milk may or may not have fallen into poultry — eating poultry with milk is forbidden by rabbinic law), one adopts the more lenient course (לְהָקֵל).

Rambam, in his principles (*Sefer HaMitzvos*), rules that a person who violates any rabbinic decree has violated the Torah law of לֹא תָסוּר — "You shall not diverge." *Ramban* rejects this view, and asks: If every rabbinic decree is also a Torah law, the rule should be that even in a סָפֵק — "doubt" — regarding a rabbinic decree one should say take the more stringent course, for in essence every rabbinic decree is part of the Torah law.

Meshech Chochmah, though, justifies *Rambam's* view, using the following logic. The Torah wished, in addition to the eternal laws laid out in it, that the Sages should also institute various safeguards and decrees. The latter, though, were meant to be temporal, and if a *beis din* greater in number and wisdom than the one that made a certain decree would decide to annul that decree, it would be annulled. As long as any decree has not been annulled, though, one is required to observe it under the Torah law of לֹא תָסוּר, so that the Torah should not become two or more Torahs, with each group keeping its own decrees. The *mitzvah* here is to listen to the decrees of the Sages, but that does not mean that the words of the Sages are directly in accordance with what Hashem wants. Therefore, if a later *beis din* arises and shows that the first had erred, or that the decree that was made by the *beis din* was one that the Jewish people simply cannot live up to, the later *beis din* has the right to annul the decree. These decrees have no sanctity in themselves, but only derive their power from the fact that they were said by the Sages.

II.

The Regime of the King and the Regime of the People

In both *Sanhedrin* and *Sifri*, *Chazal* tell us that Israel was commanded that when they entered *Eretz Yisrael* they should appoint a king, and this is one of the 613 *mitzvos*. This seems to stand in contrast with the prophet Shmuel's attempts to prevent the people from having a king (*I Shmuel*, chs. 8-12). *Chazal* and various commentators explain Shmuel's opposition, as will be shown below. All agree that the Torah command is what determines matters, and that is why there is an obligation to appoint a king. As to Shmuel's opposition, there were reasons, based either on the way or the time that the demand was made, which led Shmuel to be opposed to it.

The one commentator who disagrees with all the rest is Abarbanel, who holds that Shmuel's opposition was the correct course to be followed, and there is no obligation to appoint a king. Abarbanel answers all the attempts to show the contrary, and also shows how the words of *Chazal* can be in keeping with his view. Incidentally, Abarbanel also has an interesting view of the whole institution of the monarchy, both in general and in Jewish terms. He explains and clarifies his view in two major discussions, in our *parashah* and in *Shmuel*. Below, we will present his interesting approach.

~§ Arguments and Views Which Cannot
Be Substantiated

Chazal and different commentators spent a great deal of effort in explaining Shmuel's reservations about the whole institution of the monarchy, for his opposition appears to be contrary to a specific *mitzvah* in the Torah. Five basic answers are given for this opposition, but Abarbanel answers each.

The first view is that of *Chazal* in *Sifri*, that at the time of *Shmuel*, the Jews asked for a king in order to have him lead them to idolatry, as we see in the verse (*I Shmuel* 8:20), "We too will be like all the other nations." So too did Hashem say (ibid. v. 8), "Since the day that I brought them out of Egypt up to this day they have forsaken Me and served other gods."

Abarbanel brings proofs from *Tanach* against this argument. Had they wanted a monarchy only to worship idolatry, why did Hashem fulfill their demand? And why did He say (ibid. 9:16):

> Tomorrow, about this time, I will send you a man out of the land of Binyamin, and you will anoint him to be captain over My people Israel, that he may save My people out of the hand of the Philistines: for I have looked upon My people, for their cry has come unto Me.

From this we see that the purpose of the monarchy was to bring salvation to Israel, and for no other reason. So, too, did Hashem say to Shmuel (ibid. 8:9), "Now listen to their voice; but warn them and tell them the laws of the king." There is no hint here against idolatry. When the people wanted to be "like all the other nations," they were simply referring to having a king to lead them into battle and to judge them, and not for idolatry.

The second opinion is that of *Chazal* in *Tosefta Sanhedrin* 20b, that Israel were punished for saying, "We too will be like all the nations" (ibid. v. 20). This was the fault of the ignorant among the people. It appears, says Abarbanel, that this view of *Chazal* was what *Rambam* had in mind when he stated (*Hilchos Melachim* 1) that their sin was because they asked complainingly, and not for the sake of a *mitzvah*. Abarbanel argues against this too, for in the Torah, too, we see that it states (*Devarim* 17:14), "when ... you say, 'I will set a king over me, like all the nations that are about me.' " What difference is there between the words in *Shmuel* and those in *Devarim*? Shmuel, when he warned the people, told them (*I Shmuel* 12:17), "Your wickedness is great, which you have done in the sight of Hashem, in asking for yourselves a king."

Thus, we see that he was angry at the very fact that they asked for a king, and not at the purpose behind this request — that the king judge them just as was the case with the other nations.

The third view is that of *Ran* in his *d'rashos*, that their sin was that they asked for "a king to judge us" (ibid. 8:5). Had they asked for a king without defining his duties, Shmuel would not have had any complaints and would have accepted their request, but the right to judge the people is given only to the judges and not to the king. Abarbanel rejects this view as well, for the reasons mentioned above. After all, Shmuel complained to the people (ibid. 10:19), "You have this day rejected your God, Who saves you out of all your adversities and your tribulations; and you have said unto Him, 'But set a king over us.' " We thus see that what bothered Shmuel was the very fact that they wanted a king, and not what they defined as his role. When they asked for a king to judge them, they were not interested in having him judge them on a day-to-day basis, and having him becoming involved in disputes between neighbors or between husband and wife, but to see that justice prevailed in the land, even outside the judicial framework. This is a duty assigned to the king under the Torah regime.

The fourth view is that of *Ramban* in *Parashas Vayechi*, that their sin consisted of scorning Shmuel's rule and seeking a new ruler, even though Shmuel was a judge and prophet of Hashem. One can claim, says Abarbanel, that the people were justified in rebelling against Shmuel's leadership because he did not rebuke his sons when they sinned, as had been the case with Eli before him (ibid. ch. 2), but one cannot compare the cases of Eli and Shmuel. The sin of Shmuel's sons was that they took bribery, and this sin took place in secrecy, without Shmuel knowing about it, unlike the sins of Eli's sons, which were apparent to everyone. Eli's sons were *kohanim* and they sinned in their work of the sacrifices, while Shmuel's sons were only judges, whose duties ended as soon as their father removed them from their positions.

Abarbanel argues against this view as well, using a question which can be used against all the different views given above. If there is indeed a *mitzvah* to appoint a king, why didn't Yehoshua and the elders appoint a king straight after they entered *Eretz Yisrael*?

The fifth view is that of a non-Jewish scholar, Don Paulo of Bourges. According to him, there are two types of kings: a constitutional monarch and an absolute monarch. The first is the one that the Torah wrote about, telling the king to write for himself *Mishneh Torah* and to read it all the days of his life (*Devarim* 17:18-19). The second is a despotic king, who arbitrarily makes up whatever laws he feels he needs to administer his kingdom. Israel wanted a king of the second type, and that was why they said, "We too will be like all the nations" (*I Shmuel* 8:20); namely, that the king would make his own laws and practices. On this demand, Hashem said (ibid. v. 7), "they have not rejected you (Shmuel), but they have rejected Me." That was why Hashem commanded Shmuel to tell the people what it would be like living under a despotic ruler, who would treat everyone's property whichever way he wished, and would steal from all as he needed. That was why Shmuel said to the people (ibid. 12:14), "both you and the king that reigns over you shall follow Hashem your God"; in other words, that the people should seek a king of the first kind, who would accept the authority of Hashem's laws. Indeed we find that Shaul was punished because he refused to submit to the words of the prophet.

But this view is opposed by Abarbanel from the verses themselves. We are told very clearly in *Shmuel* that the people were punished for asking for a king, and not for anything else. Hashem said (ibid. 8:7), "they have rejected Me, that I should not reign over them." Shmuel told the people (ibid. 12:17), "your wickedness is great, which you have done in the sight of Hashem, in asking for yourselves a king." Israel, too, answered (ibid. v. 19), "we have added evil unto all our sins to ask for a king for ourselves." We thus see it was for this alone that Hashem was angry with them. In addition, the people asked for a king because they had rejected Shmuel's despotic sons. How can we then imagine that they would ask for a despotic king who would disregard the law? Furthermore, which fool would want a despotic king over him? The despotism of tyrants comes only later. At first there is no doubt that they do not show themselves as despots. Again, if they wanted such a king, they would have appointed him themselves, and would not have come to Shmuel to demand that he should be the one to appoint a king over them.

⊷§ Monarchy Is Bad for the Whole World

There are scholars of the other nations who claim that the relationship between the king and his nation is that of the heart and the body, and the relationship between the Prime Cause and the creation. According to them, monarchy is based on three essential elements: a) unity; b) continuity; c) continual ability.

Abarbanel does not agree with this view. According to him, it is certainly possible to have a collective leadership that comes to a mutual agreement about a unified view. The leadership can also be changed once every year, and as a result the ruler will be afraid of the person who succeeds him, and he will act justly. Why shouldn't the ruler be limited by a just constitution? A solitary ruler is liable to go astray because of stupidity, desire or anger. We see that countries that are ruled by kings are filled with all types of detestable things. The country is filled with brigandage. On the other hand, where countries are ruled by judges who rule for a limited time span, there is justice. As long as Rome was ruled by the consuls it withstood any tests, but as soon as the emperors took over, it declined. The state of Venice had been supreme, as had Genoa and Florence. None of these had a king, but instead a collective leadership, and these were states which sought justice and conquered other lands through their wisdom and understanding.

The king, says Abarbanel, harms his nation and brings disaster upon it. Abarbanel finds support in the words of *Rambam* in *Moreh Nevuchim* (3:10), that both the king and the sea have no limits to their anger, and one who walks among them is only a step away from death. The spirit which prevails in them is either the stormy winds of the sea or the stormy temper of the king.

> In reality, there is no value to a state in having a king, either in terms of its political structure or in terms of the unity of its people. The kings attained their positions by violence. They were chosen to be servants to their nations, but afterwards took over the nations. From their midst arose this festering disease, that a single man should arise and tyrannize his people, and lead them like donkeys.

Abarbanel's views on the monarchy are the sharpest in our literature against an absolute monarchy, and against any tyrannical regime and rule by one individual.

๛ The Monarchy Among the Jewish People

Even if we assume, says Abarbanel, that there is value among other nations in having a king, Israel has no need for one. According to those in favor of the monarchy, it has three roles: a) to wage war; b) to pass laws and establish courts; c) the ability, where necessary, to punish people outside the conventional parameters of law and justice. All of this applies only to the other nations, which do not have Torah and *mitzvos*, but with Israel the conditions are entirely different. All these three duties are carried out by Hashem or through those who do His will. Hashem wages war, and it is He who fights for the people, as Moshe said (*Devarim* 33:29), "Who is like unto you, O Israel, a people saved by the Lord, the Shield of your help, and Who is the Sword of your excellence! Your enemies lie to you; and you shall tread upon their high places."

Moshe gave us laws which he had received from Hashem, and we have no right to add to or to detract from them. The king has no right to make a new law. Rather (*Devarim* 17:18-19), "he shall write for himself this *Mishneh Torah* . . . and he shall read it all the days of his life in order . . . to observe all the words of this Torah and these statutes, to do them." Where there is warranted need to punish a person beyond what the *halachah* calls for, this right is given to the Sages, and *Chazal* tell us in *Sanhedrin* 46: "The *beis din* (Torah court) gives lashes and (other) punishments both in accordance with the *halachah* and not in accordance with the *halachah*, so as to safeguard the Torah." In addition, Hashem tells us that if a judge declares a guilty person innocent, the person will be punished by Hashem. The prophet Yeshayahu said (*Yeshayahu* 33:22), "Hashem is our Judge, Hashem is our Lawgiver, Hashem is our King; He will save us." This verse includes the three functions of the king: justice, legislation, and waging war.

Even if we assume that the other nations of the world need a monarchy, says Abarbanel, the institution is totally superfluous among the Jewish people. History has shown that most Jewish kings rebelled against Hashem, led Israel astray, and caused the nation to go into exile. That was not true for the judges of Israel, all of whom were men of valor and feared Hashem; and not a single one of them rebelled against the yoke of Heaven.

Chazal tell us in *Zevachim* 102: "Ulla said, 'Moshe Rabbenu wished to receive the monarchy and it was not given to him, as it states (*Sh'mos* 3:5), "Do not draw הֲלֹם — close," and הֲלֹם refers to the monarchy.'" *Chazal* did not mean to tell us that Moshe wished to be the king and that Hashem rejected it, but that Moshe investigated what the monarchy consisted of, and Hashem told him that it would be better for him to remain a prophet and judge. That is also the meaning of the prophet Hoshea, who stated (*Hoshea* 13:11), "I shall give you a king in My anger." This is not, as *Ramban* interprets it, a reference to the kings of the other nations, but that is the way the prophets regarded the entire institution of the monarchy, regardless of the nation and the king involved.

✒ The Appointing of a King

As opposed to various other *poskim* and commentators who state that the appointing of a king is one of the 613 *mitzvos*, Abarbanel holds that this is only רְשׁוּת — "permitted," but not required. The *mitzvah* only begins when Israel decides that it wants to have a king. At that time, the Torah tells us that the people cannot choose whomever they want.

Rather, the king is to be the one (*Devarim* 17:15) "that Hashem your God chooses." When the Torah states (ibid. v. 14), "When you come to the land which Hashem your God gives you, and possess it and dwell in it, and shall say, 'I will set a king over me, like all the nations that are about me,' " that is just a description of what will occur in the future. Hashem says that a time will come when Israel, out of ingratitude to Hashem, will ask for a king for themselves, and not because he is needed to lead them into battle, because by then they will have taken possession of the land. If this occurs in the future, the Torah commands us to observe two *mitzvos*: a) that the king must be chosen by Hashem through His prophet; b) the king must be a Jew. "From among your brethren shall you set a king over you" (ibid. v. 15).

In any event, these two *mitzvos* are dependent on the option to appoint a king. This *parashah* resembles that of *yefas to'ar* (*Devarim* 21:10-14), where a soldier is permitted to seize a heathen woman in the midst of war, but is not, of course, required to do so.

Abarbanel proves, using five proofs, that the very demand to have a king is רְשׁוּת (optional) and is not obligatory. a) If appointing a king is a מִצְוָה, why does the Torah say that they should *ask* for one? It would be more appropriate to state that they should honor their king, not that they should ask if they must appoint one. b) The Torah states (*Devarim* 17:14), "When ... you shall say, 'I will set a king over me, like all the nations that are about me.' " If it was a *mitzvah*, why was it stated in this way, which is the opposite of the command by Hashem (*Sh'mos* 23:24) not to emulate the ways of the non-Jews? c) *Chazal* in *Sanhedrin* 20 said, "Israel were commanded three *mitzvos* to be performed upon entering *Eretz Israel*: to appoint a king over them, to destroy the seed of Amalek, and to build the *Beis HaMikdash*." *Chazal* base the obligation of choosing a king on the verse (*Devarim* 17:15), "You shall set a king over you that Hashem your God chooses," and not on the verse (ibid. v. 14), "When you come to the land which Hashem your God gives you ... and shall say, 'I will set a king over me, like all the nations that are about me.' " This implies that verse 14 is just telling us what will occur in the future and is not a *mitzvah*, the *mitzvah* being having Hashem choose the king (v. 15), and not the appointing of a king. d) If there is a *mitzvah* to appoint a king, we have two positive *mitzvos* here — the appointing of a king, and having the choice made by Hashem — yet nowhere do we find that these are counted as two separate *mitzvos*. e) When Shmuel rebuked the people for wanting to choose a king, why didn't they simply answer that they wanted to fulfill a *mitzvah* of the Torah?

From all of this, we see there is no *mitzvah* to want a king, and what the Torah tells us here, as in the case of *yefas to'ar* (ibid. 21:10-14), is that should the people's *yetzer hara* (evil inclination) get the better of them, they are to act in accordance with the Torah's guidelines.

The whole institution of the monarchy is harmful to any nation, and all the more so in the case of Israel. That was the reason, in the days of Shmuel, when the people wanted to have a king, that Hashem became angry at them and said to Shmuel (*I Shmuel* 8:7), "they have not rejected you, but they have rejected Me." Once, however, that Israel had done *teshuvah*, Hashem sent His emissary, Shmuel, to appoint Shaul over them, and afterwards David, for this was not a forbidden action. Hashem was most concerned that the choice of the king be made by Him. That is what Shmuel meant when he told the people (ibid. 12:20), "Do not fear: ... do not turn aside from following Hashem, but serve Hashem with all your heart." In other words, Shmuel was telling the people that there was nothing wrong, in itself, in choosing a king, provided that it was done through Hashem. If that was the case, the king would be of great aid to the people, and if not, then (ibid. v. 25), "you shall be consumed, both you and your king." Hashem chose David because he feared Hashem. Hashem sent Shmuel to anoint David, so as to publicize and make clear that Shmuel's opposition to the institution of the monarchy was not a matter of principle, but was meant to stress that the king must be chosen by Hashem.

Abarbanel gives three reasons why Hashem did not leave the choice of the king to the people themselves, but that He Himself chose the king. a) The entire institution of the monarchy is a harmful one, and it should only be instituted where this is essential. The people cannot tell when this becomes essential; only Hashem can determine that. b) The people choose a person by his outward appearance, but Hashem sees into the heart, as Yirmiyahu said (*Yirmiyahu* 17:9), "The heart is deceitful above all things, and sick: Who can know it?" c) If people are given the right to choose, there will be major disagreements and clashes, because everyone will want to be king.

It is interesting that in spite of Abarbanel's fierce opposition to a monarchial system, he is equally opposed to rebellion even if the king is not acting as he should. One of Abarbanel's reasons for this stand is that as the people did not choose the king, the people cannot remove him from his position, and once he is appointed one is forbidden to undermine his rule.

III.

"As He Plotted to Do to His Brother"

he law of עֵדִים זוֹמְמִין — literally "scheming witnesses" — is classified by *Chazal* as a *chiddush* (unique innovation), namely, something which is beyond the realm of normal logic. *Rashi* in *Chullin* 11 comments on the *gemara* which states that only if the defendant is not executed are the scheming witnesses executed, whereas if the defendant is executed, the scheming witnesses are not executed. *Rashi* gives as the reason for this that the Torah states (*Devarim* 19:19), "as he plotted to do to his brother," and not "as he did to his brother."

Rambam, too, in *Hilchos Eidus* 20:2 states:

> If the person they testified about was killed and afterwards [these witnesses] were proved [by other witnesses] to be schemers, they are not killed based on *kal vachomer* (*a fortiori* reasoning, i.e., as they would be killed if the person they testified against had not been killed, they should certainly be killed if the person they testified against was killed as a result of their testimony), for it states, "as he plotted *to do*," implying that [he is executed only if] he has not yet done it.

Chazal, though, in *Sifri*, deduce this rule from the fact that the Torah states, "as he plotted to do *to his brother*," implying that "his brother" must still be alive for the scheming witnesses to be given the death penalty.

Rashi in *Makkos* 5 explains that "to his brother" implies that the brother must still be alive, but many commentators are surprised at *Rashi's* words, for there are many places in *Tanach* where we have reference to a "brother" who is dead, such as (*Bereishis* 4:10), "the voice of your brother's blood cries out to Me from the earth." Likewise we find: "When our brothers died" (*Bamidbar* 20:3). And there are numerous other cases such as this.

Rashash on *Sanhedrin* 10b explains that "his brother" means "his brother in *mitzvos*," namely another person who is capable of performing *mitzvos*, and that excludes a dead person.

It is true that we have a similar deduction to that used by *Rashi* in

Yevamos 8, where we are told that when the Torah states (*Vayikra* 18:18), "You shall not marry a woman and her sister," we deduce from the word "sister" that the prohibition against marrying one's wife's sister only applies as long as one's wife is alive. *Rashi's* choice of deducing the law from "his brother," implying "that his brother is still alive," is still surprising; why didn't he simply use the deduction of "as he plotted," rather than "as he did"?

Torah Temimah therefore explains that when the *gemara* states, "that his brother is still alive," it is indeed referring to the deduction of "as he plotted," rather than "as he did." If his brother was already killed, then it is already "as he did," and not "as he plotted." Thus, when we are told that his brother is still alive, that implies that it is still at the plotting stage.

Malbim explains this along similar lines. Plotting implies a serious thought to do wrong to somebody. The Torah commands us to punish these witnesses for the evil of their plans and not for the deed itself (the reasons for this will be explained below). מְזִמָּה (*Devarim* 19:19: זָמַם — "plotted") is a particularly loathsome type of plot, with the two witnesses not even present where they claimed to have been, but a lie in general is not known as מְזִמָּה. *Chazal* said, " 'You shall do to him as he plotted to do to his brother' (ibid.) — his brother is alive." In other words, the plot was directed against the defendant, and he is still alive. Thus the deduction is not from the word "his brother," but from "as he plotted."

R' David Zvi Hoffmann states that from the verses themselves we can see that זָמַם — "plotted" — applies only to thought but not to action, for it states in *Zechariah* 1:6, "as the Lord of hosts thought (זָמַם) to do unto us, according to our ways, and according to our doings, so has He dealt (עָשָׂה) with us." Thus we see clearly that there is a difference between זָמַם, which refers to thought, and עָשָׂה , which refers to deed. Thus we see that זָמַם refers to a thought which has not yet been put into effect.

Chazal in *Makkos* 5 tell us the *Tzadokim* (Sadducees) explain the word זָמַם to mean an action that has been carried out, and they claim that a witness is killed only if, as a result of his false testimony, another person was killed; if that person was not yet killed, the witness is not killed. Later in the same *Gemara* passage, the *chachamim* state that the witnesses are not killed unless both of them have been proved to be schemers. On this, R' Yehudah ben Tabai says, "I should see the consolation (a euphemism for "I should not see the consolation"- a form of curse) if I did not myself kill a single עֵד זוֹמֵם (scheming witness)" — i.e., where only a single one was proved a schemer, and that was done to refute the *Tzadokim* (to show clearly that the *halachah* was not in accordance with the *Tzadokim*), for the *Tzadokim* hold that scheming witnesses are only killed if the person they testified against was killed. Thus, if R' Yehudah would not ensure that the man was killed, the *Tzadokim* would take it as proof that they are right, and that the witness was not killed because the man he had testified against was still alive. R' Shimon ben Shatach said, "May I see the consolation if you did not shed innocent blood, for the *chachamim* said, 'scheming witnesses are not killed until both are proved schemers.' "

Avnei Shoham asks why R' Shimon ben Shatach accused R' Yehudah ben Tabai of shedding innocent blood, for R' Yehudah knew that according to *halachah* this witness did not deserve the death penalty, but in spite of this he had ordered the witness killed "to refute the *Tzadokim*." This is in keeping with *Rambam's* ruling in *Hilchos Sanhedrin* 24:4: "The *beis din* (Torah court) puts to death a person who does not deserve the death penalty, and this is not in order to violate Torah law, but to make a safeguard for the Torah." R' Yehudah ben Tabai also made such a safeguard, so why did R' Shimon ben Shatach then accuse him of shedding innocent blood?

Avnei Shoham answers this question logically. R' Yehudah ben Tabai wanted to disprove the claim of the *Tzadokim* that only a person who has killed another by false testimony is killed. The *Tzadokim*, though, do not agree with the *chachamim* that both witnesses must be proved schemers before the witnesses can be killed. According to the *Tzadokim*, even if a single witness was proved a schemer he is to be put to death. Thus, when R' Yehudah ben Tabai had the single witness killed to show the *halachah* is not in accordance with the *Tzadokim*, he was, in essence, corroborating their view that even when only one of the witnesses is proved a schemer he is killed. That was exactly what R' Shimon ben Shatach meant, when he stated, "The *chachamim* said, 'scheming witnesses are not killed until both are proved schemers.' " The emphasis here is on the word "*chachamim*," in that R' Shimon ben Shatach in essence told R' Yehudah ben Tabai, "By doing what you did, you were not acting in accordance with the *chachamim* but rather in accordance with the *Tzadokim*; so what have you accomplished?"

Gan Raveh proves from the language of the Torah itself that the *chachamim* are correct. It states in *Sifri* that the *Tzadokim* deduce from the fact that the Torah states, נֶפֶשׁ בְּנֶפֶשׁ — "a soul for a soul" (*Devarim* 19:21) — that the witness is not killed unless the person he had testified against was put to death. The *chachamim*, though, hold that "a soul for a soul" means that the witness is not put to death unless his testimony had resulted in the person being sentenced to death (i.e., in order to be executed, the witness must be proved a schemer after the death sentence is passed but before it is carried out). *Gan Raveh* explains that had the Torah written נֶפֶשׁ תַּחַת נֶפֶשׁ — "a soul instead of a soul," the *Tzadokim* would be able to explain that this refers to a person who is no longer alive, as is the meaning of the word תַּחַת in every place, as in (*Bereishis* 4:25), "She called his name Sheis, for she said, 'God has given me other seed instead of (תַּחַת) Hevel, for Cain killed him.'" So, too, does it state (*Bereishis* 36:36), "Hadad died, and Samlah ruled in his place (תַּחְתָּיו)." Here, however, the Torah states נֶפֶשׁ בְּנֶפֶשׁ — "a soul for a soul," and the letter בְּ which joins the two words indicates that both men are still alive, as we see in the verse (*Vayikra* 27:10), "if he shall change a beast for a beast (בְּהֵמָה בִּבְהֵמָה), then it and the exchange shall be holy," and in that case both animals are still alive. So, too, do we see that when a person strikes out another's eye, it states (*Sh'mos* 21:24), עַיִן תַּחַת עַיִן — "an eye instead of an eye," where one eye no longer exists. Here though, according to *Chazal*, the person the witnesses tried to have killed is still alive, and that is why the Torah states נֶפֶשׁ בְּנֶפֶשׁ — "a soul for a soul," rather than נֶפֶשׁ תַּחַת נֶפֶשׁ — "a soul instead of a soul."

ᓬᏸ When Are the Witnesses Killed?

Rambam states that the law that עֵדִים זוֹמְמִין — "scheming witnesses" — are killed only if the person that they had testified against is still alive was handed down as an oral tradition, but in spite of this, there are numerous explanations of it among the *rishonim* and *acharonim*. Below, we will give some of these explanations. (R' Yehudah Copperman, director of the Jerusalem *Michlalah* for women, has published a pamphlet containing a rich selection of material on this topic.)

R' Ovadiah of Bartenura has a simple and logical reason to explain this. (My brother-in-law, R' Yitzchak Levi, points out that it is also found in *Ba'al HaTurim*.) Had we killed the witnesses after the person they had testified against had been killed, we would have had a never-ending cycle. Relatives of the person who had been killed could bring scheming witnesses to testify against the first witnesses and have them killed, then relatives of the witnesses that had been killed could bring scheming witnesses, and so on. This would result in a desecration of Hashem's name, a desecration of the *beis din* (Torah court), and bloodshed. Therefore the Torah enacted a simple safeguard to prevent such a state of affairs from occurring.

Ramban holds that here the Torah shows its own justice, which is different from the justice of human logic. The fact that the Torah believes the latter witnesses over the former (i.e., when two witnesses accused a person of committing a certain crime and then two other witnesses come and testify that the first two witnesses were not at the scene of the crime as they were all together in another place, the Torah states that the second set of witnesses is believed, and the first set is killed as scheming witnesses) is a *chok* ("statute"), a decree of the King — a law that human reason cannot understand. Thus, if the witnesses succeeded in having the person they accused put to death, they are not killed if contradictory witnesses come along, for had the person put to death not been evil and worthy of the death penalty, Hashem would not have allowed the death penalty to be carried out, as it is said, "I shall not acquit the wicked" (*Sh'mos* 23:7). Thus if a person was executed it is a sign that "he died by his sin" (*Yechezkel* 18:18). If he had been righteous, Hashem would not have abandoned him to the hands of the court, as it is written, "Hashem will not abandon him to his hand and will not convict him when he is judged" (*Tehillim* 37:33). Furthermore, Hashem would certainly not allow the judges of Israel to shed innocent blood, for "justice belongs to God" (*Devarim* 1:17).

Abarbanel, quoting R' Chisdai, holds that this law was meant to uphold the reverence for the *beis din*, because the very foundations of the legal system are shaken if the judges' authority is undermined by having two witnesses killed after the court had used their testimony to have another person killed. Therefore there is no choice but to come to terms with what was done already.

Other commentators add that while a person has the free will to kill another person if he wishes, one cannot warp the free will of another person and have him act as one's agent to kill another person, and have that agent do the evil that the first person wanted to do. One cannot, therefore, accept the premise that the witnesses tricked the *beis din* into killing an innocent man. In such a case, we say the person who was killed deserved the death penalty.

Rabbenu Bachya gives an explanation by *Ri*, which is difficult to understand. Once two witnesses killed a person, they cannot be killed, because it is their word against the word of the new witnesses who claim that they plotted their testimony. Thus, we have two witnesses against two. On the other hand, if the person against whom they testified is still alive, there are three (the person they testified against and the two later witnesses) against the two original witnesses. This interpretation is surprising, because the *halachah* states that even if there were 100 original witnesses and then two other witnesses came and testified that the original witnesses had not been in the place they claimed to be, all 100 original witnesses are put to death. R' Chavel wishes to explain that only regarding witnesses do we say that "two are the same as a hundred," but not regarding one of the people involved in the case itself (e.g., the defendant). It is difficult to accept this logic.

Chinuch says almost the exact opposite in *Mitzvah* 524, quoting "a certain sage." The Torah believes the witnesses and does not believe those about whom testimony is being offered. There is no doubt that if two proper witnesses testify that three specific people killed someone, the two witnesses are believed, and not the three people who have been charged. Thus, when the second pair of witnesses comes to testify about the first pair (and claims that the members of the first pair must be lying because they were with the members of the second pair in a different place at the time the crime was committed), the first witnesses are no longer considered to be witnesses but defendants, and thus the second pair of witnesses is believed against the first pair.

Tumim in *Choshen Mishpat* 38 has a beautiful interpretation. As long as the person charged with the crime is alive, if a second set of witnesses arrives to claim the first set is lying, the person charged with the crime would not dare say that the witnesses are lying unless he was telling the truth, because otherwise he would be sentencing a set of innocent witnesses to death. Thus, when the second set of witnesses comes and the defendant too states that the first set is lying, that is proof that the first set of witnesses must indeed have lied. If, however, the person was put to death, we have no idea what his reaction would have been after the second set of witnesses arrived. He might well have admitted his guilt, in order not to have two innocent people die, even though he would have seen no reason earlier to admit that he was guilty. As a result we are in doubt, and the court cannot kill a person when there is a doubt present, as it is written, "The congregation shall judge ... and the congregation shall acquit" (*Bamidbar* 35:24-25).

HaKesav VeHaKabalah takes this view further. In general, if a second set of witnesses arrives before the defendant is killed, the presumption is that the second set is more reliable than the first, and the first set of witnesses is put to death. If, however, the person was already put to death, where the first witnesses had to be physically involved in the person's death, as it is written, "the hand of the witnesses shall be upon him first, to kill him" (*Devarim* 17:7), there is a counter-presumption — that the witnesses would not have been involved in killing the person if he was innocent. Therefore, as we have one presumption against another, the first witnesses are not killed.

Aperion has a convincing view of this *parashah*. If a second set of witnesses comes to claim that the first set was elsewhere at the time of the crime, we should logically say that it is a case of two witnesses against two. On *Eiruvin* 36, though, *Ritva* says that where there are two

חֲזָקוֹת — "presumptions" — which contradict one another, one follows the חֲזָקָה of the object which is under discussion. Therefore, as long as the defendant is still alive, he is the object under discussion and he is presumed to be innocent. That means the first witnesses are false and are put to death. If, however, the person had already been put to death, then the object under discussion is the first set of witnesses, and they are presumed to be innocent.

One of the *acharonim* gives a clever answer to the question. If the witnesses wanted to have an innocent person killed, they should be killed. There is a perfect symmetry in this: They wanted to kill a person who had done nothing, and they too are killed even though they have done nothing, in the sense that the person they wanted to kill is still alive. If, however, the person was already killed, then there would be no symmetry if they would be killed, for they would have killed an innocent man, while killing them would mean that two guilty men were killed. Hence their execution would not fulfill the commandment, "You shall do to him as he plotted to do to his brother" (ibid. 19:19). Of course this is only cleverness, for there is no doubt that if they are guilty they deserve the death penalty.

Let us mention here the view of *Nitzotzei Or* by R' Reuven Margolios. The entire law of עֵדִים זוֹמְמִין — "scheming witnesses" — is a *chiddush* (unique innovation) of the Torah, i.e., a law which we would not have deduced by rational means, for why should we believe the second pair of witnesses any more than we believe the first pair? If all that the first set of witnesses has done was to speak, the *chiddush* tells us that the speech of the second pair of witnesses is accepted over the speech of the first pair. If, however, the person charged has already been killed, where the first witnesses were physically involved in killing the person ("the hand of the witnesses shall be upon him first"), the words of the second witnesses cannot convict the first witnesses, for the *chiddush* does not extend to having the *words* of the second set of witnesses take precedence over the *words and deeds* of the first set; why, then, should we favor the second set over the first?

More than all the above, it appears that the most logical explanation of this *halachah* is the simple one, that the Torah allowed only a single set of witnesses to be killed, so as not to have the *chiddush* extend too far, for there is no doubt that one set of witnesses must be guiltless. This reason is contained in the view of Bartenura which we brought above, that killing the witnesses after the first person was killed would just lead to repeated bloodshed.

The reason we brought above, that the Torah does not allow witnesses to be killed after the first person was killed so as to preserve respect for the *beis din*, has a basis in *Chazal*, for we find that major prohibitions of the Torah are sometimes violated in order to maintain respect for the *beis din*. Thus, for example, if a *beis din* ruled that a certain person is not a *kohen*, even if it erred, he does not revert to his former status of *kohen*, even though this means that now he might violate Torah prohibition such as marrying a divorcee or becoming ritually impure (*tamei*) by contact with the dead.

◂§ You Were with Us

The law of עֵדִים זוֹמְמִין — "scheming witnesses" — only applies if the second group of witnesses claims, "You (the first witnesses) were with us," thus claiming that the first witnesses were simply lying in testifying that they had seen what they claim to have seen. As opposed to this are עֵדִים מַכְחִישִׁים — "contradictory witnesses" — such as where one group claims that the defendant killed a person whereas the second set claims that someone else was the killer. In the second case, the second set of witnesses cancels out the first, but no set of witnesses is punished. *Chazal* deduce this in *Makkos* 5 from a verse in the Torah. This law, though, requires an explanation. Why should "scheming witnesses" be punished but not "contradictory witnesses"?

Ramban explains that in the case of scheming witnesses, testimony is about the witnesses themselves and not on any specific detail of their testimony. The first set of witnesses is then not believed to say that it is telling the truth, for had the second set of witnesses wished to have them falsely convicted, they could have claimed that the first set killed someone or desecrated Shabbos.

Penei Yehoshua on *Makkos* 5 explains this matter further. Had the second group of witnesses wanted to have the first group convicted, they could have testified against each one of the witnesses separately, claiming for example that each one had desecrated *Shabbos*, rather than testifying that "you both were with us." In such a case, we would have believed the second set of witnesses rather than each individual of the first set of witnesses, for no person is trusted to testify about himself. This explanation is found in *Ramban*, *Chinuch* and Abarbanel.

If the second set of witnesses contradicts the first set, and we don't know whom to believe, we have the one cancel out the other. However, if the testimony of the second group does not relate to the incident itself, but rather to the fundamental possibility that the first set could have witnessed the crime, we believe the second set, just as we would have believed them if they had claimed that the two first witnesses had desecrated Shabbos.

R' David Zvi Hoffmann questions this idea. He asks: What is the difference if the second set of witnesses claims that the first witnesses were with them, or if it would state that the accused or the person killed was with them? In either event, if the testimony of the first group is considered to be testimony about itself, then we should say in the latter case as well, for their testimony is always for their own benefit.

Abarbanel brings another explanation of this *halachah* in the name of *Ran*. It is more logical to accept the testimony of the second set of witnesses which claims that "you were with us," because the first witnesses did what they did under the impression that no one saw them, whereas if the second set was lying, it would be afraid that the first set would bring witnesses from the street in its defense.

R' David Zvi Hoffmann also argues against this logic. The second set will lose nothing if the first set brings witnesses that the first was indeed where the crime took place, because the second set would not face the death penalty unless a third set of witnesses would come and claim about the second set, "you were with us." R' Hoffmann therefore comes up with his own unique interpretation as follows: If the second set of witnesses are liars and wish to save the accused, they have accomplished nothing by saying, "you were with us." After all, they are not contradicting the act itself, and other witnesses may come and testify that the first set of witnesses were indeed where they claimed to have been at the time of the crime, and this way the accused would again be guilty. It would be better for the second set of witnesses to testify that the accused was with them in some other place, and then, even if other witnesses come to testify about the murder, they will not be believed more than this set, because two witnesses are the same as a hundred witnesses. Therefore, when the second set of witnesses claims, "you were with us," it is reasonable to assume that it is telling the truth.

This topic, though, still needs further clarification.

IV.
Those Who Are Exempted from War

The war discussed in our *parashah*, in which various groups of people are sent back from the front for different reasons, is a מִלְחֶמֶת רְשׁוּת — a "voluntary war" (as opposed to מִלְחֶמֶת מִצְוָה — a "*mitzvah* war"). In a *mitzvah* war, there are no exemptions, and every person is required to go to war: "even a bridegroom from his room and bride from her *chuppah*."

Radvaz and other *poskim* see the latter as a symbolic rather than *halachic* statement by *Chazal*, for when the bridegroom goes out of his room, the bride's *chuppah* is automatically terminated, but this does not under any circumstances mean to imply that women go to war. It is possible, says *Radvaz*, that in a *mitzvah* war the women supply food and drink to their husbands at the front.

In the "voluntary war" in our *parashah*, though, not only are women exempt, but so are many classes of men for economic reasons, trepidation, or, according to R' Yose in *Sotah* 44, fear that the sins which they have committed may result in their being injured or killed. These exemptions apply only in a voluntary war, even though the Sanhedrin is the body which makes the decision whether to go to war.

Rambam does not include war to conquer *Eretz Yisrael* in subsequent generations as a *mitzvah* war, for, as *Ramban* explains in his comments on *Sefer HaMitzvos*, *Rambam* does not include this type of war among the 613 *mitzvos*. According to *Rambam*, *Hilchos Melachim* 5:1, there are three types of *mitzvah* war: a) the war against the Seven Nations of Canaan (even the wars of the Chashmona'im [Hasmoneans] would not be included in this category, though they might conceivably be included in the third category below). b) The war against Amalek. c)To save Israel from an enemy attack.

As we mentioned, *Rambam* does not mention a war to conquer *Eretz Yisrael* in the category of *mitzvah* war. Nor does *Ramban* mention a preventive war, "to reduce the heathens in order to prevent them from attacking." There is, in fact, a controversy among *Chazal* (*Sotah* 44) as to whether this type of war is considered to be voluntary or *mitzvah*.

Most of the wars in Israel since the War of Independence have been preventive wars or wars in defense against an enemy attack. The 1973 war was a *mitzvah* war according to all accounts. The status of the War of Independence would be a dispute among the Sages. According to *Ramban*, it would be considered to be a *mitzvah* war, whereas wars to expand the borders of Israel are voluntary wars according to all views.

Below we will discuss the exemptions given in a voluntary war to a considerable number of the prospective soldiers. We generally assume that the exemptions mentioned in the Torah were meant either to make things easier for certain individuals under specific conditions, or to ensure that the morale of the others is not affected by people that are fearful or cowardly, or to ensure that the troops that go out to fight are not sinners, for sinners can bring about evil both upon themselves and upon everyone else, as we will explain below.

Sifri, though, gives a different reason for these exemptions, one to which it is worth paying attention. According to *Sifri*, these exemptions are for the benefit of the hinterland, or the people that stay behind and don't go out to war: "so that the cities of Israel should not be desolate." As *Malbim* explains it, the purpose of this law is to ensure that the cities will be populated, so that the enemy will not be able to launch a surprise attack on these cities and destroy the country.

Oznayim LaTorah, though, explains *Sifri* to be referring to a preventive war, where the object is to prevent the enemy from attacking first by reducing their forces. One should not say, "Why should we provoke the enemy, who will not take pity on us if we fall into his hands, and why should we go to war?" *Sifri* therefore adds: "so that the cities of Israel should not be desolate." If you do not go out to war against the enemy while you still have the power to do so, the enemy will attack you, will destroy your land and leave your cities desolate. Therefore you have no choice but to win. A situation where there is no alternative available gives you no choice but to emerge victorious, as when Yoav saw fighting in front of him and behind him, and exclaimed (*II Shmuel* 10:12), "Be of good courage, for our people, and for the cities of our God."

During the time of the *Beis HaMikdash*, a number of groups of people were exempted from the duty to serve in the army, either for the reason that *Malbim* gave in explaining *Sifri*, or in accordance with the reason given by Abarbanel and other commentators. According to these commentators, by sending away these people, the commanders would boost the morale of those who remained, for they would see how great was the faith of their leaders, who had no compunctions in sending prospective soldiers back to their homes.

In the case of Gideon, in *Shoftim* (7:2), we are told, "The people that are with you are too many." Similarly, with Yehonasan, we read in *I*

Shmuel (14:6), "there is no restraint for Hashem to save by many or by few." While every Jew is commanded to fight Hashem's battles by using natural means, in the end salvation comes from Hashem, regardless of the numbers.

It is interesting that *Rivash* explains the verse, "do not fear" (*Devarim* 20:3), as referring to sending home all those who are exempt. Send all these types of people back, and, in spite of that, deliverance will come.

◅§ To Stand Firm in Battle

The other commentators explain "do not fear" (ibid.) according to the literal meaning of the words. The people must remain strong in waging war and must trust Hashem, as in the words of *Chinuch*: " 'Do not fear.' Each member of Israel must place his trust in Hashem, and not fear for his body, at a time when he can bring glory to Hashem, blessed be He, and His nation."

Rambam, in *Sefer HaMitzvos*, *Negative Mitzvos* 58, states that the commandment, "do not cringe before them" (ibid.), is a לָאו — a negative commandment. *Ramban* disagrees and says that this is merely a promise (i.e., "you will not cringe before them"), but *Ramban* too explains that here we were commanded about two things:

> that their hearts should not be faint and that they should not fear their enemies. Furthermore, they should not trust their own strength to think in their hearts, "we are strong and mighty men of war." Instead, their hearts should be directed only to Hashem, and they should think that (*Tehillim* 147:10), "He does not delight in the strength of the horse: he does not take pleasure in the legs of a man."

The Torah commands us to have faith in Hashem, and to stand steadfast in the field of battle.

The Torah uses four different expressions to tell us the commandment not to fear: "Do not be faint hearted (אַל יֵרַךְ לְבַבְכֶם); do not fear (אַל תִּירְאוּ); and do not panic (וְאַל תַּחְפְּזוּ); and do not cringe before them (וְאַל תַּעַרְצוּ מִפְּנֵיהֶם)." *Rashi*, echoing *Chazal*, explains that this means that one should not be afraid at the noise of war which the enemy produces in four different ways in order to terrify the opposing army.

Ibn Ezra, though, says that these four expressions include not to be afraid in one's heart; not to run away; not to collapse; and that any person "afraid" (ibid. v. 8) to kill or "faint hearted" (ibid.) at the thought of being hurt should "go back to his home" (ibid.).

Ha'amek Davar explains the words "do not be faint hearted" as meaning "do not be afraid to do evil to your enemies when you capture them"; "do not fear" — to take whatever actions are necessary for a soldier to take; "do not panic" — do not act impetuously without thinking, but rather think out your actions in advance; "and do not cringe" — do not be a defeatist by surrendering when you think the situation is not a good one. Later, too, in *Devarim* 31:6, *Ha'amek Davar* explains that "do not fear" and "do not cringe" means not to break the will of the army troop and not to surrender to the enemy, and by the same token not to be overcome by despair. This is a warning to Israel that when a troop feels it is in a situation where it has no alternative except to surrender, it may not do so. *Ha'amek Davar* also deduces from the verse, "he will not melt his brothers' hearts as his heart" (*Devarim* 20:8), that a person is permitted to put his life in danger even though one is generally required to do everything possible to preserve his life. The proof of this is that every voluntary war has an element of mortal danger, and yet in spite of this, the Torah permitted the king of Israel to engage in such a war at will, even though this obviously includes danger to himself and to his nation.

Based on the factors mentioned above, and in accordance with the meaning of the verses, *Rambam* rules in *Hilchos Melachim* 7:15:

> After a person enters into a war, he should trust to Hashem Who saves Israel in its time of distress. He should know that he is waging war for the unity of His name, and he should place his soul in his hand (i.e., he should be willing to risk his life), and should not fear or be afraid. He should not think of his wife or his children, but should erase their memory from his heart. He should forsake every other concern for the war. Whoever begins to think (about such matters) in the war and causes fear in himself is transgressing a negative commandment, as it states (ibid. v. 3), "do not be faint hearted; do not fear; and do not panic; and do not cringe before them." Not only that, but all the blood of Israel depends on him. If he does not emerge victorious and does not fight with all his strength, it is as if he shed the blood of everyone, as it states (ibid. v.8), "he will not melt his brothers' heart as his heart."

In *Yad HaChazakah* as in *Sefer HaMitzvos*, *Rambam* regards not to become afraid in the war and not to think of anything but the victory as a negative commandment. *Rambam* explains these verses as a religious and national obligation; that one must fight with all his strength and dedication, even in a מִלְחֶמֶת רְשׁוּת, a voluntary war.

≈§ "He Shall Speak to the People"

Before the soldiers are to go out to fight, they are addressed by the כֹּהֵן
מְשׁוּחַ מִלְחָמָה — the "kohen anointed for the battle" — who offers them
words of inspiration and encouragement. Chinuch says that at the time
of war, the soldiers need encouragement, and as people will generally
pay more attention to an important person, the Torah commanded that
the person to offer the inspirational message should be a kohen, who is
of the chosen group within Israel.

According to Ha'amek Davar, the kohen must use not only the text
given in the Torah, but must add inspirational words of his own, this,
according to Ha'amek Davar, being a special commandment in the
Torah: "He shall speak to the people" (ibid. 20:2). Thus, the kohen must
offer a warning to the soldiers to be especially careful not to commit any
sins at the time that they are in danger and when the Ark is in their
midst, and must give other such words of encouragement and
admonition, based on the circumstances at the time.

But even the text prescribed by the Torah to be recited by the kohen
contains words of emunah — "faith" — coupled with encouragement
and inspiration. The kohen begins by saying, "Hear O Israel" (ibid. v.3),
that being the proclamation of the Oneness of Hashem (ibid. 6:4). Thus,
according to R' Samson Raphael Hirsch, the kohen must instill emunah
in the soldiers, so that they should place their trust in Hashem. (Rabbenu
Bachya has a similar comment, when he states that "it is through the
merit of 'Hear O Israel,' this being the secret of [Hashem's] unity, that
they emerge victorious.")

In Sotah 42, R' Shimon bar Yochai states that the kohen tells the
people that even if all they did was to recite the Shema every morning
and evening, they will not fall victim to their enemies. Maharatz Chajes
explains that R' Shimon bar Yochai's statement is in keeping with his
view in Menachos 99, that even if a person only says the Shema in the
morning and evening, he has fulfilled the obligation of (Yehoshua 1:8),
"This Book of the Torah shall not depart out of your mouth."

One is forced to say that R' Shimon bar Yochai's view disagrees with
that of R' Yose HaGelili, for R' Yose states that one who is afraid
because of the sins he has committed should return home from the battle
front, and, as Chazal tell us, according to R' Yose this category would
include even a person who speaks between putting on the tefillin of the
arm and that of the head. According to R' Shimon bar Yochai, on the
other hand, the saying of the Shema alone is enough to protect the
warriors.

An alternate interpretation of R' Shimon's statement is that he is referring to the battlefront itself, and once they are there, the soldiers are protected by saying the *Shema* twice a day.

Chazal also interpret the other statements of the *kohen* as both offering encouragement and inspiring *emunah* among the soldiers. A full description of what the *kohen* is to say and its inspirational meaning is to be found in *Sotah* 42-44. Each verse is meant to instill a spirit of bravery in the soldiers so that they will fight valiantly and will not allow themselves to be taken prisoner.

Abarbanel sees three basic themes by which the *kohen* inspires the army before the battle: a) He instills a sense of national pride in the soldiers. People that are not proud of their country run away from the battle, but you, "Hear O Israel!" (ibid. 20:3) you are the valiant fighters for Hashem, for you have battled with an angel and with man (this last allusion is to what the angel told Yaakov after their battle, when he renamed him Israel — *Bereishis* 32:28). You are perfectly suited to do battle, in order to honor your past and your glory. b) "Today you are approaching battle" (*Devarim* 20:3). You yourselves chose this fate. You decided, of your own good will, to go and fight. It is therefore proper for you to honor that decision that you took, and do not retreat or fear anyone. c) "Today you are approaching battle *against your enemies*" (ibid.). Your enemy will not pity you if he captures you, as *Chazal* tell us in *Sotah*:

> "Against your enemies" and not "against your brothers." This is not a battle of Yehudah against Shimon or Shimon against Yehudah, where, if you fall into their hands, they will take pity on you. You are going against your enemies, and if you fall into their hands they will not pity.

There are innumerable interpretations of the words of the *kohen*, all of which explain how it is his task to instill courage and bravery in the troops, and primarily to instill *emunah* in them so that they should know that Hashem is fighting for them so as to have their enemies fall by the sword, and to ensure that every single one is saved, and none should fall. This is the way *Ramban* explains the verse (*Devarim* 20:4), "For Hashem your God is He that goes with you, to fight for you against your enemies, to save you."

⋙ The Declarations and the Exemptions

After the *kohen* has finished offering his inspirational message to the soldiers, the various exemptions are announced: for a man who has built a house and not yet dedicated it, has planted a vineyard and not yet enjoyed its fruits, betrothed a woman (*eirusin*) but has not yet consummated the marriage (*nisu'in*). This declaration is made by the *kohen*, and is then repeated by an officer (*shoteir*). Afterwards (*Devarim* 20:8), "the officers shall speak further unto the people, and they shall say, 'What man is there that is fearful and faint hearted? Let him go and return unto his house.'" This last declaration is made by an officer and is then repeated by another officer.

The difference between the two declarations is that the first permits a person to complete a task which he has begun (building a house, reaping the crops of a vineyard, etc.), the reason for this, according to R' David Zvi Hoffmann, being that the Torah values the rights of the individual above that of the community. This general declaration of the Torah policy is made by the *kohen*. The second declaration, on the other hand, which caters to those people who are overcome by their fears, is not given by the *kohen* but by an officer.

The above interpretation is not in keeping with that of *Rashbam*, *Ramban*, Rabbenu Bachya and other commentators, who explain the meaning of the words of the Torah, "lest he die in battle (... and another man will dedicate the house" — ibid. v. 5) as fear, as the person is afraid that he will lose his home, his vineyard or his wife. According to these commentators, though, the question arises as to what difference there is between the first declaration and the second. R' David Zvi Hoffmann asks, correctly, why the Torah uses the expression, "speak further" (וְיָסְפוּ — ibid. v. 8), when the two are so similar. It is also strange that these *rishonim* do not accept the interpretation of *Sifri* on "lest he die in battle," namely, that he may have sinned and may therefore not be worthy of completing his deeds, as is mentioned among the curses listed in *Vayikra* Chapter 26 and *Devarim* Chapter 28; if this is so, he may adversely affect his brothers as well.

Abarbanel has a different interpretation. It is unreasonable to think that a person will be concerned about what will happen to his house or vineyard after his death. Rather, the reason for the Torah's allowing people in the first category to return is because it wished to allow them to finish the *mitzvah* which they have begun. A person who builds a house, for example, is required to put a מַעֲקֶה — "parapet" — around the roof (ibid. 22:8). One who plants a vineyard can be מְחַלֵּל it in the forth year (he may take the crops of the fourth year and redeem them with money, after which the money is used to buy food in Yerushalayim), so that that marks the completion of the vineyard. Similarly, a man who marries must fulfill the *mitzvah* to "be fruitful and multiply" (*Bereishis* 1:28, 9:1). These people are sent home lest they die and do not complete the *mitzvah* which they have begun. The person is distressed that he has not completed the *mitzvah*, and that is why he is commanded by the Torah to return home and complete it.

The concept of being sent home because of fear is also not the same among the commentators. According to R' Akiva in *Sotah*, this is taken literally, as a person who is afraid to go to war. According to R' Yose, though, this refers to a person who is afraid because of the sins which he has committed.

It is interesting that *Sifri* and *Yerushalmi* require a person wishing to be exempted from battle to bring witnesses to corroborate his statements, and, according to R' Yose, this means to bring witnesses that he has sinned.

Rambam rules that the *halachah* is in accordance with R' Akiva, and totally ignores R' Yose's opinion that "fear" means fear of the sins the person may have committed. *Rambam* also differs from the other commentators in that the declarations about exemptions are made twice: a) before they cross the border b) after they are arrayed for battle in the field. What forced *Rambam* to explain this differently from *Sifri* and the other commentators, who say there was only one declaration, at the time that they crossed the border? *Rambam* evidently had a source that we do not have. The commentators on *Rambam* deal with this question at great length. There are those who say that the source is to be found in accordance with what *Tosefta* says in *Sotah* 7:10: "What does he say at the border? that he should go and hear the words of the *kohen*." According to this, the soldiers are given advance preparation by being told at the border that they will be going to the battlefield, where the *kohen* will announce the various types of exemptions.

Ki Seitzei – כי תצא

I.

A Double Portion to the Firstborn

The law of giving one's firstborn a double portion in his inheritance is not found in the Torah until this point, where it is introduced regarding a man who has two wives, one of whom he loves and the other whom he hates (*Devarim* 21:15-17). According to Abarbanel, we find a hint to this law in a number of places in the Torah. Thus, for example, in *Parashas Vayechi* we are told that Yaakov told Yosef (*Bereishis* 48:22), "I have given you one portion above your brothers," as a result of the birthright having been taken from Reuven and given to Yosef. We also find this hinted at in regard to the daughters of Tzelafchad, according to the interpretation of *Chazal*. It states in *Bamidbar* 27:7, 'you shall surely give them a possession of an inheritance among their father's brothers," which, as *Rashi* explains, refers to the standard portion that their father inherited, while the second part of the verse, "and you shall cause the inheritance of their father to pass unto them," refers to their father's birthright portion.

According to Abarbanel, our *parashah* simply comes to tell us that not only in the case of a single wife is one forbidden to transfer the birthright to a son who is not the firstborn, but this is even true with two wives, and even if one of the wives is beloved and the other is hated. It is interesting that *Tosefes Berachah* here also discusses the fact that the Torah is referring to the firstborn receiving a double portion as if it were a well-known law; yet *Tosefes Berachah* does not mention Abarbanel's comments on this point.

Ramban in *Parashas Vayeishev* (*Bereishis* 38:5) states that the law of *yibum* (i.e., that if a man dies childless, his brother marries his deceased brother's wife) was also in effect before the giving of the Torah.

There are other places where the Torah merely alludes to a *halachah* incidentally. Thus we find in *Parashas Mishpatim* (*Sh'mos* 21:4), "If his master has given him a wife," teaching that a Hebrew slave can be given a non-Jewish female slave as a wife. Similarly we find (ibid. v. 9), "If he has betrothed her unto his son," which teaches that purchasing a female Jewish slave gives marriage rights to her owner or his son (i.e., either of them may marry her using her purchase price as the betrothal gift). Similarly, it states (ibid. 22:16), "he shall pay money according to the dowry of virgins," which shows that there was a fixed dowry amount which was well known. The same applies to the *get* that a husband gives his wife if he divorces her. The Torah never states what this is exactly, but it merely states (*Devarim* 24:1), "He will write her a bill of divorcement." According to *Tosefes Berachah* the same is true for the double portion which the firstborn receives. This law was known and practiced even before the Torah was given, and here the Torah simply comes to reinforce and affirm the law.

Abarbanel explains that the special right of the firstborn to his father's property is related to the superiority granted to the firstborn by the Torah in general. Hashem is the Prime Cause of all, and that is why the Torah treats the first of everything as important. Thus, it commanded that the first of everything be consecrated to Hashem, including the first dough, the first shearing, etc., and the special rights granted by the Torah to the firstborn also come to stress this principle.

Abarbanel also gives a simpler explanation. The firstborn takes the place of his father. It is as if he proclaims to his parents that there is continuity in the family. Because of their joy, the parents award their firstborn son additional rights.

Chizkuni has an interesting, but also surprising, explanation for the preference given to the firstborn with the birthright. Originally, the firstborn were not to be given any portion in the land, because they were meant to serve Hashem (the position later taken over by the *kohanim* and Levites). After this right was taken from the firstborn and Hashem commanded that the Levites were not to receive a portion for their tribe in *Eretz Israel*, their birthright went over to the firstborn, and thus the firstborn take a double portion — their own portion and that of the Levites.

The Gaon of Brashov asks a question on this interpretation. If that is so, why do the firstborn deserve double? At the outset, they were not supposed to receive any land. Afterwards, they received the portion of the Levites, but that was just one portion, and not a double portion. He leaves the question unanswered.

Ba'al HaTurim finds an interesting hint in the Torah to show that the firstborn gets a double portion. In the Torah, the word for "firstborn" is written as בְּכֹר. Each of these letters represents a double: ב is twice 1, כ is twice 10, and ר is twice 100.

◆§ Is It a Negative and Positive Mitzvah or only a Positive One?

According to *Rambam* in *Sefer HaMitzvos*, *Mitzvah* 248, there is only a positive *mitzvah* here, as stated in the verse (*Devarim* 21:17), "he shall acknowledge the son of the hated" [as firstborn], but the previous verse, "he cannot make the son of the beloved the firstborn," is not a negative *mitzvah*.

Ramban, on the other hand, holds that the latter verse is a negative *mitzvah*, and a person who does not give his firstborn the birthright transgresses both a positive and a negative *mitzvah*.

Sifri appears to follow the view that it is only a positive *mitzvah*. Thus *Sifri* states:

> "He cannot make the son of the beloved the firstborn." He cannot [do so], but one might imagine that if he does so then it is valid. It therefore states "he cannot make the son of the beloved the firstborn"; if he did so, it is not valid.

Malbim explains *Sifri* above, in that there is a difference between stating "he shall not make him the firstborn," and the way the Torah actually writes it, which is, "he cannot make [him] the firstborn." According to *Sifri*, even if the father takes such a step, the step has no meaning.

It would seem that the above is in accordance with the view of Abaye, who holds that if the Torah forbids a person (by a negative *mitzvah*) to take a certain action, and he then proceeds to take that action, the action is valid. We thus need a special verse to tell us that in this particular case, unlike under general conditions, the father's action has no effect, and the oldest son still receives the birthright. According to *Rava*, though, who holds that if a person takes an action forbidden by Torah law his action is not valid, the verse above seems superfluous, because in any event the father's decision would not take effect. From this, *Malbim* proves that *Sifri* holds that there is no negative *mitzvah* involved here, but only a positive one, as

Rambam stated. That is why the Torah must inform us that if the father takes such a step, it has no validity.

Ramban in our *parashah*, following in the footsteps of *Targum Onkelos*, states that the words לֹא יוּכַל (translated above as "he cannot") implies a negative *mitzvah*, just as in other verses which use this same Hebrew construction, as for example (ibid. 12:17), "You may not eat the tithe of your wheat within your gates," and (ibid. 17:15), "You may not set a stranger over you." This expression is meant to stress that under no circumstances should one permit oneself to perform these actions.

The Torah links this prohibition in our *parashah* to the case of a man having two wives, one of whom he loves and the other whom he hates. According to *Sifri*, the Torah teaches us, incidentally, דֶּרֶךְ אֶרֶץ — "proper behavior."

According to R' David Zvi Hoffmann, the דֶּרֶךְ אֶרֶץ that is being taught here is that the Torah is not pleased with a man taking two wives, even though as far as *halachah* is concerned this is permissible. Thus we have here a hint at the *takkanah* — "decree" — of Rabbenu Gershom Me'or HaGolah against marrying more than one wife.

Ba'alei HaTosafos and Abarbanel, on the other hand, state that what the Torah wished to stress here was the progression that will occur if a man marries a *yefas to'ar*, a gentile woman captured in war, even though under certain circumstances this action is permitted by *halachah*. From this we see, says *Midrash Tanchuma*, and this is repeated in our *parashah* by the *Ba'alei HaTosafos*, that עֲבֵרָה גוֹרֶרֶת עֲבֵרָה — one sin draws another in its wake. Taking a *yefas to'ar* results in a person having more than one wife. As a result, there is strife in the house.

Abarbanel sees an even greater punishment here. This *yefas to'ar* will be "hated," and in the end, "the firstborn son will be born from the hated one." The firstborn son will be a rebellious one, and his father will try to transfer the birthright to another son, but he won't be able to do so, and will regret his whole life that it is this son who will receive the double portion.

Abarbanel goes on to state that it is just in this case, where one of a man's wives is hated by him, that Hashem will give her the firstborn, as we see in the verse (*Bereishis* 29:31), "Hashem saw that Leah was hated, and He opened her womb," giving her Reuven, the firstborn.

Or HaChayim also explains the verse categorically, that the firstborn son will be born to the wife that is hated.

The source of both of these is *Sifri*, that states, "The Torah is telling us that the firstborn son will be that of the hated wife." *Sifri* deduces this from the fact that the Torah states (*Devarim* 21:15), וְהָיָה ("the firstborn son *will be* to the hated one"), and not וְאִם יִהְיֶה — "*if* the firstborn son will be ..." Thus we see that the Torah is telling us of the progression of events which will occur. In spite of this (ibid. v. 16), "he cannot make the son of the beloved the firstborn." In this case, we can understand quite clearly why the Torah gives a negative commandment and prohibits the father to transfer the birthright to the son of the beloved wife; for the birth of the firstborn to the hated wife is a punishment for hating her. Therefore he is forbidden to perpetuate this hatred and use the punishment itself as another expression of his preference for the other wife.

There are commentators, such as *Da'as Zekeinim MiBa'alei HaTosafos* and *S'forno*, who are astonished at Yaakov, who was not concerned about this prohibition and transferred the birthright from Reuven, the son of the hated wife, Leah, to Yosef, the son of the beloved wife, Rachel. *S'forno* states that one is forbidden to transfer the birthright from one son to another only if the reason for doing so is that one hates the mother of the firstborn, but is permitted to do so if the reason is that the firstborn sinned. Thus, in the case of Reuven, the Torah explains that Yaakov did so not out of hatred of Leah, but (*I Divrei HaYamim* 5:1), "because he desecrated his father's bed, his birthright was given to the sons of Yosef the son of Yisrael."

Abarbanel holds that Yaakov did what he did at Hashem's command, but without such a command one is forbidden to transfer the birthright from the firstborn to another son. According to Abarbanel, it is also possible that when the Torah in our *parashah* mentioned the beloved and hated wife, it was meant to teach us that Yaakov's case was a one-time occurrence, based on Hashem's command, but other people cannot act that way in similar circumstances.

✑§ During the Lifetime of the Firstborn

Ramban on our *parashah* states that when the Torah tells us (*Devarim* 21:16), "he cannot make the son of the beloved the firstborn before (עַל פְּנֵי) the son of the hated," this only applies if the firstborn is still alive, because the phrase עַל פְּנֵי always is used in reference to a person who is alive, such as (*Bamidbar* 3:4) "in the sight of (עַל פְּנֵי) Aharon their father." So too do we find (*Bereishis* 11:28), "Haran died before (עַל פְּנֵי) his father Terach." Therefore, says *Ramban*, it appears to him that this law applies only as long as the firstborn is alive, but if the firstborn son died before his father, even though his (the firstborn's) sons would by law inherit his double portion in his father's estate, the father has the right to determine that the double portion will go to another grandson.

In *Sefer HaMitzvos*, Ramban does not repeat this law. *Tur* also interprets the Torah this way, but does not bring any such *halachah* in his *Arba'ah Turim*. On the other hand, *Ketzos HaChoshen* 281 states that this is the *halachah*.

R' Chavel, in his commentary on *Ramban*, brings proof to *Ramban's* view from *Minei Targima*. *Chazal* in *Bava Basra* 126 state: "One who says, 'so-and-so is my firstborn son, but he may not take a double portion' ... he has said nothing" (i.e., his statement has no validity). *Chazal* here stress, "my firstborn son," and do not state, "so-and-so who is a firstborn." We can conclude from this that this law applies only to "my firstborn son" specifically, but not to "my grandson," the implication being that if he wants to exclude his grandson, son of his firstborn, from receiving a double portion, he has the ability to do so.

Many, though, are puzzled by *Ramban's* proof based on the words עַל פְּנֵי, for not everyone agrees that the verse, "in the sight of (עַל פְּנֵי) Aharon their father," means that Aharon was alive. That is the view of only R' Yitzchak in *Bamidbar Rabbah*, the end of Chapter 2, but R' Chiyye bar Abba says there, "after his death." Thus we see that there is a dispute about whether עַל פְּנֵי refers to a person who is alive or whether it is a reference to one who is dead, and one cannot, therefore, reach a decision regarding *halachah* from that source.

On the other hand, *Divrei Shaul* brings support, through a hint, to *Ramban*, in that it states in regard to Esav (*Bereishis* 25:32), "I am going to die, and what use is the birthright for me?" We see from this that if Esav would die, there would not be any guarantee that his son would receive the birthright, and that was why Esav despised the birthright and sold it to Yaakov.

Using this principle laid down by *Ramban*, that once the firstborn dies, his father can assign the birthright of the grandsons whichever way he feels, *Torah Temimah* answers the question raised above as to how Yaakov transferred the birthright from Reuven to Yosef. This transfer referred to receiving a double portion in *Eretz Israel*. At the time that *Eretz Israel* was divided up at the time of Yehoshua, Reuven was no longer alive, and thus Yaakov had the right to transfer Reuven's double portion as he desired. This is what the Torah stresses in the verse (*I Divrei HaYamim* 5:1), "because he desecrated his father's bed, his birthright was given to the sons of Yosef," namely, that the transfer was not from Reuven to Yosef, but from Reuven's sons to Yosef's, after the brothers were already dead, and according to *Ramban* that is permitted.

Torah Temimah nevertheless remains with an unanswered question in regard to *Ramban*, as to whether a person may transfer the birthright of his firstborn while the firstborn is still alive, provided the actual transfer is to take place after the firstborn dies, as was the case with the transfer of the birthright from Reuven to Yosef.

A comment is made in the name of *Gra* on the verse (*Devarim* 21:15), "if ... they have born him children, the beloved [wife] and the hated [wife]." On this, *Gra* points out that the Torah mentions the beloved as being the first to give birth. Why then is the son of the hated wife the firstborn? From this, *Gra* (as brought in *Divrei Eliyahu*) concludes that the child who was the first conceived, even if he was not the first one born, is considered the firstborn. Thus, the Torah is referring to a case where the hated wife was the first to conceive, but the son of the beloved wife was born first, because the hated wife gave birth in the ninth month, while the beloved wife gave birth in the seventh month. (R' Zvi Domb, *shlita*, chief rabbi of Hod Hasharon, pointed out that *Divrei Shaul* 3:52 disproves this statement alleged to have said by *Gra*, and shows that the birth is what counts toward the birthright.)

Ha'amek Davar states that he heard this statement in the name of *Gra*, but does not believe that *Gra* said it. The law is the opposite: The firstborn depends on the date of birth, regardless of the date of conception. *Ha'amek Davar* goes on to say that this also explains why the Torah states (ibid.), "If a man has two wives, *the* one (הָאַחַת) beloved, and *the* other (וְהָאַחַת) hated," rather than merely stating "one (אַחַת) beloved, and one (אַחַת) hated." This shows that the husband did not marry both at the same time. Rather, he married the beloved one first and the hated one later. Even though the beloved wife conceived first, she gave birth after nine months, while the hated one gave birth after seven months, so that hers was the first child born. The law is nevertheless that the child born first has the birthright, because it goes by birth, not conception.

It would appear that this is an ancient dispute. Ibn Ezra on the verse (ibid. v. 17), רֵאשִׁית אֹנוֹ (literally "his first strength"), indicates that it is the first conception which counts. *HaKesav VeHaKabalah*, though, shows that רֵאשִׁית אֹנוֹ refers to the first child born, and the meaning of the expression here is not the same as in *Bereishis* 49:3.

◦§ The Firstborn to the Hated Wife

The Torah (*Devarim* 21:15) uses the word לַשְׂנִיאָה ("to the hated one") with a *yud* rather than לַשְׂנוּאָה with a *vav*. *Ha'amek Davar* explains this according to the simple meaning of the verse, that this woman is not hated for herself, but that the first wife *made the second hated* (הִשְׂנִיאָה) by her husband; that is why the first did not give birth to the firstborn.

Chazal, though, say that this woman was hated in her own right, and this refers to a woman that a man was forbidden to marry under a לָאו — "a negative *mitzvah*." (Certain women, such as close blood relatives, are forbidden to be married under a prohibition of *kares*, and even if a man attempts to marry a woman in this category there is no valid marriage. Other women, such as a divorcee to a *kohen*, are forbidden by a לָאו, and in such a case the marriage, though forbidden, is valid. — trans.) This is the language of *Chazal* in *Kiddushin* 68: "Can there then be a beloved wife before Hashem and a hated wife before Hashem?" As *Rashi* explains it:

> Is the love or hatred of the husband important to Hashem that the Torah had to write (ibid. v. 16), "he cannot make the son of the beloved the firstborn before the son of the hated"? Rather, this refers to a woman who is beloved in her marriage — i.e., of a permitted marriage — and a hated wife is one hated in her marriage — i.e., a forbidden marriage. On this the Torah states (ibid. v. 15), "If a man has," which teaches that where the prohibition is one for which the penalty is lashes — i.e., a לָאו — the marriage is valid.

One would imagine that one can ask a question on this *gemara* from another *gemara* in *Bava Basra* 130:

> One who says, regarding a person who is entitled to inherit him, that that person will inherit everything instead of the other heirs, his statement is valid. So too with a person who transfers his inheritance from his son to his daughter, his statement is valid.

Here we see that if a person transfers his inheritance because of personal love or hatred, his action is valid, implying that the love or hatred of the father is indeed "important to Hashem." This question, though, does not undermine the words of *Chazal*, because the transfer of the birthright of the firstborn is forbidden by the Torah, and of course the fact that the father hates his firstborn is not enough to enable him to invalidate that law. Therefore the Torah must have mentioned the "hatred" for some other reason. From this, *Chazal* deduced that the Torah wishes to tell us that even though the marriage is "hated" — i.e., forbidden by a לָאו, nevertheless it is valid.

Chasam Sofer states that the deduction by *Chazal* that this is referring to a hated woman because of a prohibited marriage is due to the fact that the Torah mentions a beloved and a hated wife. As the Torah is dealing with the transfer of the birthright, why did it need to bring in the concepts of "beloved" and "hated"? The reason for this must be because the Torah wished to teach us a new law, that one is forbidden to transfer the birthright from a firstborn that one hates, and even if the hatred is the result of a sin. *Chazal* tell us in *Kesubos* 53: "One may not transfer the birthright from a bad son to a good son, because he (i.e., the bad son) may have good children." Here, however, where the son is hated because of a prohibited marriage, all future generations of the man's children will have the same hated status, and thus no good children will come out of future generations. One might therefore have said that in such a case one is permitted to transfer the birthright. The Torah therefore tells us that one is not able to transfer the birthright even in such a case.

II.

The Punishment of the
בֵּן סוֹרֵר וּמוֹרֶה — The Rebellious Son

The whole topic of the בֵּן סוֹרֵר וּמוֹרֶה, the rebellious son, adds a new direction to the ethics of the Torah. We are taught that a person should not only be judged based on his actions, but also on the results of his actions, or the influence of his actions on the community.

R' David Zvi Hoffmann wishes to relate this law to the law of honoring one's father and mother. According to *Chazal*, even though the rebellious son's parents do play a role in punishing him because he disobeyed what they told him, they are nevertheless limited to complaining about his gluttony and excessive drinking. The actions for which the son is punished no doubt involve humiliation of his parents; *Ramban* mentions this aspect as well.

The Torah gives the father and mother the right to punish the son, or to forgive him. This is an indication that this matter relates directly to them. In reality, though, the sin for which the son is punished involves other matters as well in which the aspect of honoring one's father and mother is almost invisible. It appears, as we will explain below, that this law is related to the question of educating the son, which the father and mother are commanded to do, but the terrible punishment imposed on the son is extraordinary within this framework, and there are other elements involved as well.

Very few of the commentators have analyzed all the aspects involved in this striking law. In any event, this is one of the *mitzvos* of the Torah which teaches us new concepts in morals and education. It is true that *Chazal* and the *poskim* noted numerous limitations in the enforcement of this law, but in spite of these limitations, according to the *poskim* this law was an actual one.

There are opinions in *Chazal* (*Sanhedrin* 71) that the case of the rebellious son never occurred and will never occur, and the purpose of having it in the Torah is to learn the *halachah* and receive a reward for doing so. According to R' Yehudah, this law cannot ever be carried out in practice, as, according to him, the mother must be identical to the father in voice, appearance and height. And of course that is simply impossible. R' Shimon, too, holds that such a case never occurred and will never occur. According to R' Shimon, though, this is not because of a limitation in reality, but because it is so unlikely: "Is it just because he ate a *tartimar* of meat and drank a *log* of Italian wine that his father and mother will take him out to stone him?" R' Shimon cannot imagine a case where the father and mother will arrange to have their son stoned. According to R' Shimon, though, the Torah does grant the father and mother permission to carry out the law in all its severity.

Yet R' Shimon's statement seems puzzling. Granted that all the boy did was eat some meat and drink some wine, but *Chazal* state: "the Torah penetrated to the ultimate plan of the rebellious son, who, after disposing of all his father's possessions and not finding more, will go to the road junction and rob people." Why then does R' Shimon minimize the sin of the rebellious son? The answer appears to be that while R' Shimon sees the theoretical possibility of this law being enforced and the logic behind its enforcement in terms of avoiding future sin, he cannot imagine that the father and mother will implement the law, and it is they who must be the ones to bring the charges. As a result, R' Shimon sees this *parashah* as serving to teach the parents their obligations, so that they should understand to what extent they have the obligation to educate their children. Thus the parents will not reach a stage where there is a conflict between their ethical obligations and their love for their children. This *parashah* is meant as a warning to the parents, so that they should realize what the end of their child will be if they do not give him the proper upbringing. If the parents understand the nature of this warning, they will be rewarded for educating their children properly in Torah and in *Yiras Shamayim*.

Indeed, *Maharsha* in his commentary on the *aggadah* portion of *Sanhedrin*, writing on R' Shimon's statement, follows along these same lines:

> It is clear that, according to R' Shimon, the Torah required the death penalty for [the rebellious son's actions], for the Torah penetrated into the ultimate plan [of the son], as it states later. However, what [R' Shimon] says is that the parents will never be able to fathom [their son's] ultimate plan, and will take pity on him and not have him taken out to be stoned for a single *tartimar*. Why then was this [*parashah*] written? so as "to study it and receive a reward," meaning that *the parents* should study the *parashah* and realize that the Torah fathomed such a son's ultimate plans, and that such a son is worthy of being stoned. This is as it states: "What *zechus* — "merit" — do women have? It is that they raise their sons to study Torah."

Rabbenu Bachya introduced another educational principle on this topic. According to those who state that there was never a case of a rebellious son who was stoned under this law, the Torah wishes to teach us how much love of Hashem a person must have, even to the extent of being willing to sacrifice his son on the altar of love of Hashem. There is no greater love than that of a parent for a child, but here we see that that love must be suppressed when it comes in conflict with love of Hashem. This is the lesson that we must "study and receive a reward for" in this *parashah*. From that point of view, says Rabbenu Bachya, this *parashah* resembles that of the *akeidah* — Avraham's bringing Yitzchak to be sacrificed, and the two have a common conclusion, the conclusion being only an educational one, for in fact Hashem did not allow Avraham to sacrifice Yitzchak, but taught him how far the love of Hashem must extend.

Kli Yakar holds that "study it and receive a reward" refers here to the sons, and not to the parents. The Torah wanted the sons to hear the *parashah*, so that they would be afraid of descending into gluttony and alcoholism. That is why in this *parashah* it states, "and all of Israel will hear and be afraid," (*Devarim* 21:21) and, unlike other *parashiyos*, does not go on to state, "and they will not sin any more" (ibid. 17:13). The purpose of this *parashah* is so that the sons should hear and draw the necessary educational conclusions. The fact is, though, that such a case never occurred, and will never occur.

The above, of course, is in accordance with the Sages who hold that the entire *parashah* was only written so that one can "study it and receive a reward." R' Yonasan, on the other hand, testified that he himself had been at the grave of a rebellious son. The Mishnah, too, holds that it is entirely possible that this law will be enforced, and that a son will be killed because of what he will eventually turn out to be if left alive now. As the Mishnah says, "Let him die blameless rather than to die guilty."

Rambam, too, and the others who give lists of the 613 *mitzvos* place this law as one of the 613, and *Rambam* even has chapters in *Hilchos Mamerim* to clarify the laws involved and the way the law is to be carried out.

R' Simchah Zissel of Kelm, in his *Or RaShaZ*, explains here the great importance of the *mitzvah* of educating one's children in the Torah ways. If a person killed someone but there were no eyewitnesses, that person is not killed, whereas a rebellious son is killed because of the fact that in the future he will become a highway robber. The Torah gave the parents full authority in such a case. They have the right to hand the son over to be killed, so as to fulfill the *mitzvah* of educating one's children.

The obligation to educate one's child appears in our *parashah* as a supreme value. The parents have the right not to hand their son over, but by the same token they have the right to insist that the law be enforced. Thus all of Israel should hear and fear how great this obligation is.

◆§ The Individual for the Community

This terrible punishment, based on the obligation to educate one's children, has resulted in interpretations by many commentators. *Sifri* extends the meaning of the words סוֹרֵר וּמוֹרֶה, stating that the son turns away from (סוֹרֵר) the Torah, and is opposed to (מוֹרֶה) the words of the prophets.

Ibn Ezra, too, explains that the סוֹרֵר וּמוֹרֶה "is against Hashem and against his fathers, if they feared Hashem." According to Ibn Ezra, סוֹרֵר implies that the son does not keep the positive *mitzvos*, while מוֹרֶה implies that he violates the negative ones. Later on, Ibn Ezra defines the סוֹרֵר וּמוֹרֶה as a heretic, who seeks only the pleasures of this world.

Abarbanel too describes the סוֹרֵר וּמוֹרֶה as turning aside (סָר) from the proper path, and teaching (מוֹרֶה) others how to sin, and showing (מוֹרֶה) them his crimes.

All of these explanations, though, are not in accordance with the *halachah*, which defines the sin of the סוֹרֵר וּמוֹרֶה as eating a specified amount of meat and drinking a specified amount of wine which he stole from his father's house and consumed elsewhere, in a way which would get him used to a wanton life. Thus we see that the only reason for which the son can be punished is for his eating and drinking, and in accordance with the view of the Sages that he will eventually come to robbing people at the highway junctions.

One can still ask about this law, for the *halachah* is that a person who kills another is killed by סַיִף — "the sword" — whereas the rebellious son is killed by stoning. If the son is killed now for the fact that he will eventually be a murderer, why isn't the penalty that of סַיִף? None of the commentators has found a simple answer to this question. *Tosafos* holds that the son is stoned because that is the punishment he would have received had he cursed his father or mother. *Rosh* and *Chizkuni* hold that the son will rob people on *Shabbos* as well, and therefore he receives the same punishment as a person who desecrates *Shabbos*. *Maharsha* holds that *Chazal* did not mean that the person will necessarily be a highway robber, but that he will commit various serious crimes whose punishment is stoning, and that is why he receives this most severe of all punishments. In any event, the Torah considers the rebellious son, who has committed a relatively small crime, as eventually coming to commit the most serious crimes. He is not given this punishment, however, until he was caught once, was lashed, and then repeated the offense.

With all of this, the severe punishment that the rebellious son receives evokes various thoughts among the commentators. *HaKesav VeHaKabalah* explains that when the Torah states here, "you shall destroy the evil from your midst" (*Devarim* 21:21), it is an explanation of the severity of the punishment. Evil will spread and expand unchecked, unless one nips it in the bud.

(As a general rule, whenever the Torah wishes to impose a punishment for an act, there are two references to that act, one of them known as the אַזְהָרָה — the "warning" — where the Torah states that the act is forbidden, and another the עֹנֶשׁ — stating the punishment to be received if one violates the law. — trans.) *Chinuch* explains the severity of the punishment for eating and drinking in accordance with the view of *Chazal*, that the warning to the rebellious son is contained in the verse, "you shall not eat on the blood" (*Vayikra* 19:26). In *Mitzvah* 248, *Chinuch* states that the prohibition contained in this verse is meant to tell us that one should not be a glutton and a drunkard when one is a youth, under the conditions outlined for the rebellious son. According to him, the source of the *mitzvah* is that most sins are committed as a result of excessive eating and drinking, as in the verse (*Devarim* 32:15), "Yeshurun waxed fat and rebelled," and in the same verse: "You became fat, thick, bejowled; and he abandoned the God Who made him."

Chazal, too, said: "filling the belly is an evil deviation" (מָלֵי כְּרֵסֵהּ זִינֵי בִּישֵׁי), meaning that a full belly will bring people to commit serious sins. The explanation for this is that food is the sustenance of the body, while contemplation about the soul and about the *mitzvos* are the sustenance of the soul, and the body and soul are complete opposites of one another. Therefore, when the material predominates, the spiritual is somewhat weakened. That is why there were numerous sages who ate only exactly what was necessary. That is also why the Torah stresses that one should not indulge in excessive food and drink, for this can result in the soul becoming sick and eventually being lost. And that is also why the Torah warned us so strenuously in the case of the rebellious son, and imposed the death penalty. Furthermore, the Torah warns the young man about the severity involved at the very outset of his adult life, just as he is entering the first three months of puberty and begins to be obligated to guard his soul. That is why the law of the rebellious son applies only for the first three months after the young man becomes an adult *halachically*. The intention is to have the young man learn a moral lesson that will last him the rest of his life. Since food is a constant need throughout man's life, and he cannot live without it, the Torah did not make him liable for this *mitzvah* throughout his entire life. Instead, it teaches him the moral lesson at the first opportunity, so that it will govern his behavior at all times.

According to *Chinuch*, this *mitzvah* comes to teach us not to indulge too much in the material, and not to eat or drink excessively. In order to teach us this lesson, the Torah chose the young man who has just become an adult, and limited the application of the law to the first three months after that time. The lesson is taught by informing us of the punishment involved, which is no less than the death penalty. From this we will learn not to indulge the flesh too much, for that brings about a shrinking of the soul.

The above explanation is similar to that of *Ramban*, that when a person indulges excessively in eating and drinking, he violates the law of "you shall be holy" (*Vayikra* 19:2), as well as that of "you shall serve Him and cling to Him" (*Devarim* 13:5), which cannot be fulfilled when one is indulging the body to excess. *Ramban* adds that the sin of the rebellious son also includes the sin of acting disrespectfully towards one's father and mother. All of this, though, does not seem sufficient to explain the severity of the punishment, and *Ramban* adds that, in accordance with *Chazal*, the son is not killed because of the greatness of his sin, but rather because his being put to death will be a lesson for others. *Ramban* lists four similar cases where a person is condemned to death, not because of his sin itself, but so that his death will prevent destruction to society. In all of these matters, the Torah states, "and all of Israel will hear and fear," to stress that the death of these people is independent of their deeds, and is meant to serve to teach the others.

The laws where the Torah uses this concept of "all of Israel will hear and fear" include: a) our *parashah* (*Devarim* 21:18-21); b) the *zaken mamreh* — "rebellious elder" (ibid. 17:8-13) whose refusal to accept the ruling of the *beis din* is not enough for him to deserve the death penalty, but whose death will serve to remove disputes and arguments in Israel; c) עֵדִים זוֹמְמִין — "scheming witnesses" (ibid. 19:15-21), who tried to have a person killed but didn't succeed, and who are killed so as to dissuade others from testifying falsely; d) a מֵסִית ("instigator") — a person who attempts to get others to leave Hashem. Such a person is killed even if he did not succeed in what he set out to do, but is killed so that others will learn from this (ibid. 13:7-12).

Thus we see that the rebellious son is punished for the good of the community. The individual is punished severely because of the great damage that his existence can eventually cause to the community, and, as we noted above, his is not the only case where this occurs.

❧ Limitations on the Law of the Rebellious Son

Even though, according to *halachah*, the law of סוֹרֵר וּמוֹרֶה, the rebellious son, does apply, there are so many limitations involved in it as to make it extremely uncommon. First of all, it applies only in the first three months after a boy reaches *halachic* manhood, for the Torah says he is a בֵּן סוֹרֵר וּמוֹרֶה, a rebellious *son*, and after the first three months he is considered to be a "father." The implication is that if a woman had conceived from him immediately after he became an adult, by the end of three months, her pregnancy would be noticeable, and the son would then be considered to be a "father."

Another limitation is that his rebelliousness refers only to eating and drinking, and not to other sins. It is a *chok* — a law which human reason cannot understand — that the law applies only to sons and not to daughters, even though, according to R' Shimon, a girl, too, would be suitable to be a סוֹרֵר וּמוֹרֶה for she too can eat and drink to excess and wind up corrupting society by turning to prostitution; the Torah nevertheless excluded girls from this law. (*Rambam* states that girls are not drawn to excessive eating and drinking, and the commentators find it difficult to reconcile his views with those of R' Shimon.)

If either parent is not living, a boy cannot be a סוֹרֵר וּמוֹרֶה. The parents have the option to press charges if they wish, but are not obliged to do so. If either parent does not want to press charges, the boy cannot be convicted. If either parent had a limb amputated, is deaf, or lame, the boy cannot be a סוֹרֵר וּמוֹרֶה. The gluttony and excessive drinking is limited to meat and wine, and there are minimum quantities that need to be consumed before charges can be pressed. The boy must steal the meat and wine from his father's house and consume them elsewhere, in order for him to be able to be convicted. The meat and wine must be consumed in the company of worthless individuals. These are but some of the numerous limitations before a boy can be executed as a סוֹרֵר וּמוֹרֶה, all of which ensure that a case such as this will be extremely rare.

Nevertheless, in spite of these limitations, both *Chazal* and the *poskim* hold that the law is possible, and it serves as an educational and moral lesson, as quoted above in the name of *Ramban*. This idea is amplified by R' Yehudah Leib Chasman in *Or Yahel*, who writes that the well-known statement, כָּל יִשְׂרָאֵל עֲרֵבִין זֶה לְזֶה — "all Israel are responsible for one another" — does not only mean that those who did not sin are punished for the sins of those who did sin, but also that the sin of those who do sin is great, and they receive a severe punishment in order to protect society, so that a thirteen-year-old boy must understand what the Torah demands of him when it states, "You shall be holy" (*Vayikra* 19:2) — and if he doesn't understand it, he is punished by being stoned.

The law of סוֹרֵר וּמוֹרֶה is also limited in place. *Meshech Chochmah* quotes *Tosefta Nega'im* that the law is not in effect in Jerusalem. He explains that the reason for this is that in Jerusalem they ate the meat of so many sacrifices: the *todah* (thank offering) and *shelamim* (peace offering), as well as eating *ma'aser sheni*, the tithe of produce that could only be eaten in Jerusalem, so that it could not be considered a sin if a boy indulged in gluttony. Other commentators, though, state that the reason for this is that the holiness (*kedushah*) of Jerusalem protects a person, just as a boy cannot be convicted of being a סוֹרֵר וּמוֹרֶה if he overindulges at a *se'udas mitzvah* — a meal to mark a festive religious occasion such as a *bris milah* or wedding. Eating for a *mitzvah* instills *kedushah* in the body, and does not cause a person to be a glutton.

That is why, in *Maseches Sanhedrin*, *Rashi* explains that the wine which is specified for the סוֹרֵר וּמוֹרֶה comes from Italy. A food product grown outside *Eretz Yisrael* is liable to introduce *tum'ah*, spiritual impurity, into one's body, whereas food grown in *Eretz Yisrael* introduces *kedushah* into the body.

Bach, in *Tur Orach Chaim*, writes that the *kedushah* of *Eretz Yisrael* is influenced by the *kedushah* above, and the produce of *Eretz Yisrael* draws this *kedushah* from the *Shechinah*, Divine Presence, which is immanent in *Eretz Yisrael*. Thus the concluding benediction after eating of fruit is וְנֹאכַל מִפִּרְיָהּ וְנִשְׂבַּע מִטּוּבָהּ — "we will eat of its produce and be satisfied with its goodness" — so as to stress the *kedushah* which enters our bodies through the fruit of *Eretz Yisrael*.

III.

The Mercies of Man and the Mercies of Hashem

hazal in the Mishnah, *Berachos* 33, tell us, "One who says, 'Your mercies extend even to a bird's nest' (i.e., regarding the law that the mother bird must be sent away before the chicks are taken — *Devarim* 22:6-7) ... is silenced." According to one opinion in the *gemara*, the reason for this is that "he considers Hashem's attributes to be רַחֲמִים — 'mercy.'" As *Rashi* explains this:

> He did not do it for the sake of mercy, but to impose on Israel laws which are decrees (i.e., unfathomable by man), to let all know that they are His servants, who observe His *mitzvos* and His decrees, even in those areas which Satan and the non-Jews may criticize.

One who delves into *Rashi* will see that he is not rejecting the idea that the *mitzvah* of שִׁלּוּחַ הַקֵּן — "sending the mother bird from the nest" — has an element of mercy by Hashem toward His creatures, but he rejects those who wish to interpret this as the sole reason for the *mitzvah*. The problem with explaining שִׁלּוּחַ הַקֵּן this way is that a person may then insist that each *mitzvah* must have a reason, and if one cannot find such a rational reason, the *mitzvah* should not, Heaven forbid, be kept. Even where a person knows the reason for a particular *mitzvah*, he must not perform it because he understands the reason, but because that is what Hashem commanded us. If a person follows this course, he will observe also those *mitzvos* which are questioned by the *yetzer hara* (evil inclination) and by non-Jews.

This is also the way *Maharsha* understood the words of *Chazal* in his commentary on the *aggadah* of the *gemara*.

On the other hand, there are a number of places where *Chazal* explain the reason of שִׁלּוּחַ הַקֵּן as being a matter of mercy. *Midrash Rabbah* too, at the beginning of our *parashah*, states that, "just as

Hashem has mercy on man, so too does He have mercy on animals ... and so too is He filled with mercy for birds, as it states (*Devarim* 22:6), 'If you should come across a bird's nest.' " So too are we told in *Chullin* 80 on the verse (*Mishlei* 12:10), "A righteous one knows the soul of his beast," that "R' Berachiah said in the name of R' Levi, This refers to Hashem, who wrote in His Torah (*Devarim* 22:6), 'You shall not take the mother with the young.' "

Many commentators ask about the contradiction between this and the statement in *Berachos*, which seems to imply that one is not to regard the *mitzvah* as being related to mercy. However, based on our interpretation there is no contradiction. Of course we can see Hashem's mercy in this *mitzvah*, but *Chazal* wanted people not to regard various *mitzvos* as being based on considerations such as mercy, but to consider them all as decrees from Hashem, regardless of whether the person understands the *mitzvah* or not. If a person considers the *mitzvos* to be based on the fact that Hashem is merciful, he will come across certain *mitzvos* where this is not obvious, and then the person may, Heaven forbid, fail to observe those *mitzvos*.

Tosafos Yom Tov, on the first chapter of *Berachos*, differentiates between considering the *mitzvah* of שִׁלוּחַ הַקֵּן as merciful in one's prayers, and doing so in the interpretation of the *parashah*. Other commentators also follow this approach.

R' Tanchum Rubinstein, in his commentary in *Rambam La'Am*, *Hilchos Tefillah* 9, sees *Rambam* as implying this same difference, for *Rambam* states, "One who said this in his pleading ..." According to R' Rubinstein, a person who makes this statement in his prayer is worse than one who does so as Torah interpretation, because if one makes this statement as part of a prayer, he is saying it as a definite fact. On the other hand, if one says it as interpretation, there are "seventy facets to the Torah," and this is but one of the different possibilities to explain the topic.

In his commentary on the Mishnah, *Rambam* states that the *mitzvah* of שִׁלוּחַ הַקֵּן is a *mitzvah* for which there is no logical explanation, and one is forbidden to consider that the reason is mercy. Had the reason for the *mitzvah* been mercy, we would not have been permitted to slaughter fowl for food. According to this view, it is difficult to explain various statements by *Chazal* that this *mitzvah* is an example of Hashem's mercy. This requires further study.

As opposed to *Rambam* in his commentary on the Mishnah, *Rambam* in *Moreh Nevuchim* 3:48 states that there is a definite element of mercy in many *mitzvos*, such as when the Torah permits slaughtering animals for food:

> The *mitzvah* of slaughtering an animal is essential, because man's natural sustenance is from the seeds and plants of the earth, and from the flesh of living creatures. The best of meat was permitted for us to eat. That is something of which no doctor has doubts. Since the obtaining of good food requires the slaying of animals, the Torah demands that the death be in the easiest possible manner, i.e., by proper slaughtering, and not by stabbing it or by cutting off a limb while the animal is still alive.
>
> ... So too is one forbidden to slaughter the young before the eyes of its mother, because the distress of animals is very great at this. There is no difference between the distress of man and the distress of animals, because the love and tender mercy of the mother toward its young is not a matter of intellect, but of visualization which is a power found in most animals, as it is in man.

Rambam also follows along this path in explaining sending away the mother bird before taking its young. He regards this, as well, as an instance of mercy in Creation,

> because the eggs upon which the mother roosted and the young chicks which need their mother are not suitable for food, and when one sends away the mother and it goes elsewhere, it will not be distressed at the taking of its young. In most cases, [sending away the mother] will be reason to leave everything behind, because what the person would take would not be suitable for food.

Rambam does not ignore the words of *Chazal* in *Berachos*, which state that, "One who says, 'Your mercies extend even to a bird's nest' ... is silenced, because he considers Hashem's attributes to be רַחֲמִים — 'mercy.'" *Rambam* attributes this statement to those who are opposed, in principle, to any logical explanation of the *mitzvos*. On the other hand, there is the view, which *Rambam* also supports in *Moreh Nevuchim*, that one is not only permitted but is obliged to explain the reason for the *mitzvos* logically. According to this view, the *mitzvah* of שִׁלּוּחַ הַקֵּן is a clear instance of mercy. In general,

Rambam does not determine the *halachah* based on a theoretical discussion, and that is why, in *Mishneh Torah, Hilchos Tefillah*, he rules that if a person claims the *mitzvah* is due to Hashem's mercy, he is silenced. Nevertheless, when he wishes to explain the *mitzvah* on the theoretical level, he adopts the view that this is an instance of mercy.

Meleches Machsheves uses *Rambam's* views to explain the verses of the Torah. It is true that the slaughtering of animals and fowl for meat should have been forbidden due to considerations of mercy. Indeed, Adam was forbidden to eat meat. Later generations, though, became weaker, and that was why the flesh of living creatures was permitted as food. When the Torah states, "you shall surely send the mother away" (*Devarim* 22:7), it refers to the aspect of mercy, but when the verse continues, "so that it may be good for you and you will have length of days," the Torah goes on to explain why one may nevertheless eat meat, where there is clearly no mercy involved. The Torah wanted man to have "length of days," and that is impossible by having only a vegetarian diet, and that was why it permitted the eating of meat.

Kesav Sofer also regards שִׁלּוּחַ הַקֵּן as being based on mercy. He explains the Torah's promise, "you will have length of days," in accordance with what *Chazal* tell us in *Pesachim* 113, that those who are merciful have no real life, because they are always merciful and yet are unable to help someone in distress. The Torah therefore promises a person who is merciful in this instance, that he will have "length of days" and that "it will be good" for him, because he will be able to save another person in distress. This, of course, is much more relative to *d'rash* (homiletics) than it is to *p'shat*, the plain meaning of the verses.

Ramban, who is generally not too eager to give logical explanations of the different *mitzvos*, does not totally negate *Rambam's* view that שִׁלּוּחַ הַקֵּן is based on mercy. What *Ramban* does, though, is to shift the focus; the attribute of mercy should not be ascribed to Hashem, Who gave the Torah, but to man, who received the Torah. One cannot attribute any human emotions such as mercy to Hashem, and that was why *Chazal* were so opposed to those who claimed that שִׁלּוּחַ הַקֵּן is an example of Hashem's mercy. On the other hand, Hashem established lofty moral values in His *mitzvos*, so that man would be imbued with them. Based on this, *Ramban* explains the words of *Chazal* in *Bereishis Rabbah*: "What difference is it to Hashem if a person slaughters from the throat or from the back of the neck? Rather, the *mitzvos* were given to refine Israel." We cannot attribute any human emotions to Hashem, and therefore, as far as He is concerned, there is no difference how an animal is slaughtered. In Hashem's supernatural hierarchy of values, there are no such distinctions. But Hashem gave the Torah to Israel in order to refine them and to implant in them lofty moral and ethical values. That was why He permitted the slaughtering of animals for food, but only in a way which would impart mercy in our characters. There are many *mitzvos* related to this idea in regard to eating and slaughtering. By its nature, killing an animal can be an action close to the barbarism of Amalek, and there is the danger that the cruelty involved may spread to man through his actions. That was why the Torah required humane acts even in the killing of animals, as a counterweight to the cruelty of the action itself. This counterweight includes not killing the mother and its child on the same day (*Vayikra* 22:28) and other such *halachos*.

Ha'amek Davar explains that the special aspect of mercy involved here is that of the mother bird. The mother bird could have fled to save its life, but didn't do so and was willing to die for its children, thus showing exceptional mercy. One is forbidden to abuse the mother's mercy, and to grab it just at the time that it shows this extraordinary quality.

Oznayim LaTorah also explains the essence of this *mitzvah* in similar terms, and explains that the source of this interpretation can be found in *Rambam, Hilchos Shechitah*, where *Rambam* states: "The Torah forbade one to hunt [the mother bird] only when it is unable to fly away because of its young, for it hovers over them to ensure that they are not taken, as it states, 'and the mother is sitting upon the young'" (*Devarim* 22:6). In other words, one is forbidden to exploit the pure love of the mother bird for its young just at the time that this love binds the mother to its place, and makes it easier for man to capture it. Hunting the mother at that time is despicable and is forbidden.

✑§ The Continued Existence of the Species

Ramban gives an additional, natural explanation for the *mitzvah* of שִׁלּוּחַ הַקֵּן. Hashem wants every species to continue to exist, and does not want any species to be wiped out. It is true that Hashem permitted the slaughtering of animals for food, but if a person kills both the mother bird and its young, or the mother animal and its young on the same day (*Vayikra* 22:28), it appears as if he is destroying the entire species.

Rabbenu Bachya also follows along the same lines, and sees this as the basic reason for שִׁלּוּחַ הַקֵּן. He states that the reason why the Torah promises "length of days" (*Devarim* 22:7) to a person who observes this *mitzvah* is because this is a reward of מִדָּה כְּנֶגֶד מִדָּה — "measure for measure." As the person has helped ensure the "length of days" of the particular species involved, Hashem rewards the person with "length of days."

Using the above, *Chasam Sofer* explains the statement by *Chazal* that: "If you observe (the *mitzvah* of) שִׁלּוּחַ הַקֵּן, I (i.e., Hashem) will reward you with children." As by your actions you have ensured the continued existence of a species, Hashem says, I will see to it that your species will also continue to exist, and I will grant you children to live after you.

Chezyonos HaRamah says that this is the meaning of *Chazal* (*Berachos* 33) that "One who says, 'Your mercies extend even to a bird's nest' . . . is silenced." This *mitzvah* is not because of mercy. As far as mercy is concerned, it might be better to kill both the mother and its young together, so that neither should witness the death of the other. The reason for the *mitzvah*, though, is to ensure the continued existence of the species, and the reason why the Torah insists that the mother be kept alive is so that she will continue to propagate the species.

Abarbanel has a somewhat similar approach, with certain differences. Hashem wants to ensure continuity in His Creation, and to prevent anything from terminating before its time. Thus He permitted the picking of fruit, but forbade chopping down the tree upon which the fruit grows (*Devarim* 20:19-20). By the same token, the Torah permitted the taking of the young, but forbade one to take the mother bird which can give birth to more young and ensure continuity in Creation.

Chazal in *Chullin* deduce from a verse that this *mitzvah* applies only when a person happens to come across a nest by chance, but not to ducks and other birds which come to one's home, because those are meant to be used for human consumption and taking them does not disturb the continuity of the Creation. So too are we told that this law only applies to the kosher species of birds, the reason for this being that the non-kosher species are considered to be the equivalent of those species of trees which do not bear fruit, and which may be chopped down.

The Torah states, "in order that it will be good for you and you will have length of days" (ibid. 22:7). The purpose of the *mitzvah* is to maintain the continuity of Creation, so as to ensure man's continued supplies and existence, so that his days will be lengthened as a result. Thus, according to Abarbanel, the continuity of existence is the purpose of the *mitzvah*, and not, as other commentators have it, the continuity of species. The two interpretations are closely related, but not identical.

Chasam Sofer has an interesting interpretation. The Torah means to stress the cruelty of Esav, and Yaakov's prayer (*Bereishis* 32:12), "Lest he come and strike me, the mothers with the children." The promise of "that it be good for you" parallels the promise of Hashem to Yaakov, to which Yaakov refers in the continuation of his prayer, "and You said, I will do good to you." *Chasam Sofer's* grandson, R' Yosef Naftali Stern, comments that this idea is hinted at in *Midrash Rabbah* on *Parashas Vayishlach*, where it states, " 'Lest he come and strike me, the mothers with the children,' and You have stated (*Devarim* 22:6), 'You shall not take the mother with the young.' "

⋞§ The Mitzvah of שְׁלוּחַ הַקֵּן in Kabbalah

The kabbalists, who also give reasons for the *mitzvos* in their own way, follow *Zohar's* path in explaining the *mitzvah* of שְׁלוּחַ הַקֵּן, sending away the mother bird (*Devarim* 22:6-7). The mother bird, which is chased away from her chicks, wanders crying and full of distress throughout the world, and arouses pity upon itself and upon others that are harmed as it is. As a result, Hashem's pity is aroused toward the nest that was abandoned, toward *Knesses Yisrael* (i.e., the Jewish people) that wanders without rest among the nations, and over the fact that the *Shechinah* is so far from its dwelling place.

Imrei Yosef of Spinka says that when *Chazal* (*Berachos* 33) tell us that "One who says, 'Your mercies extend even to a bird's nest' ... is silenced," that is only if the person is referring to Hashem's mercy as being the reason for the *mitzvah*, because Hashem's *mitzvos* are all decrees that man cannot fathom. If, however, a person concentrates in prayer on the *mitzvah* of שְׁלוּחַ הַקֵּן to arouse Hashem's mercy and pity toward the empty nest of *Knesses Yisrael*, he may do so and will be blessed for it. Based on this, *Imrei Yosef* goes on to explain a seemingly astounding passage in *Berachos* 33:

> A certain person prayed in the presence of Rabbah and said, "You (Hashem) took pity on the bird's nest. Take pity and have mercy on us." Rabbah said, "How this wise man knows how to

appease his Master!" Abaye said to him, "Did we not learn in the Mishnah that he is to be silenced?" (The answer is that) Rabbah was testing Abaye.

This passage seems strange, for how would Rabbah say something against *halachah*, even if he meant to test Abaye? Couldn't he have tested him in another fashion? Rather, says *Imrei Yosef*, Rabbah knew that the man who was leading the prayers wished to arouse Hashem's pity, as the kabbalists do, and that was why he praised the man, for this is indeed a good way to pray. Abaye, though, thought that the man's statement was made in accordance with the view that this was an example of Hashem's mercy. "Rabbah was testing Abaye." Rabbah wanted to find out how perceptive Abaye was: whether he could sense the man's intentions and distinguish between kabbalistic intentions and those of ordinary interpretation. From Abaye's comment, Rabbah realized that Abaye understood the man to have adopted the approach of interpreting the *mitzvah* in terms of Hashem's mercy, and Rabbah saw that Abaye apparently was not acquainted with the kabbalistic interpretation.

Using this as an introduction, one can possibly answer the question of a number of *acharonim* on *Chavas Ya'ir* 66, who asks whether the *mitzvah* of שִׁלּוּחַ הַקֵּן applies only if a person wishes to take the young, or whether it applies in all circumstances, whenever one finds a mother bird sitting on its young. All find this question surprising, because *Ran* on *Chullin* 140 states clearly that if a person does not wish to take the young, he is exempt from this *mitzvah*. According to the above discussion, though, it is possible that *Ran* agrees with those who interpret the *mitzvah* as being due to Hashem's mercy and His pity toward His creatures. Therefore, wherever the person does not need the young, he is forbidden to chase the mother away and cause her distress. On the other hand, according to the kabbalists, one would be required to chase the mother away regardless, because by doing so, one arouses Hashem's mercy toward the world.

∞§ Against the Heretics

I myself have studied intensively the words of *Chazal* regarding "he is silenced." Had it not been for the explanation given by the *gemara*, I would have said that *Chazal* regarded a prayer such as that given by this person ("Your mercies extend even to a bird's nest") as smacking of heresy, or more specifically, Christianity, whose adherents were trying to infiltrate Judaism in those days. The version of *Rif* and *Rosh* of the Mishnah in *Berachos* 33 is:

> One who states, "May the Good Ones bless you," that is heresy; one who says, "Your mercy extends to a bird's nest" or "Your name is remembered for the good" or *"modim, modim"* (i.e. repeating the word *modim* — "we thank" — twice in the prayer, which *Chazal* see as a person implying that there are two Gods) is silenced.

Tosafos in *Megillah* 25 explain that "the Good Ones" implies that there are good Gods, namely, more than one. In other words, that is heresy, or more specifically, Christianity, which is based on the trinity.

It thus occurred to me that the entire Mishnah may be referring to Christianity. *Chazal* were afraid that such a statement about the bird's nest might be a concealed Christian prayer, in terms of a reference to "the father and the son." "Your name is remembered for the good" (וְעַל הַטּוֹב יִזָּכֵר שְׁמֶךְ) has the letters of the Nazarene, although in different order. And of course the last two, about "the Good Ones" and *modim, modim*, as we explained, refer to plural gods. Thus the entire Mishnah is a reference to heretics who tried to covertly insert their ideas into the Jewish prayers. This is only a thought, which requires further support from other sources, and is only a hypothesis at this time.

⋖§ שִׁלּוּחַ הַקֵּן and Honoring One's Parents

R' Samson Raphael Hirsch in *Chorev* explains the educational aspect of the *mitzvah* in order to understand the nature of Creation and the way it acts. While the Torah permitted man to take whatever is fitting for his enjoyment, he is nevertheless obligated to have regard for Hashem's creatures when they are engaged in completing the act of Creation. If you happen to have the opportunity to take a bird for your own enjoyment, but see that it is engaged in the work for which it was created, then *at that time* you must honor it as a servant of Hashem. Do not take it at the time it is performing its task (*Bereishis* 1:20-22) of propagating its species. You may pick it up to show your right to it, but you must immediately set it free, in order to honor the work of Hashem which it performs when it fulfills its purpose. If you are able to honor this holy work of the purpose of Creation, Hashem will then honor you as His faithful servant. Then you will look into yourself and realize that you too have a positive role to play in the world, and through that, you will feel happy and will have length of days. This law resembles that of honoring one's parents, which stems from a person's appreciation of the role his parents play in keeping mankind alive.

R' David Zvi Hoffmann also devotes space to comparing the *mitzvah* of שִׁלּוּחַ הַקֵּן and that of honoring one's parents, the observance of both of which are linked by the Torah to having "length of days" (*Devarim* 22:7; *Sh'mos* 20:12). What the Torah wishes to teach us is that one must respect the relationship between the parent and child even among animals and birds. If a person takes the young and sends away the mother bird, he must regard this as an act of self-sacrifice by the young in order to save their mother.

Oznayim LaTorah points out that the non-domesticated kosher species of animals (חַיּוֹת) and all kosher species of birds have the same *halachah* after slaughtering: In both cases the blood must be covered with earth. There are differences between these animals and the birds, though, in two other *halachos*: regarding sending forth the mother before taking the young, which applies only to birds; and not slaughtering the mother and child on the same day, which applies only to domesticated species of animals. Birds differ from animals in that while animals give birth to young that resemble them, birds lay eggs, which the mother bird protects even though they are not even alive yet. The mother sits on the eggs for weeks on end until the chicks hatch and she can see birds that look like her. Thus, the mother feels great distress when the eggs or chicks, for which she has been sacrificing her life, are taken from her. The Torah (*Devarim* 22:6) stresses twice "the chicks or the eggs" to teach us how great the love of the mother bird is, that she is willing to sacrifice her life for something which doesn't even look like her. Normally, when a person approaches a bird, it tries to fly away, and why does the mother bird stay here even though she puts her life in danger? It is because she loves her young even to the point of sacrificing her own life. The Torah therefore decreed that a person should not exploit this good quality of the bird to capture it. You have the right to try to trap birds by any method you want, but not when they are offering their own lives to protect their young.

Ki Savo – כי תבא

I.

Submitting to Hashem's Will

According to *Rambam* in *Moreh Nevuchim* 3:39, the purpose of the *mitzvah* of *bikkurim* — "first fruits" — (*Devarim* 26:1-11) is to stress man's total submission to Hashem, and his appreciation of Hashem's goodness. The first fruits of the land were chosen to express this basic principle, because whatever is first is always precious to a person, as we see in the verse (*Hoshea* 9:10), "as the first ripe fruit in the fig tree at the beginning of its season." So, too, do we find this idea in the verse (*Yeshayahu* 28:4), "as the first fruit before the summer; which one no sooner looks upon, and while it is yet in his hand, he eats up." Hashem commanded that these first fruits be brought as a gift to Him, in appreciation for all His kindness. At that time, when the person is rejoicing, he must remember and make mention of his days of poverty, so that he will more fully appreciate Hashem's mercies. The person must also show signs of submission and humility by bringing the *bikkurim* on his shoulder, as a symbol of his insignificance and to serve as a reminder of our poverty in earlier times.

There are numerous times when the Torah tells us, "You shall remember that you were a slave in the land of Egypt." Hashem understands man's nature, whereby, when a person becomes well-off and has a leisurely life, he has the tendency to become conceited, to rebel, and to leave the proper path, as we see in the verse (*Devarim* 8:12-14), "Lest you eat and be satisfied ... and your heart become haughty and you forget Hashem you God," and (ibid. 32:15), "But Yeshurun waxed fat, and rebelled." The Torah therefore teaches us to bring our *bikkurim* to Hashem each year, and to remember our dismal past, so that now, too, we will submit to Hashem.

Akeidah also explains the *parashah* along these lines. He states that after we come to *Eretz Yisrael* and inherit and settle into it for many years, we must take great care to ensure that we don't have any delusions to the effect that (ibid. 8:17) "my strength and the might of my arm made me this wealth." We and our descendants should not forget all the great deeds which Hashem did for us in bringing us to *Eretz Yisrael*. Thus, by bringing the *bikkurim* each year, we will always remember that (*Tehillim* 24:1) "the earth is Hashem's, and all in it," and it was He who gave us what we have and granted us all our success. It is when we bring the *bikkurim* "from your land" (*Devarim* 26:2) that we must realize that it is not our land, but the land "that Hashem your God is giving to you" (ibid.). By bringing the *bikkurim*, we demonstrate that we have not forgotten for a moment the source of our salvation and blessing, and we thank Him for His gifts and blessings. The reason the *bikkurim* are brought in a large, public procession, as mentioned in *Chazal*, is in order to publicize to all that we have accepted the yoke of heaven. *Chinuch* and other commentators also follow a similar approach.

R' Yitzchak Breuer, in his *Nachaliel*, eloquently sums up the various interpretations:

> The *bikkurim* brought every year are an unparalleled demonstration of a happy and blessed nation living on its land in quiet and security. It is a demonstration of the sovereignty of Hashem over the nation, which each year accepts anew, with bended knee and with bowed head, the land from its God. In that tremendous national joy, the nation offers up its confession, a national confession stemming from national joy.

Kli Yakar has an interesting observation, when he notes that just as in our *parashah*, also in the *parashah* regarding the king, the Torah stresses that "you will possess [the land] and dwell in it." In both cases, there is reason to fear that people will become excessively proud, "Yeshurun waxed fat, and rebelled." The king that will arise after the land is inherited and settled may begin to think that the Jewish people is no different from any other nation. By the same token, the people may begin to believe that it was the power of their sword that gave them the land. The Torah therefore demands that both must visibly demonstrate their submission to Hashem.

HaKesav VeHaKabalah also explains the *parashah* along similar lines, and states that the reason we must bring our first fruits to Hashem is as a sign of our submission to Him, so that we will know that we are no more than sharecroppers working the land, and that we must bring the best portion to the Owner (i.e., Hashem) of the field.

⇜§ "You Shall Come to the Kohen"

On the verse, "You shall come to the *kohen* who will be in those days" (*Devarim* 26:3), *Rashi* comments, "You have none other than the *kohen* in your generation as he is," or, in other words, the Torah tells us that we must accept the leaders (in this case, the *kohanim*) of each generation as they are. The question then arises as to why the Torah made this statement specifically in regard to *bikkurim*, first fruits. The reason for this is evidently that as the *bikkurim* are meant to have us express our subservience to Hashem and as the *kohen* represents Hashem in this, one might think that the *kohen* must be a *talmid chacham*, an accomplished scholar, a person who stands out above the others. The Torah therefore tells us that one does not need such a superior type of *kohen* to accept the *bikkurim*, for the *bikkurim* are meant for Hashem.

This is also the way *S'forno* explains the verse (ibid. v. 4), "He [the *kohen*] will place it before the altar of Hashem." As *S'forno* puts it, this verse is meant to stress that the gift is not to the *kohen*, but to Hashem. The *kohen* is only Hashem's messenger, and he later receives the *bikkurim* as a gift, together with the other gifts that the *kohanim* are given.

There is a beautiful interpretation, along the lines of *d'rush*, by Aperion. At the end of Tractate *Bikkurim*, there is a dispute between R' Yehudah and the other Sages. According to R' Yehudah, the *bikkurim* are given only to a *kohen* who is a scholar, whereas the other Sages say that they are to be given to all the *kohanim* that have the *mishmar* — those whose turn it is to serve in the *Beis HaMikdash*, and these *kohanim* then divide up all the *bikkurim* among themselves. R' Yehudah's view is that since the *bikkurim* are not used in the *Beis HaMikdash* service as such, we are afraid that if a *kohen* who is not a scholar would receive the *bikkurim*, he would not treat it with the proper sanctity, while the other Sages hold that as the *bikkurim* are brought into the *Beis HaMikdash* courtyard, even *kohanim* who are not scholars will take the proper precautions. The truth is that one does not give *terumah* (agricultural tithes) and such other gifts meant for the *kohanim* outside the *Beis HaMikdash* except to a *kohen* who is a scholar, as stated in *Chullin* 130b:

R' Yochanan said, "How do we know that one does not give the gifts to a *kohen* who is an ignoramus (*am ha'aretz*)? (We deduce this from a verse,) as it states (*II Divrei HaYamim* 31:4), Moreover, he commanded the people that dwelled in Jerusalem to give the portion of the *kohanim* and the Levites, so that they might hold fast to the Torah of Hashem.' Whoever holds fast to the Torah of Hashem has a portion, and whoever does not hold fast to the Torah of Hashem does not have a portion."

It would appear that this is a Torah (as opposed to rabbinic) law, as it states (*Devarim* 18:3), "This shall be the law of the *kohanim*." Thus, as *terumah* and other gifts to the *kohanim* can be given only to a *kohen* who is a scholar, one might have imagined that the same should be true for the *bikkurim*, as R' Yehudah says. We are therefore told by *Rashi* that "this refers to the *kohen* in your generation as he is," namely that even if he is not a scholar one may give him the *bikkurim*, in accordance with the view of the Sages who opposed R' Yehudah's view.

Ramban is surprised at *Rashi's* commentary and asks what *Rashi* is trying to add. Whom else should the person bring the *bikkurim* to than the *kohen* of his days? We can understand why we must be told that one must come to the judges of one's time, even if the judge of one's own generation is not as great as those of previous generations, as it is written "you shall come . . . to the judges who will be in those days"(ibid. 17:9), but in regard to *kohanim* such a statement is superfluous, says *Ramban*, because what alternative is there than to bring the *bikkurim* to the *kohanim*?

Mizrachi, though, sees no basis for *Ramban's* question. There is no difference between a *kohen* and a judge. Just as one might have thought that one does not go to the judge of one's own generation if his scholarship does not match that of earlier generations, one might equally have thought that one does not bring *bikkurim* to the *kohanim* if they are not sufficiently righteous.

Because of his own question above, *Ramban* explains that the Torah meant to prohibit a person from bringing a *kohen* from the place where the person himself lives, so as to give that *kohen* the *bikkurim*.

Chizkuni has a similar approach. The Torah came to warn us that a person may not wait until the time when a *kohen* that he wants is officiating, and then bring the gifts. The person must bring them to whichever *kohen* is fulfilling the duty in the *Beis HaMikdash* at the time.

Avnei Shoham has a novel interpretation, which appears to be accurate. When the Torah states, "to the *kohen* who will be in those days"(ibid. 26:3), it wishes to teach us that *bikkurim* are brought only when there is a *kohen gadol* (High Priest). *Avnei Shoham* quotes *Targum Yehonasan*, "to the *kohen* when there is a *kohen gadol* in his days."

Ibn Ezra also explains "in those days" as implying that the obligation to bring *bikkurim* applies only if there is a *kohen gadol*. *Tosafos* in *Kesubos* 105b also quotes *Seder Eliyahu Zuta*: "Did Elisha then eat *bikkurim*? After all, there was no *Beis HaMikdash*, no altar, and no *kohen gadol*." Thus we see that the *mitzvah* of *bikkurim* applied only when there was a *kohen gadol*.

As noted, the origin of this novel interpretation is *Targum Yehonasan*, but there is still room to discuss the issue, because we do not find any *poskim* (and we find almost no commentators) who hold that bringing *bikkurim* requires the existence of a *kohen gadol*.

⋖§ "I Have Stated Today"

S'forno explains the phrase "I have stated today" (*Devarim* 26:3) in regard to the *bikkurim* as meaning, "Through the act of bringing the first fruits, I have declared and publicized that I thank Hashem for the gift of the land." *Ramban*, too, states that the very act of bringing the produce is the "statement" that the person makes.

Torah Temimah explains that according to its use in the Torah, the word הַגָּדָה can imply a proof. Thus we see a verse (*I Shmuel* 24:18), "you have showed (הִגַּדְתָּ) this day that you have dealt well with me." Similarly, when David grieved excessively for Avshalom, Yoav said to him (*II Shmuel* 19:7), "You have proven (הִגַּדְתָּ) this day that you have no [regard for] princes or servants." In other words, David had proven this fact by mourning excessively. Thus, the very act of bringing the *bikkurim* is the strongest proof that a person can bring that he thanks Hashem for having given us *Eretz Yisrael*.

HaKesav VeHaKabalah has an interesting explanation of this *parashah*. The word הִגַּדְתִּי is derived from the Hebrew root גַּד, which means good fortune. The person thus proclaims, "I am overjoyed that Hashem brought me to this land. I am not complaining, but, on the contrary, wish to proclaim to everyone how happy I am about this."

S'forno ties the statement that the person makes, "I have come to the land" (*Devarim* 26:3) with the *mitzvah* of *bikkurim*. "I am just a stranger in this land. I 'have come' to it from afar. You, Hashem, are the master of all, and that is why I will bring You my gift, just as every sharecropper does with his yield."

Oznayim LaTorah takes this a step further.

"I have come to the land" — I was not among those who declared, "Let us make a leader and return to Egypt" (*Bamidbar* 14:4). "I have come to the land" — I did not try to become rich, but rather I became rooted in the land of my forefathers, and I earn my living from working the land. I have thereby fulfilled the *mitzvah* of Hashem: "The first of all the produce of the land that you bring from your land" (*Devarim* 26:2) — the first fruits of your land, which you brought forth with your sweat, with plowing, with sowing, and with weeding. After all that effort, you must understand that Hashem your God gave you the land, and it is through that action that it is yours, and not because of conquest. "The land that Hashem swore to our forefathers to give to us" (ibid. v. 3) — that is our only right to this land, and we have no other right. You must bring *bikkurim* of your hard labor to Hashem, to show that your work also belongs to Him, and is nurtured at its source by His benevolence.

◄§ "You Shall Answer and Say"

In accordance with the view of various commentators who see the *bikkurim* as an act of submission to Hashem, *Or HaChayim* explains the word וְעָנִיתָ — "you shall answer" (*Devarim* 26:5) — in terms of עֲנָוֹת (humility) — reciting one's words with a broken heart. *Tiferes Shlomo* and other Chassidic works have a similar approach. A person must be humble when he makes the declaration when bringing the *bikkurim*. *Chazal* in *Sotah* 32 deduce from a *gezerah shavah* — the use of the same word or phrase in two places in the Torah — that the word וְעָנִיתָ teaches us that the declaration must be in Hebrew.

Yerushalmi deduces from וְעָנִיתָ that it is possible for another person to say the declaration aloud, and for the person bringing the *bikkurim* to repeat the declaration after him. *Rashi* and *Tosafos* learn from וְעָנִיתָ that a person is required to make the declaration in a loud voice.

Ibn Ezra says that it is possible that when the *bikkurim* were brought, the *kohanim* would ask the person: "What is this?" The person would then respond by making the declaration.

Abarbanel explains that the person had to make the declaration in the form of שִׁירָה — singing the praise of Hashem. Indeed, *Chazal* tell us that the *bikkurim* need to be accompanied by song, and they may have learned this from the word וְעָנִיתָ, as does Abarbanel.

HaKesav VeHaKabalah, though, holds that *Chazal* learned the need for song from the words בְּכָל הַטּוֹב — "for all the good" (ibid. v. 11) — as we see in the verse (*I Melachim* 8:66), שְׂמֵחִים וְטוֹבֵי לֵב — "joyful and glad of heart." There is nothing which arouses pleasantness and joy as does song.

Meshech Chochmah notes that the text in the Torah reads, "For all the good which Hashem your God gave to you and to your household" (*Devarim* 26:11). *Chazal* in *Gittin* 47 learn from the word "your household" (וּלְבֵיתֶךָ) that a person must also bring *bikkurim* from the assets belonging to his wife. Thus we see that בֵּיתֶךָ is a reference to one's wife. Furthermore, *Semak* writes that if a woman took a vow not to hear song, her husband can annul that vow, because that is considered to be an affliction. From this we see that one of the main things that is "good" for your "household" (wife) is song. Thus, when the Torah states, "for all the good ... to your household," it is a reference to song.

Avnei Shoham has a beautiful, novel explanation. *Chazal* in Berachos 48b state:

> R' Meir says, "How do we know that just as a person must recite a blessing for something good, he must also recite a blessing for something bad? It is deduced from the verse, 'which Hashem your God gave you.'"

Various commentators attempt to find the source for this *halachah* (see *Rashi* there). According to *Avnei Shoham*, though, the source of this blessing is from the *bikkurim*, where it states, "You will rejoice with all the good which Hashem your God gave you" (*Devarim* 26:11), whereas in regard to curses, we are told, "You will eat the fruit of your womb, the flesh of your sons and daughters, that Hashem your God gave you" (ibid. 28:53). Thus, R' Meir deduces that one must recite a blessing for the bad just as for the good because of the fact that in both cases — the blessing and the curse — the Torah uses the identical language: "which Hashem your God gave you."

◆§ An Aramean Wanted to Destroy My Father

In bringing the *bikkurim*, the person bringing them tells the story of our past, and mentions the very first miracle which occurred to Israel (*Devarim* 26:5), "An Aramean wanted to destroy my father." According to *Chazal*, as also brought by *Rashi* on this verse, Lavan the Aramean wanted to uproot all by destroying Yaakov. This way, there would be no Jewish people.

Ibn Ezra, though, finds this explanation difficult, because if that were the meaning, the Torah should have stated אֲרַמִּי מַאֲבִיד אָבִי, rather than the way the actual text appears: אֲרַמִּי אֹבֵד אָבִי; as it stands the Torah text implies that he himself would be destroyed! In addition, what connection is there between this part of the verse, of the Aramean destroying our father, and the continuation of the verse, which states that our fathers went down to Egypt? As a result, Ibn Ezra explains that this confession is our way of expressing our thanks to Hashem, Who gave us the good land, after we had nothing and were destitute. According to Ibn Ezra, the words mean, "When my father (Yaakov) was in Aram, he was a 'destroyed' and destitute man" and had nothing. After that, "he went down to Egypt" to live in a foreign country. Now, though, we have a good and broad land, after Hashem took us out of Egypt. *S'forno* and *Chizkuni* also explain the verse as does Ibn Ezra.

HaKesav VeHaKabalah, on the other hand, says that the *trop* (melody markings) on the verse is in accordance with *Rashi*, because the *trop* divides the verse into two sections: אֲרַמִּי ("an Aramean"), and אֹבֵד אָבִי ("[wanted] to destroy my father"); whereas according to Ibn Ezra and those who follow along the same line, the words should have been divided into אֲרַמִּי אֹבֵד ("a poor Aramean"), and then אָבִי ("[was] my father").

Abarbanel explains that Lavan the Aramean was the one who, by his actions, caused Yosef to be sold to Egypt and Yaakov to go into exile in that land. It was Lavan's evil ways which caused the feuding between Yaakov's sons, which led them to eventually sell Yosef to Egypt. Yaakov's sons would simply not have been able to act that way if there had not been a drop of their grandfather Lavan's blood in their veins.

Rashbam explains the word אֲרַמִּי (Aramean) to refer to Avraham. In other words, Avraham was lost and in exile from Aram, as Hashem had told him, "Go from your land" (*Bereishis* 12:1). According to *Rashbam*, the confession said at the *bikkurim* then tells us that our forefathers came from another country.

Alshech explains that it was Lavan the Aramean who gave Leah to Yaakov rather than giving him Rachel, as had been agreed between the two men. As a result, the firstborn was not Rachel's son, but Leah's son, Reuven. It was the jealousy of the brothers which brought upon us the exile in Egypt.

This *parashah* is also repeated in the *Haggadah*. Abarbanel, in his commentary on the *Haggadah*, states that on the night of the *seder* we have to thank Hashem for all the good which He did for us, not only in Egypt, but ever since that time as well. That is the reason we say the same confession at the *seder* as was said when the *bikkurim* were brought. As we sit with the *k'arah*, the *seder* plate, in front of us, we should feel as if we are bringing *bikkurim*.

One might venture a simple explanation of the *Haggadah*. The purpose of the *Haggadah* was to lift up the spirits of the Jewish people after the exile by the Romans, and to tell us that Hashem will yet redeem us, as He did when we were in Egypt. The use of the word אֲרַמִּי (*Arami*, "Aramean") also reminds us of the word רוֹמָאִי (*Roma'i*) — "Roman" — and this was a hint to the people that even though Rome had destroyed the Second *Beis HaMikdash*, Hashem will redeem us from this exile as well, as He has redeemed us from all other exiles.

II.
Memorial Tablets for the Torah and Emunah

The *parashah* which commands Israel to set up the stone tablets after crossing (*Devarim* 27:1-8) the Jordan is a *parashah* which needs to be explained. The Torah gives this *mitzvah* twice. At first, it states (ibid. v. 2), "It shall be on the day when you shall pass over Jordan unto the land which Hashem your God gives you, you shall set up great stones, and plaster them with plaster," and this is followed by (ibid. v. 4,5,8),

> It shall be when you have gone over the Jordan, you shall set up these stones, which I command you this day, in Mount Eval, and you shall plaster them with plaster. There shall you build an altar unto Hashem your God ... You shall write upon the stones all the words of this Torah very plainly.

Rashi explains the verses in accordance with the way the *mitzvah* was carried out by Yehoshua, as we see in *Yehoshua*, Chapter 4, where he commanded that twelve stones be taken from the place where the *kohanim's* feet stood firm, and these were taken to the first place that the Jews camped after crossing the Jordan. The purpose of the stones was to publicize the miracle and to tell the future generations what had happened to Israel when they crossed the Jordan.

Yehoshua also commanded that an additional twelve stones be put up in the Jordan River itself, "where the kohanim's feet stood firm" (Yehoshua 4:9). At the end of the parashah, it states that Yehoshua put up in Gilgal the twelve stones that Israel had taken with them. In Yehoshua Chapter 8, though, we are told that Yehoshua set up the altar at Mount Eval, as Moshe had commanded, and it was there that he wrote the Torah on the stones.

According to Chazal in Sotah 35, the stones of Mount Eval and the stones of Gilgal were the same ones. On the day they crossed the Jordan, they traveled sixty mil (approximately 60 miles) to Shechem, and set up the altar on Mount Eval. Afterwards, on that same day, they dismantled it, and brought the stones to Gilgal.

From the above, we see that there were a total of 24 stones, twelve that they set up in the Jordan and twelve that ultimately rested in Gilgal.

In our parashah, too, Rashi explains the verses in accordance with the above. The first verse (Devarim 27:2) thus refers to the twelve stones which were set up in the Jordan. Then they took out twelve other stones from the Jordan, and it was on these that they wrote the Torah. Rashi, though, adds that, "There were thus three types of stones, twelve in the Jordan, and a like number in Gilgal, and a like number in Mount Eval, as we see in Sotah 35."

Mizrachi and various other commentators are surprised at Rashi's comment that there were three sets of stones, when, after all, there were only two sets, for the stones of Mount Eval were moved to Gilgal. What is even more surprising is Rashi's reference to Sotah. It is true that the gemara there states that there were three sets of stones, but that is because the gemara there includes the set of stones that Moshe set up in the plains of Moav. As Rashi doesn't mention this set, he should have said there were two sets of stones. This question has not yet been answered.

Maharal, in Gur Aryeh, tries to explain that Rashi is referring to the three times that stones were set up, thus including the two times that the same stones were set up in Mount Eval and thereafter in Gilgal, but excluding the stones set up by Moshe. This answer, though, appears to be forced. After all, Rashi uses the language of the gemara in Sotah, which states "three sets of stones," and he even refers us back to Sotah, where the stones of Mount Eval and Gilgal are considered to be a single set. This question on *Rashi* is already brought in *Chizkuni*.

◆§ Only as a Hint

Abarbanel is the only one among the commentators on the Book of *Yehoshua* who states that there were three sets of stones: Those set up in the Jordan, those taken out of the Jordan and placed in Gilgal as a sign and memorial, and a different set of stones that was set up in Mount Eval. After the case of Achan, who took war spoils against Hashem's orders, Hashem made the following declaration (*Yehoshua* 7:11), "They have transgressed My covenant which I commanded them." As a result, Yehoshua saw the need to set up an altar in Mount Eval and to pronounce a curse on those who violated the Torah. This view is not in keeping with that of *Chazal* in *Sotah*.

Abarbanel also argues with *Rashi* as to the nature of the stones that were set up in the Jordan. According to *Rashi*, these stones were placed in the river, at the place "where the *kohanim's* feet stood firm," to replace the stones taken from there, so that the *kohanim* would not have to stand in the mud.

Ralbag has a different interpretation of this. The stones were placed there as a sign that a miracle had occurred in that place, and it was there that the waters had split.

Abarbanel has another interesting interpretation. The twelve stones set up in the Jordan were not set up one next to the other, but rather one on top of the other, so that they would serve as a memorial that everyone would be able to see. Abarbanel explains the words, "where the *kohanim's* feet stood firm" (ibid. 4:9), as meaning in the place where the *kohanim* had stood, i.e., to commemorate the place where the miracle had occurred, and the stones were placed one on top of another so that all would see where the place was. "And they are there to this day" (ibid.) — namely, they were visible for all to see, and if they had been placed one next to the other, who would be able to see them under the water?

If *Rashi* would hold like Abarbanel, we could understand why he stated that there were three sets of stones, but in *Rashi's* commentary on *Yehoshua* and on the *gemara* in *Sotah*, he states clearly that there were only two sets of stones, and this requires further study.

Meshech Chochmah also expresses surprise at *Rashi's* words, that the verse (*Devarim* 27:2), "you shall set up stones," means to set them up in the Jordan, because this is not stated specifically in the verses. Why then did *Rashi* say what he did? To answer this, *Meshech*

Chochmah uses a philosophical approach. *Rambam* states in a number of places that the miracles did not occur in order to strengthen our faith, but because Israel needed them. Now, we are told in *Yerushalmi Shevuos* Chapter 6 that Yehoshua sent three letters to the Seven Nations before attacking them. One of these letters offered to make peace with these nations, if they wanted this. If they had agreed to make peace, Israel would have crossed the Jordan by natural means, using boats, and would not have needed the miracle of the river splitting. In order to allow these nations to have full free will in their decisions, the Torah did not write about placing the stones in the Jordan, because had the nations made peace, there would be no miracle and no reason to place the stones in the Jordan to mark a miracle. The fact that Hashem knows what will happen does not affect a person's free will, but if Israel had known in advance, that would have affected the other nations' free will. That is why the stones in the Jordan are only hinted at, but there is no specific statement to that effect.

⊷ The Torah Was Engraved in Seventy Languages

One should add here the explanation of *Oznayim LaTorah* on the question as to why Israel were commanded, on the day they crossed the Jordan, to walk a distance of sixty miles to Mount Eval, in the midst of enemy territory, and to build an altar there, to write the Torah on its stones, and to return that day to Gilgal. *Oznayim LaTorah* gives three reasons for this: a) to let everyone know that the Jewish people had come to *Eretz Yisrael*, not as foreign conquerors, but as commanded by Hashem, as stated in the Torah engraved upon the stones of the altar in the center of the country, in Shechem. They were commanded to do this even before they unsheathed their swords to begin the battle. b) When Avraham came to Canaan at Hashem's command, his first trip was from Shechem to Elon Moreh. There he built an altar to Hashem, Who had appeared to him and promised him the land (*Bereishis* 12:6-7). Hashem thus wanted Avraham's descendants to follow the same path, to come to Shechem, and to build an altar as a sign that Hashem had kept His promise. c) They came to Shechem, the place where *Eretz Yisrael* had been promised to Avraham, in order to demonstrate to all that the promise of the land to the Jewish people depended on the observance of the Torah.

Ramban explains a verse in our *parashah* along similar lines. Thus we are told, "You shall write upon them all the words of this Torah when you cross, so that you may come to the land that Hashem your God gives you" (*Devarim* 27:3). You are to engrave the words on the stones, so that you and all the people will know that you came to *Eretz Yisrael* in order to observe the Torah, and that is what gives you the right to the land which you conquered.

Kedushas Levi says that this will also explain why the Torah was engraved on the stones in seventy languages, as we see in *Chazal's* comment on the words, בַּאֵר הֵיטֵב — "very plainly" (ibid. v. 8) — that this means in all seventy languages. The Torah serves as the document upon whose basis we were given the land, and it was written in all seventy languages so that all the inhabitants of the world would know that *Eretz Yisrael* belongs to the Jewish people and no one else, for only Israel received the Torah, and no one else.

Various commentators, though, wonder how it was possible to write the entire Torah, and in seventy languages yet, on twelve stones. *Ralbag* says that if the altar at Mount Eval was as large as the altar in the *Beis HaMikdash*, there was enough room on it to write the entire Torah, but still not enough room to write it seventy times, and this was simply a miracle. R' Sa'adiah Gaon says that all that was written on the stones was a list of the 613 *mitzvos*. *Ramban*, on the other hand, says that the entire Torah text was written on the stones, but these were either enormous rocks, or it was a miracle.

Oznayim LaTorah has a beautiful interpretation of the words of *Chazal* in *Sotah* 34, where we are told that Abba Chalafta, R' Eliezer bar Masia, and Chanania bar Chachinai discussed these stones, and estimated that "each one weighed forty *se'ahs*." According to *Oznayim LaTorah*, this was a measurement of size, this being the size necessary for the entire Torah to be written on the twelve stones. These Sages were experts in the size of letters and in the amount of space the entire Torah takes. The reason there were three of them present was because *halachah* requires a *beis din* of three to make decisions regarding appraisals. Thus, according to this, the Torah was written on the twelve stones entirely within the realm of nature.

R' David Zvi Hoffmann holds that the only thing that was written in seventy languages was the prohibition against idolatry, for that is the most fundamental law that all of mankind requires, for, as *Chazal* tell us, practicing idolatry is equivalent to violating all of the rest of the Torah together.

HaKesav VeHaKabalah, quoting his son, has a similar interpretation. "All the words of this Torah" (*Devarim* 27:3) refers to the *parashah* that includes all the rest of the Torah. This is similar to the way *Chazal* interpret the verse, "you shall remember all the *mitzvos* of Hashem" (*Bamidbar* 15:39), which, *Chazal* tell us, refers to reading the *Shema*, for the *Shema* includes accepting the yoke of heaven and forsaking idolatry. Here too, "all the words of this Torah" refers to the *parashah* that includes all of the Torah, namely the first two paragraphs of *Shema*. One may be able to see a certain amount of support for this from what the Torah writes in regard to *hakhel* (*Devarim* 31:12), "that they may hear, and that they may learn, and fear Hashem your God, and observe to do *all the words of this Torah*," even though the portion of the Torah that was read was only from the beginning of *Devarim* until the *parashah* of *Shema*. (And see *Sotah* 41.)

HaKesav VeHaKabalah adds that, without the tradition handed down to us by *Chazal*, one would have been able to explain that the verses meant that the entire Torah was written on parchment, and then the parchment was glued onto the stones. This, however, is not the view of *Chazal*.

Among *Chazal*, there is a dispute as to what actually occurred. According to R' Yehudah, the Torah was written on the stones, after which the stones were plastered, whereas according to R' Shimon they were first plastered and then the Torah was written upon them. The *gemara* then asks: According to R' Yehudah that the stones were plastered after the Torah had been written on them, how could the other nations have learned the Torah from these stones, for the writing was no longer visible? R' Yehudah answers that Hashem gave the other nations extra wisdom, so that they sent their scribes, who peeled off the plaster and then copied the text, "and it was because of this that it was decreed upon them to go down to the pit of destruction."

Maharsha, in his commentary on the *aggados*, states that it is only according to R' Yehudah that the other nations were doomed, because their wise men copied the Torah and brought the copies home to their people. As their people had the Torah, they should have studied it, and their punishment came for not having done so. According to R' Shimon, though, the other nations did not send their wise men to peel off the plaster and to copy the Torah, because the Torah was written on the plaster, and was visible to all. The masses were thus not able to study the Torah, because it had not been copied and brought to them, and thus they do not deserve a severe punishment.

Oznayim LaTorah, though, points out that we are told by *Chazal* that Hashem went to all the seventy nations of the world and offered them the Torah and they all refused it. Why, then, did He give them the Torah a second time, in the form of the text written on the stones? This question is really to be found in *Tosafos* on *Sotah*, regarding the fact that they were consigned to the pit of destruction. *Tosafos* asks: Should they have been consigned to the pit of destruction regardless, because Hashem had offered them the Torah and they had refused it? *Tosafos* answers that the punishment is for not having learned after they already had the Torah in their hands.

One should also note that *Chazal* tell us that even though the non-Jews did not receive the Torah, they copied it and had it in their possession. This undoubtedly refers to the cultural and spiritual values of the non-Jews, whose source is ultimately the Torah. Hashem gave the non-Jews the powers of discernment so that they would send their scribes to find out whatever they could from the Jews. They took everything, but did not use it. That was why their fate was decreed.

Panim Me'iros 1:33 discusses R' Yehudah's statement that they wrote the text before covering it with plaster. Doesn't this violate the prohibition against erasing Hashem's name? He concludes that this is not considered to be erasing Hashem's name, because it was possible to peel off the plaster, as the wise men of the non-Jewish nations did. This was, therefore, no more than covering the name. *Panim Me'iros* then asks what purpose the plaster served and answers that the plaster was needed to protect the writing, so that it would not be wiped off by the rain.

On this, *Oznayim LaTorah* asks: Doesn't rain wash away plaster, and how would this plaster protect the writing? Furthermore, they crossed the Jordan on the tenth day of *Nissan*, and by then the rainy season was finished in *Eretz Yisrael*. He therefore explains that the plaster was placed on the text because if they had left the text open it would be considered to be teaching the Torah to non-Jews, which is forbidden, as we see from the statement of *Chazal* that the day that the Sages translated the Torah into Greek was like the day that the Golden Calf was made. Hashem did not want the Jews to expose the Torah to the non-Jews, and that was why He ordered that the writing be covered with plaster, but he gave the non-Jews the wisdom to peel the plaster off and to expose the writing underneath.

As to the question of *Oznayim LaTorah* that the plaster would be washed away by the rain, Abarbanel interpreted this not to refer to regular plaster, but to gypsum (i.e., plaster of Paris). Rabbenu Bachya, too, says that the plaster referred to was gypsum.

⊷ In Place of a Memorial

Abarbanel has a novel interpretation of our *parashah* and of *Yehoshua* Chapter 8. According to him, the fact that the Torah mentions twice in our passage (*Devarim* 27:1-8) the setting up of stones and the writing of the Torah on them is to teach us that there would be a voluntary action as well as an obligatory *mitzvah*. The first part is an introduction to the *mitzvah*, while the second is the statement of the *mitzvah* itself. There was a custom among the nations at the time that every king or nation that conquered another nation would thereafter set up a memorial made of stones, upon which it would inscribe the name of the king and the year in which he conquered the land. Thus we find that throughout Italy and Spain, wherever the Romans conquered any area, they set up memorials which exist to this day. Hashem knew that Israel too would set up such stones, and would write upon them the great deeds and miracles which they had seen after they crossed the Jordan, so that these would serve as memorial monuments for all to see. Hashem therefore commanded that those same actions which others took as a sign of their pride and haughtiness should be taken by Israel for a *mitzvah* purpose, and in order to perpetuate the words of the Torah.

The beginning of the *parashah* (ibid. v. 2) states, "On the day when you cross the Jordan ... you shall set up stones." That is not a command, but a description of how the Jews would undoubtedly act after they emerged victorious. They would certainly set up memorials of stone. "You shall write upon them all the words of this Torah when you cross." In essence, Hashem told them: You will certainly write down those sections of the Torah dealing with the conquest of *Eretz Yisrael* and crossing the Jordan. You will certainly write down the Exodus from Egypt, what happened to you in the desert, the wars against Sichon and Og, and everything that happened to you when you crossed the Jordan. That you will do on your own, just as the other nations do. After the Torah states this, it goes on to explain the *mitzvah*. "It shall be when you have gone over Jordan, you shall set up these stones, which I command you this day" (ibid. v. 4). You must perpetuate these things in the manner that I command you to do. Build an altar of stones, offer sacrifices, and eat there, and write the Torah and the *mitzvos* on the stones. That is the memorial you have been commanded to set up.

III.

The Significance of the Curses in Devarim

hazal find numerous differences between the curses in the tochechah ("rebuke") of *Vayikra* (ch. 26) and those in the tochechah of *Devarim* (ch. 28). In *Bava Basra* 88, *Chazal* state that there are more curses in *Devarim* than in *Vayikra* (there are 98 or 99 in *Devarim* and half that number — 49 — in *Vayikra*. R' David Zvi Hoffmann finds it difficult to fathom how *Chazal* calculated these numbers, and decides that this needs further study). In spite of this, *Chazal* tell us in *Megillah* 31 (cited as *halachah* by *Hagahos Ma'monios*, *Tur*, and *Shulchan Aruch* in *Hilchos Tefillah*) that the latter curses are milder than the first in two ways: a) The curses in *Devarim* are addressed to the individual, while those in *Vayikra* are addressed to the community, because the language used there is in the plural. b) The first curses were stated by Hashem, whereas the second were said by Moshe.

In *Parashas Devarim*, we discussed the statement by *Chazal* that Moshe said things "on his own." It appears that *Chazal* sought to find ways of lessening the impact of the second set of curses, because in content they are more severe. Thus we are told in *Midrash Tanchuma*: "When Israel heard the hundred minus one curses in this *parashah*, their faces turned pale, and they said, 'Who can withstand these?' But then they investigated and found that the second set of curses was said in the singular, and there is no threat against the community as a whole, unlike the first curses."

Maharsha in his commentary on the *aggadah* in *Bava Basra* explains that the first curses were said before the Jews entered *Eretz Yisrael*, and at that time, the principle that all Jews are responsible for one another was not yet in effect. The latter curses, on the other hand, were said as they were about to enter the land, and then all became responsible for one another, just as where a person acts as a guarantor for a loan taken out by his friend. This interpretation is counter to all the others, and makes the latter curses far more severe in nature.

Maharsha in *Chiddushei Aggados* also quotes *Zohar* that the curses in *Devarim* referred to the Second *Beis HaMikdash*. This view was discussed at length in our section on the curses in *Vayikra*, and we will explain this further below.

Ramban uses this assumption to explain the difference between those things said "by Hashem" and those said by Moshe "on his own." In the First *Beis HaMikdash*, the *Shechinah* — "Divine Presence" — was visible to all, and that is why the reference is to the statements "by Hashem," whereas in the Second *Beis HaMikdash* there was only Hashem's Glory, but not Hashem revealing His *Shechinah*. Thus the expression, that Moshe spoke "on his own," stresses to us that in the Second *Beis HaMikdash* the *Shechinah* was no longer there.

There is also another clear difference between the curses in *Devarim* and those in *Vayikra*. In *Vayikra*, the curses were given in various stages, implying that if the people would repent at any given stage, the following stage of the curses would not come to pass. In *Devarim*, though, all the curses are given together, without any breaks. At the end of these curses, we are told, "besides the covenant which He made with them at Chorev" (*Devarim* 28:69), and there already it states that the punishment would be in accordance with the severity of the sin involved.

The various commentators analyze the nature of the curses, but we will devote our discussion to their attempts to relate them to actual events, and to see how the curses were fulfilled in Jewish history.

৬৯ The Actualization of the Curses

Abarbanel begins his commentary on the *tochechah* ("rebuke") as follows:

> It is proper that we should know that the curses in this *parashah* were not meant as a threat and an exaggeration, but came through the spirit of Hashem, so that we should know what would happen to us, and all of them (the curses) were fulfilled in those generations which sinned.

This approach is also used by *Ramban* and *Akeidah*, as we will see below.

R' David Zvi Hoffmann has another approach. It is true that he too relates this or that detail to a specific historical event which occurred in the past. For example, the verse, "Hashem will return you to Egypt in ships ... and you will be sold there to your enemies as slaves" (*Devarim* 28:68), which many commentators find hard to place in history, is given by R' David Zvi Hoffmann as a reference to the events of the Second *Beis HaMikdash*, in that before the destruction of the *Beis HaMikdash*, Titus sent 17,000 Jewish rebels to perform slave labor in Egypt. At the same time, R' Hoffmann states that "there is no need to say that the prophecy refers to a specific historical event."

The earlier commentators, though, did explain these verses based on historical events which occurred at various times. Their views were brought briefly in *Parashas Bechukosai*. We will bring additional ideas along these lines here.

As we mentioned in regard to the curses in *Vayikra*, *Ramban* and Abarbanel argue as to whether the first curses applied only to the First *Beis HaMikdash* and the second curses to the Second *Beis HaMikdash*, or whether both sets of curses applied to both destructions. These differences also reflect a difference in viewpoints, as to whether the time of the Second *Beis HaMikdash* was considered to be a time of redemption, or whether it was merely a continuation of the destruction of the First *Beis HaMikdash*, albeit a time of relative calm.

Ramban holds that the Second *Beis HaMikdash* period marked the end of the exile of the First *Beis HaMikdash*. It is true that the Second *Beis HaMikdash* was not a full redemption, because most of the Jews did not return to *Eretz Yisrael*, they did not repent fully, and there were even times when they were subservient to Persia and Greece, but in spite of that, this period was different from the previous one, and marked the end of the first exile. It is because of this view that he explains that the curses in *Vayikra* refer to the First *Beis HaMikdash*, whereas the curses in *Devarim* refer to the Second *Beis HaMikdash*. The first curses mention (*Vayikra* 26:30) "your high places" and "your (graven) images" (where idolatry was worshiped), and these are not mentioned in the second curses, as there was no longer idolatry at the time of the Second *Beis HaMikdash*. By the same token, the second set of curses does not mention the "sweet incense" (ibid. v. 31), because the fire that had come down from Heaven to consume the incense ceased after the First *Beis HaMikdash* was destroyed.

Again, the second set of curses mentions "a nation from far away ... whose language you do not understand" (*Devarim* 28:49), and that refers to Rome, whose language the Jews did not understand. This was unlike the language of the Chaldeans that the Jews did understand, as it states (*II Melachim* 18:26), "Please speak to your servants in Aramaic; for we understand it."

Similarly, the other verses in the second set of curses also refer to the Second *Beis HaMikdash.* "You will give birth to sons and daughters, and you will not have them" (*Devarim* 28:41) is a hint at the fact that the Jews were sent to Rome as slaves by Titus. These slaves were primarily the youth, who were thus separated from their families, whereas in the exile after the First *Beis HaMikdash* was destroyed, everyone, of all ages, left at the same time. The second exile is also hinted at in the verse, "Hashem will return you to Egypt in ships" (ibid. v. 68). It is true that the captives were sent everywhere, but the fact that this included Egypt deepened their tragedy, because it is utterly loathsome for a slave that had been freed to be returned to his previous master who had treated him mercilessly. The curses referring to the blight of the trees and crops refers to the siege of Jerusalem. After this, came the period of the complete exile, with a different character, where there would be no further blight to the crops, but other troubles would befall the people. Again, the Torah refers back to the last days of the Second *Beis HaMikdash,* when, "Hashem will lead you and your king ... to a nation you have not known" (ibid. v. 36), namely King Agrippas, who was taken to Rome. Alternately, this might be a reference to Aristobolus, who was seized by Pompey and was led away in chains. Even the terrible story of the eating of the flesh of one's sons and daughters came true in the siege of Jerusalem. The Torah passes over from the destruction to the exile, and back again. Whatever is said here is thus a reference to what happened when the Second *Beis HaMikdash* was destroyed and thereafter.

Ramban, as he does in a number of places, mentions the history of Josephus Flavius, which evidently made a deep impression on him, and he repeats various episodes countless times in his work.

◆§ The Destruction Has Continued to Our Own Days

Abarbanel begins with the assumption that, following the destruction of the First *Beis HaMikdash,* there was no "redemption." The period of the Second *Beis HaMikdash* was but a passing episode, and a way station after the destruction of the First *Beis HaMikdash.* That destruction has lasted to our own days. Since that time, the Jewish people have remained scattered throughout the world, settled in all the countries of Europe, and the people as a whole have not returned to *Eretz Yisrael.* When the Jews did return to *Eretz Yisrael* seventy years after the first exile, it was with the permission of the king of Persia. Some of the Jews took advantage of this permission and gathered together in one place. Afterwards they rebelled, and they were again evicted from the place in which they had been gathered. It is true that there was a *Beis HaMikdash* in the interim, in which they worshiped Hashem. During Herod's rule, the building was a magnificent one, but all of this was a state of freedom within slavery, because Herod and all his advisers were subservient to Rome and had no independence. Whatever authority they had was derived from a foreign power. The situation was better than it had been when all the Jews had been banished from *Eretz Yisrael*, but this was not a state of "redemption." Both the curses in *Vayikra* and those in *Devarim* refer to the single exile that we have suffered, which has stretched from the destruction of the First *Beis HaMikdash* to this day.

Abarbanel also quotes *Ralbag*, who explains the verse, "I will lay waste your *Batei Mikdash*," (i.e., more than one *Mikdash*) as referring to the synagogues and *batei midrash*, houses of learning in exile. The verse (*Vayikra* 26:38), "the land of your enemies will consume you," refers to the different exiles and destruction of communities in France, England, Spain, and the other western countries. Abarbanel says that when the Jews were banished from France, the number of those affected by calamity was twice that of the Jews who left Egypt.

Abarbanel has a number of proofs that the curses in *Devarim* refer to the First *Beis HaMikdash*, as well as to all the troubles that we have suffered from that time to the present. a) The curse (*Devarim* 28:25), "Hashem will cause you to be smitten before your enemies; you shall go out one way against them, and flee seven ways before them," was fulfilled only in the First *Beis HaMikdash*, because in the Second *Beis HaMikdash* the Jews fought like lions, and did not retreat. b) The series of misfortunes mentioned in verses 29-34 is also a reference to the First *Beis HaMikdash*, in which different people were exiled at different times. On the other hand, in the period of the Second *Beis HaMikdash*, there was only a single exile, in which everyone went into exile at the same time. c) The verse (ibid. v. 68), "Hashem will return you to Egypt in ships," was only fulfilled in the First *Beis HaMikdash*, because in the Second *Beis HaMikdash* everyone was sent to Rome. d) The curse (ibid. v. 36), "Hashem will lead you and your king ... to a nation you have not known," is also a reference to the First *Beis HaMikdash*, and refers to King Tzidkiyahu, and that is the way *Chazal* interpret this verse in *Yoma* 52. The reason this curse is given after a number of fierce curses is that there were a number of exiles before this act, which was one of the last. In the Second *Beis HaMikdash*, on the other hand, the king (whether this referred to Aristobolus or Agrippas) was exiled before the people. Other verses in the passage in *Devarim* resemble the Book of *Eichah* in content, and hint clearly at the First *Beis HaMikdash*.

According to Abarbanel, the Torah refers also to other destructions as well, and to other terrible events which occurred during the course of our history. The verse (ibid. v. 49), "Hashem will bring a nation against you from far," also refers to the Romans, who destroyed the Second *Beis HaMikdash*. Three times in this verse and the next the Torah mentions "a nation," and this refers to the three times that the Romans invaded Yehudah (Judea). The first was during the civil war between Hyrkanus and Aristobolus, when Pompey came to the aid of Hyrkanus. The second occurred when Herod fought Antigonus, son of Aristobolus, at which time a Roman general (Susius) came and took Jerusalem, and killed many people in it. Finally, the third took place when Vespasian and Titus invaded at the time that the *Beis HaMikdash* was destroyed.

This last invasion resulted in eight calamities to our nation: a) a severe famine — "he will eat the fruit of your cattle" (ibid. v. 51); b) an extended siege — "and he will besiege you in all your gates" (ibid. v. 52); c) disease as a result of the famine and distress — "Hashem will make your plagues and those of your descendants extraordinary" (ibid. v. 59). According to Abarbanel, it was as a result of this curse that Jews suffer more than other nations from various feverish diseases. Also as a result of this, the rebels at the time of the Roman siege were so obstinate; d) the decimation of the people, including many being killed by the rebels themselves — "you will remain few" (ibid. v. 62); e) the Jewish people being exiled from its land — "you will be uprooted from the land" (ibid. v. 63); f) people were converted or forced to convert to other religions — "you will worship other gods" (ibid. v. 64); g) those who had been brave became cowardly — "in the morning you will say, 'would that it was evening,' and in the evening you will say, 'would that it was morning'" (ibid. v. 67); h) the Jews were taken prisoner and sold throughout the world — "Hashem will return you to Egypt in ships" (ibid. v. 68). (Abarbanel notes that when the Torah adds, "there will be none who will buy you" (ibid.), that was more a blessing than a curse, for it means that the Jews would not be subservient slaves, but would work for the kings in those countries where they had been exiled.)

Abarbanel's interpretation reveals his broad knowledge of history. There is no fundamental difference between him and *Ramban*, except that, according to him, the curses in *Devarim* encompass both destructions, whereas according to *Ramban* the curses in *Devarim* refer only to the second destruction and the period thereafter. As noted, this also implies a difference in how these two commentators view the significance of the Second *Beis Mikdash*.

Akeidah follows in the same path as Abarbanel, and expands on the explanation of the verses, finding reflected in them various events. The obstinacy of the rebels at the time of the second destruction is to be seen, according to him, in the verse (ibid. v. 60), "He will return upon you all the sickness of Egypt," which refers to the fact that the Egyptians hardened their hearts in spite of the various plagues that Hashem visited on them:

> That was the hardened heart that characterized the irresponsible among our people, who refused to accept the Roman yoke on their necks, even though Titus offered peace and had promised and vowed to them that they would stay in their land and inheritance and continue their worship in the *Beis HaMikdash*. But they refused this and were obstinate, until they brought about the destruction of the *Beis HaMikdash*.

The verse, "you will worship other gods" (ibid. v. 64), refers to the Marranos in Spain, who were forced to accept a faith "that you did not know" (ibid.). The Jews at the time were aware of the practices of the Chaldeans, but they did not know of the idolatries of the western nations. "This refers to the thousands and tens of thousands of Jews who remained in this exile, and who converted because of the decrees against them."

That is *Akeidah's* approach throughout his interpretation of the curses in *Devarim*.

ᴗᴊ The Blessing in the Curse

The Chassidic works tend to take the curses and modify them into blessings. That was what the righteous did in each age. The major way of modifying the curses is by finding their underlying reasons. The Torah regards the curse as a necessary result of sinning, and one is thus able to annul the curse by *teshuvah* — repentance. The fact that it was, as we say in our prayers, "our sins which caused us to be exiled from our land," is what enables us to diagnose the sin, and from that point to finding a cure is but a short distance. This is like a doctor who tells his patient, "If you eat the following things, you will get sick." Obviously, the doctor is not cursing the patient to become ill, but on the contrary, is trying to prevent the patient from becoming ill, and tells him in advance what will happen if he doesn't listen to the doctor's advice.

In the middle of this terrible rebuke, in verse 58, the Torah tells us clearly that all of these curses will take place, "If you will not observe to do all the words of this Torah that are written in this book." That is the way these terrible curses are changed to blessings.

The second verse which is interpreted as modifying the severity of the curses is, "Among these nations you will find no ease, neither shall the sole of your foot have rest" (ibid. v. 65). We find that already in *Bereishis Rabbah* 33 Reish Lakish states, "Had the dove found a place to rest, it would not have returned." This curse prevents the Jews from becoming intermingled with the other nations and from becoming like them, and it was that which at various times served to keep our nation alive, and to bring back to it those who had tried to stray and to run away from their identity and fate. On this, *Akeidah* says:

> The Torah states, "Among these nations you will find no ease." Even if the Jews increase greatly among those nations, they will not find among them a resting place for the soles of their feet, because [the other nations] will always insult and humiliate them, and will consider [the Jews] to be a great danger, as has happened throughout all times. In fact, in our times it has reached the point where the smoke of their conflagration has reached the heavens throughout the Spanish kingdom and the islands of the sea. A third of them flee hither and thither to hide, and the others live in tremendous fear.

Ibn Ezra, too, explains (ibid. v. 36-37), "You will serve other gods ... and you will be a horror," as meaning that even though you serve other gods, it will do you no good; you will still be a horror, and everyone who sees you will be horrified. This is a terrible curse, but it includes a blessing within it. Had it not been for this curse, assimilation would have wreaked havoc among us, and we would not have survived until now.

One stands in amazement at the perfect accuracy in these interpretations of the Torah verses, for we have seen with our own eyes how true they are, and not only heard about it with our ears.

Nitzavim – נצבים

I.

The Covenant Between Hashem and Israel

he Sages of Aragon in Spain, according to Abarbanel, wondered at the covenant that Hashem made with Israel in this *parashah*. As we are told, this covenant was made (*Devarim* 29:14), "with him that is standing here with us this day before Hashem our God, and also with him that is not here with us this day." They ask: By what right did that generation, which had stood at Sinai, obligate all the followings generations to keep the Torah, when the other generations were not partners to that covenant?

Abarbanel answers this question at length. In summary, he says that this is similar to the case of a person who takes a loan, whose heirs are required to repay the loan after the person himself dies. Just as the person's heirs inherit his assets, they are also obligated to pay his debts. When the Jews were taken out of Egyptian slavery by Hashem, He acquired their bodies as His own possession. When Hashem gave them the Torah after they had left Egypt, He made His first covenant with them, and thereby He acquired their souls as well. Now Hashem made a covenant with the people about the acquisition of *Eretz Yisrael*. What Hashem wanted with this covenant was that they should know that they did not acquire the land through their strength and valor, but that the land was given to them by Hashem as a pledge and loan, in order to have them observe the Torah. Thus the later generations are included in the covenant not only because of the vow that their fathers took, but also because they belong to Hashem as His servants whom He acquired, with the covenant of the Torah and the inheritance of *Eretz Yisrael*. These assets are owned in common by all the Jewish people in all generations, and that is why the covenant obliges all of them equally.

According to Rabbenu Bachya, this covenant includes not only an obligation but also a right. It guarantees eternal life to Israel, and promises that they will have eternal life through the merit of the Torah.

Rabbenu Bachya sees a legal basis to obligate the later generations for the vows taken by their ancestors. The ancestors were the roots from which the children branched out. The root is what supplies the branches with life, and that is why the roots can obligate the branches.

Chazal expounded that all the souls, from the beginning of Creation until the end of days, were there at the time that the covenant was made. According to this, the verse quoted above ("with him that is standing here with us this day before Hashem our God, and also with him that is not here with us this day") refers to those who were not there in body, but were there in their souls. The word "standing" carries over to the second phrase, so that the meaning is: "and also with him that is not *standing* here with us this day." This refers to those who are "with us" (in soul) but are not "standing with us" (in body).

Maharal too, in *Netzach Yisrael*, chapter 11, discusses at length this eternal covenant which Hashem made with Israel. Whether Israel does or does not obey Hashem's commands, the covenant remains in effect eternally. Hashem promised us an eternal covenant, and that is not annulled by the sins of a generation or two. The covenant was not made with various individuals, but with the nation as a whole, those there and those not there. As a result, how can one say that those individuals who sinned caused the covenant that was made with all generations to be annulled?

Maharal explains the words of *Chazal*, "Hashem held the mountain above them like a vat," as a moral lesson to us for all generations, to teach us that we are bound by that covenant, and we should not err and think that our ties to the Torah are voluntary and dependent on our desires. It is true that the Jews said נַעֲשֶׂה וְנִשְׁמָע — "we will do and understand" (*Sh'mos* 24:7) — but in addition to that desire on their part there is also the unchangeable law intrinsic in their very being, due to the commitment of that eternal covenant.

R' Kook, too, in his *Igros Rayah*, 36, writes that the covenant was made with Israel both in terms of its being intrinsically chosen by Hashem and its free choice. The potential power of being chosen is great, but the degree to which it is revealed varies in accordance with the power of free will. Sometimes one or the other is stronger. In any event, the basic nucleus of the eternal covenant exists in the souls of Israel throughout all times.

Sefas Emes uses this idea to explain a passage in *Midrash Tanchuma* on our *parashah*. *Tanchuma* quotes *Malachi* 3:6, "I, Hashem, have not changed, and you, *Bnei Yaakov*, have not been destroyed." Commenting on this, *Sefas Emes* says that it is impossible for Israel to change. The innermost core of Israel will never change, and that was why Hashem made His covenant with them. The reason that Israel is referred to at the beginning of the *parashah* as standing ("you are standing today") is because they remain upright like the Heavenly hosts, and they too never change.

Malbim also explains the covenant in accordance with what is stated in various kabbalistic, chassidic and *d'rush* works. He concludes, based on three points, that the covenant applies to all generations: a) All the souls of the Jewish people were present, and even though the soul cannot exist without a body, the forefathers of the bodies were there and accepted the covenant upon themselves. This is similar to the seed of a plant or tree, which contains everything which will grow out of it. It is all the more true that the fathers have within them the potential of their descendants. As to those who ask how the earlier generations can obligate later generations, this refers to the souls involved, and all the souls were present. b) Forefathers are possibly not able to saddle their descendants with an *obligation*, but they can certainly take a positive step to *benefit* their descendants, by giving them a *zechus*, a right. The acceptance of the Torah and the *mitzvos* was a *zechus* for the descendants, as we see in (*Devarim* 30:19), "choose life, that both you and your seed may live." Thus, in a question of a *zechus*, the forefathers have the right to accept a *zechus* for their descendants. c) Hashem does not need the agreement of those He created in order to obligate them. When Hashem made a covenant, it was not because He needed Israel's consent; even without that consent Hashem could still impose His obligations on them. Hashem, however, wanted Israel to have the *zechus* of having voluntarily assumed the obligations of the covenant, so that they accepted it fully, with true and strong faith. As a result, these matters would become deeply embedded in the souls of the subsequent generations as well, for this strong faith would be passed on to later generations.

The eternal covenant obligates all of Israel, whether the people want it to or not. It surrounds all — the entire community and every single individual — with an embrace of blood and fire, from which one cannot escape in any way. *Chazal* in *Midrash Tanchuma* state:

> We find that when they attempted to withdraw from the yoke of the oath at the time of Yechezkel, what does it state there (*Yechezkel* 20:1)? "Certain of the elders of Israel came to inquire of Hashem, and sat before me" (i.e., before Yechezkel). They said to [Yechezkel], "If a *kohen* buys a slave, may the slave eat *terumah?*" He told them, "He may eat." They said to him, "If the *kohen* sold him to an Israelite (i.e., not a *kohen*), doesn't he leave his possession?" He said to them, "Yes." They said to him, "We too have left His possession (because we were exiled). Let us be like all the other nations." Yechezkel said to them (ibid. v. 32-33), "That which comes into your mind shall not be at all, that you say, 'We will be as the heathen, as the families of the countries, to serve wood and stone.' 'As I live,' says Hashem God, 'surely with a mighty hand, and with an outstretched arm, and with fury poured out, I will rule over you.' "

Abarbanel's commentary on *Yechezkel* is very interesting. Abarbanel refers this prophecy to his time, when many converted to Christianity in an attempt at escaping from the *mitzvos*, but they did not escape the Jewish fate, and soon found out that one cannot be released from the covenant which Hashem made with their forefathers. Abarbanel states:

> This prophecy is very powerful. It is worth paying attention to, because most of this has happened to us, and we have seen it in this bitter exile, where we live among the Children of Edom. Its meaning is without doubt, and it has been fulfilled in the exile of Rome in which we are, whereby (certain of) *Bnei Yisrael*, because of their distress, the decrees and the forced conversions by our enemies, left our religion, and decided to become members of the other religion, thinking that by this, Hashem's supervision over them would be removed. By this, they felt that they had left the obligation to observe the Torah, and as a result Hashem's anger and the punishment of His curses would not fall upon them. They would thus be like the other nations of the world, and would worship other gods. They thought they would

be left under the rule of chance and the influence of the heavenly bodies. They also felt that they would be successful in their affairs, as the other nations are successful, and they would no longer be Hashem's nation and His flock, and they would no longer be considered Jews.

This phenomenon, which Abarbanel attacks so vehemently, is familiar to us in our time of assimilation, where masses of German Jews and Jews of other lands thought that they would be able to escape the covenant of their forefathers, and that they would find refuge in the bosom of the other nations. They, however, were forced to realize how accurate were Yechezkel's words, when he said: "That which comes into your mind shall not be at all."

Abarbanel goes into a lengthy description of the results of this eternal covenant in his days, and says:

> Those who converted or who did so under duress (i.e., the Marranos) who left the (Jewish) religion, to them Hashem exclaimed, "with fury poured out, I will rule over you," where the fury resulted from their having forsaken their religion. There is a hint contained in this, that even if they or their descendants after them attempt to act completely as non-Jews, they will not be able to do so. The people of the country will always refer to them as Jews, and they will always be known under the name of Israel, against their will. They will still be considered to be Jews, and will be accused of practicing Jewish rituals secretly. They will then be burned alive. This is included in the verse, "with fury poured out, I will rule over you," that even if they wish to appear to be non-Jews, they will be Jews against their will, for the King, Lord of Hosts, will rule over them, even against their will.

This bitter prophecy was proven true, to our great sorrow, in our days, just as it was proven true in Abarbanel's days. One must be amazed at the exact definition of the situation, as given by one of our early rabbis, which was proven true in our days as well, and which made clear the eternal covenant, which can never be annulled, in both the positive and negative senses.

Abarbanel expands on this idea further to include the positive aspects of the covenant. In it we have a promise of the eternity of Israel and its ultimate redemption. This is a beacon of hope for all those who came from the loins of Yehudah, regardless of their circumstances.

This hope of all the Jewish people is sustained by the general covenant of every Jew, whether or not he is faithful to that covenant, or even if he has attempted to break away from it totally. This idea is also found constantly throughout *Maharal's* works. He stresses this especially in regard to the burning bush, at which Hashem told Moshe about the future of the nation that he was going to redeem. In his *Gevuros Hashem* Chapter 24, *Maharal* says:

It states, "I have surely seen" (רָאֹה רָאִיתִי — *Sh'mos* 3:7). *Chazal* deduced from the repetition of the words ... that Hashem explained to Moshe that He had foreseen two things, the first that they were going to come to Sinai and receive His Torah, and the second that they would sin with the Golden Calf. Thus we see that Hashem revealed in advance that He saw that Israel would sin, and no one can claim that Hashem chose Israel based on the idea that they were righteous, and only with that understanding, and that if they would sin, Hashem would have nothing to do with them. Hashem, therefore, informed Moshe how He acts; even though Israel would sin against Him, if they would cry out to Him, He would save them.

Similarly, in *Netzach Yisrael*, *Maharal* explains the reason why Avraham's *zechus* and his righteousness are not mentioned, but there is only mention of Hashem *choosing* Avraham. The covenant is not dependent on anything except for the fact that Hashem chose Avraham.

Thus, when Hashem redeemed them He said that even though they eventually sin, He nevertheless redeems them. This is the great special characteristic of Israel — that Hashem redeems them regardless. He does not look for Israel's righteousness, but only (redeems them) because He loves Israel for itself.

⋄⋗ A Natural Necessity

Akeidah develops this idea in greater depth. He asks a number of questions regarding this covenant which is in effect for all generations. Isn't that against the idea of man's free will? If man has free will, shouldn't that mean that the covenant is canceled? Also, what is the purpose of this covenant, when Hashem had stated clearly (*Yechezkel* 20:33), "with a mighty hand ... I will rule over you"? Doesn't that make the covenant superfluous? *Akeidah* also asks a number of other questions along these lines.

Akeidah then develops the idea that this covenant was a natural necessity, and Hashem instilled the covenant within us so that the Jewish people as a whole would be able to continue to exist, just as all of Hashem's creatures have a natural instinct of self-preservation, so that they do everything possible to stay alive.

This is analogous to a king who appointed a number of his ministers to high positions, provided that they remain loyal to him. After a number of generations, their descendants said, "Why should we continue to remain loyal to the king?" When they said this, the king took away his protection from them, and with this they lost their nobility; anyone who wished could now rise up and kill them. Thus no Jew may leave the covenant of Hashem, for if he would do so, he would be signing his own death sentence, as it were, and that is national suicide. When a person leaves the covenant, it is not that he is punished, but whatever happens is the inevitable consequence of his deed. This choice of the covenant cannot be annulled. The whole Jewish community cannot commit collective suicide. That is a natural law which cannot be changed. This is what *Chazal* meant when they said that at the giving of the Torah "Hashem held the mountain above them like a vat" — namely that Hashem held over the Jewish people the desire for self-preservation. Thus, later, in the time of Mordechai and Esther, when the Jews learned from their experience that this self-preservation was part of their very being, they voluntarily accepted the Torah upon themselves. They had learned that by removing the yoke of heaven they had almost been wiped out.

That is why the Torah covenant will never be annulled; if the Jews do not accept it voluntarily, they will be forced to accept it against their will, by the law of self-preservation. This idea can be seen in *Yirmiyahu* 31:34-35, where we are told, "Thus said Hashem, Who gives the sun as a light by day, and the laws of the moon and stars as light by night, Who stirs the sea and its waves roar . . . 'If those laws depart from before Me,' says Hashem, 'then the seed of Israel also shall cease from being a nation before Me for ever.' " Just as the Heavens and the earth cannot cease to exist on their own, the same is true for the existence of the Jewish people. Hashem made a covenant with the entire people not to commit collective suicide, and that is the nature of the covenant. There are different ways of removing the yoke of heaven. One type is where a person annuls the covenant, while the other is where the person simply sins. The first type cannot occur. It is the second type for which we suffer to this very day.

II.

"You Will Return to Hashem Your God"

The *mitzvah* of *teshuvah* (repentance) is one of the 613 *mitzvos* according to most of those who list the *mitzvos*. (Only R' Sa'adiah Gaon does not include it in the 613.) There is a dispute, though, as to where this is to be found in the Torah. *Semak* holds that the source is the verse (*Devarim* 30:2), "You will return to Hashem your God," which, in his view, is a command. *Rambam*, on the other hand, in *Hilchos Teshuvah* 7:5, says that "You will return to Hashem your God" is a promise, and not a command. According to *Rambam*, the source for the *mitzvah* of *teshuvah* is in the verse (*Bamidbar* 5:7), "They will confess," for *teshuvah* consists of confession.

Chinuch, like *Rambam*, holds:

> By admitting to the sin orally, the sinner's thoughts are exposed, that he sincerely believes that it is clear and apparent to Hashem what he did, and he will not treat (Hashem's) eye which sees as one which does not see. Also, by mentioning the sin, especially when he regrets it, he will be careful about it the next time, so as to ensure that he will not fail again, after he has stated orally, "I have done the following, and I was stupid in my actions."

R' Perla, in his commentary on R' Sa'adiah Gaon's *613 Mitzvos*, notes that there is already a dispute among the *geonim* about this, between Mar Cheifetz Aluf, who holds like *Semak*, and Rabbenu Shmuel ben Chofni Kohen, who holds like *Rambam*.

Ramban holds that "you will return" is both a *mitzvah* and a promise. He explains that the verse (*Devarim* 30:11), "this *mitzvah* which I am commanding you," refers to the *mitzvah* of *teshuvah*, whereas (ibid. v. 1-2), "You will return to your heart ... and you will return to Hashem your God," is both a *mitzvah* and a promise that this will occur. *Ramban* does not disagree with *Rambam* as to the components of the *mitzvah* of *teshuvah*, and he also holds that a person must make an oral confession and must resolve not to repeat the sin again. Thus *Ramban* explains the verse (ibid. v. 14), "in your mouth and in your heart to perform it," as meaning that the people must orally confess their sins and the sins of their fathers, and must return in their hearts to Hashem. They must accept the Torah this day for all future generations. The *mitzvah* itself, though, is that of *teshuvah*, as it states (ibid. v.2), "you will return."

Baal HaTurim and *S'forno* also explain that "this *mitzvah*" (ibid. v. 11) refers to the *mitzvah* of *teshuvah*. *S'forno's* interpretation is a simple one. "It is not hidden from you" (ibid.) — you do not need a prophet to teach it to you. "It is not far away" (ibid.). You do not need the distant wise men of your generation to teach you what to do. You can do *teshuvah* in every place and at every time. The Torah then repeats this idea, and states (ibid. v. 12): "It is not in heaven," that you should need a prophet, "nor is it across the ocean," (ibid. v. 13) that you should need distant wise men. Rather, it is "in your mouth and in your heart to do it" (ibid. v. 14) by yourself, by regretting the past and resolving for the future. On this, *Rambam*, *Hilchos Teshuvah*, Chapter 7, states that the Torah had already promised that in the end, Israel will do *teshuvah*.

Rambam does not include *teshuvah* as such in the 613 *mitzvos* but only lists one detail, the requirement to confess — *vidui* — as a *mitzvah*. One who studies *Rambam* will find that there are three components of *teshuvah*: a) *vidui*; b) regret; c) forsaking the sin.

Chinuch, whom we brought above, states that *"vidui"* includes all three of these aspects. Others who deal with the laws of *teshuvah* add other components. R' Samson Raphael Hirsch, in his *Chorev*, finds four components of *teshuvah*: a) admitting that one has sinned; b) repairing the sin either by a reckoning with oneself in the case of sins between man and God, or by requesting forgiveness in the case of sins between oneself and one's fellow man; c) regret for the past; d) resolving not to sin in the future. In any event, it is remarkable that *Rambam* lays the emphasis on *vidui*, and includes only it in his *Sefer HaMitzvos*, without mentioning *teshuvah* as such. It appears that *Rambam* is following in the footsteps of R' Sa'adiah Gaon and other *rishonim*, that our passage in *Parashas Nitzavim* is a prophecy about the future of the Jewish people, and does not contain commands relative to individual Jews.

Actually, *Ramban* states clearly that "this *parashah* refers to the future, because none of its contents have ever come to pass, but they will come to pass in the future." *Ramban* nevertheless sees "you will return" (ibid. v. 2) as a command, whereas according to *Rambam* it is only a prophecy regarding the future.

Rambam also deduces from this in *Hilchos Melachim* 11:1:

Whoever does not believe in the *Mashiach*, or who does not await his coming, does not only deny the other prophets, but (denies) the Torah and our teacher Moshe, for the Torah testified regarding [the Redemption], as it states (ibid. v. 3), "Hashem your God will return your exile and will take pity on you and will return and gather you."

Based on the above, *Rambam* states in *Hilchos Teshuvah* Chapter 7 that the Torah promised that Israel will do *teshuvah* at the end of their exile, and will be redeemed immediately thereafter, as it states (ibid. v. 1-3), "It shall come to pass, when all these things are come upon you ... you will return to Hashem your God ... and Hashem your God will return your exile."

Oznayim LaTorah deduces beautifully that "you will return" is not a conditional statement. The Torah does not say, "if you return," but "you will return." This is a promise to Israel that they will repent.

Toras HaMo'adim wishes to say that *Rambam* did not include the *mitzvah* of *teshuvah* in the 613 *mitzvos* because of the rule which he states in *Sefer HaMitzvos* Principle 4, that a *mitzvah* which applies to other *mitzvos* or prohibitions, or which is common to them, or which is a means or preparation for achieving other *mitzvos* but has no purpose of its own except to correct others, is not included in the listing of the *mitzvos*. *Teshuvah* too is not an independent *mitzvah* but is a means to correct the violation of the other *mitzvos*. He adds that R' Kook had stated that the reason *Rambam* did not list living in *Eretz Yisrael* among the 613 *mitzvos* is because most of the *mitzvos* of the Torah are dependent on it, and it is but a *tool* to the observance of the Torah. This view of *Toras HaMoadim* can be questioned, for by the same token one can claim that *vidui* is but a tool, and why then should it be listed among the *mitzvos*?

It appears, though, that the reason why *Rambam* did not include *teshuvah* among the 613 *mitzvos* is because, as we noted, "you will return" (ibid. v. 2), according to *Rambam*, is a promise to all of Israel, and the only *teshuvah* that the Torah lists is that of *vidui*, which, according to *Mechilta* which *Rambam* quotes, is a *mitzvah* which applies to every single Jew, whether in *Eretz Yisrael* or outside it.

Many questions have been asked by both *rishonim* and *acharonim* about what *teshuvah* accomplishes. What was especially astonishing to many of these commentators is the praise which *Chazal* heap on a *ba'al teshuvah* (penitent), to the extent that they place him above perfect *tzaddikim*. Is it fair that a person who sinned and then did *teshuvah* should be greater than people who never sinned? There are numerous answers and explanations of this. *Rambam*, in *Moreh Nevuchim* 3:36, gives a simple answer. Had there not been a *mitzvah* of *teshuvah*, there could not be such a thing as Jews that observe the Torah and *mitzvos*:

> It is impossible for a person not to err or sin, either because he errs in judgment, or because he adopts an undesirable character trait, or because he is overcome by his passions or his anger. If a person believed that he could never rectify his crooked ways he would continue repeating his error, and he might even increase his rebellious acts, as he would have no remedy. However, our faith in *teshuvah* will cause us to improve, to return to the best of ways, and to become more perfect than before we sinned.

The essence of *teshuvah* is based on recognition of the nature of mankind. Without *teshuvah*, humanity would sink deeper into sin, without any hope of repairing the damage. If Hashem created man with his nature the way it is, he cannot exist without *teshuvah* which straightens out his crooked ways. The fact that Hashem gave us *teshuvah* was not merely an act of magnanimity on His part, but a basic principle in the existence of humanity, and its moral characteristics on earth. It is a tool for the very survival of mankind.

Meshech Chochmah has an interesting point on *teshuvah*. There are numerous works about how to do *teshuvah* and the proper behavior of the *ba'al teshuvah*. *Meshech Chochmah* adds his own original interpretation. A perfect *tzaddik* may choose to follow the path of R' Shimon bar Yochai and have nothing to do with worldly matters, but a *ba'al teshuvah* must be involved in physical labor, so that he will not sink into thoughts of his former sins. The Torah tells us in regard to *ba'alei teshuvah* (ibid. v. 9), "Hashem your God will give you plenty in all the work of your hands." In *Parashas Ki Savo*, Chapter 28, where we are told of the blessings that will come to the *tzaddik* who "listens to the voice of Hashem your God," the Torah makes no mention of "the work of your hands," for the perfect *tzaddik* follows the way of R' Shimon bar Yochai and removes himself entirely from the worldly occupations. But as far as a *ba'al teshuvah* is concerned, he must act like R' Yishmael, who advises to "take part in worldly matters" (*Berachos* 35b). The *ba'al teshuvah* needs a mixture of Torah and hard work, for the combination of the two "causes sin to be forgotten" (*Avos* 2:2).

⋖§ The Types of Teshuvah and the Differences Between Them

Seven times the word *teshuvah*, in various forms, is mentioned in *Parashas Nitzavim*, and, parallel to this, we find the idea of Hashem returning, as in (*Devarim* 30:3), "Hashem will return your exile," and (ibid. v. 9), "Hashem will return to rejoice over you." The commentators see these seven references to *teshuvah* as representing different stages in it. At first, the *teshuvah* is not complete, and as a result Hashem's reward for it is incomplete as well. Then the *teshuvah* improves, eventually reaching perfection.

Akeidah and Abarbanel explain that the verse (ibid. v. 8), "You will return and hearken to Hashem's voice," refers to a higher degree of *teshuvah* than the preceding verses. As a result, the reward from Hashem is also greater, and Hashem will bless (ibid. v. 9) "the fruit of your womb (i.e., a blessing of the body) and the fruit of your land (a financial blessing), and He will return to rejoice over you" (a spiritual blessing).

The first *teshuvah* mentioned (v. 2) is the lowest level of *teshuvah*, for which Hashem will reward us by gathering in the exiles (v. 3).

R' Shlomo of Radomsk explains the verse (ibid. v. 8), "You will return and hearken," as meaning that we will merit to ascend to higher levels of *teshuvah*, and each will bring us to an even higher level.

There are *acharonim*, though, such as *HaKesav VeHaKabalah* and *Malbim*, who see the phrase "you will return" (ibid. v. 2) as not implying a complete *teshuvah*, but just the acceptance of the duty to do *teshuvah*. *HaKesav VeHaKabalah* says that when the Torah states, "You will return to Hashem your God and hearken to His voice" (ibid.), that refers to a person who has not accepted upon himself to perform all the *mitzvos*, but has only heard the voice calling him to return; in other words, the person has reached the stage of regret, as it states (ibid. v. 1), "You will return to your heart."

Malbim explains that one cannot do complete *teshuvah* outside *Eretz Yisrael*, because most *mitzvos* are dependent on *Eretz Yisrael* and on the *Beis HaMikdash*. Outside *Eretz Yisrael*, the only possible *teshuvah* is that of "You will hearken to His voice" (ibid. v. 2), which is the readiness and preparation to perform *mitzvos*. The reason the Torah states, "with all your heart and with all your soul" (ibid.), is that you will only have the desire to perform the *mitzvos*, but that desire can only be fulfilled once Hashem gathers the Jews in to *Eretz*

Yisrael from all over the world. That is why the Torah only afterwards speaks of complete *teshuvah*, stating (ibid. v. 8), "you will return and hearken to Hashem's voice and do all His *mitzvos*," in connection with *Eretz Yisrael*.

Chasam Sofer adds another idea. The Torah wants to have additional *teshuvah* in *Eretz Yisrael*, because one's *teshuvah* must take place in the place where he sinned. We sinned in *Eretz Yisrael*, and it is in *Eretz Yisrael* that we must confess our sins and do *teshuvah*.

Kesav Sofer goes a step further. He states that the Torah wished to test us, to see whether we can keep the *mitzvos* even under conditions of freedom. He says this in regard to Abarbanel's commentary on the verses here, that before He gathers in the exiles from all over the world, Hashem will ease the yoke of exile, as it states (ibid. v. 3), "and He will take pity on you."

Ramban, though, holds that the reference here is to complete *teshuvah*. The promise is that you will return to Hashem with all your heart, and you will accept the obligation for yourself and your future descendants to perform all the *mitzvos*, as Hashem commands you this day, just as the Jews did the second time they were redeemed, as it states (*Nechemiah* 10:30):

> (They) entered into oath [backed by] a curse, to walk in God's law, which was given by Moshe the servant of God, and to observe and do all the commandments of Hashem our God, and His judgments and His statutes.

Such *teshuvah* will bring about the gathering in of the exiles. The second stage, which will follow, is the cancellation of the *yetzer hara*, as it states (*Devarim* 30:6), "Hashem your God will circumcise your heart." The world is based on free will, but in the days of the *Mashiach* the ability to make the right choice will be part of man's nature. He will not desire anything which is not good for him, and he will revert to the stage of Adam before the sin of the Tree of Knowledge. So too does it state in *Yechezkel* (36:26-27), "I will give you a new heart, and will put a new spirit in you ... and I will cause you to walk in My statutes, and you shall keep My judgments, and do them."

Ramban does not tell us why there is need for *teshuvah* after this, as we see in the verse, "You will return and hearken to the voice of Hashem" (*Devarim* 30:8). *S'forno*, though, as well as *HaKesav VeHaKabalah* and other commentators, states that the meaning of "you will return (תָשׁוּב)" is not *teshuvah*, but that you will rest and find contentment, as in (*Yeshayahu* 30:15), "in rest (בְּשׁוּבָה) and ease you will be saved." After Hashem gathers in the exiles this time, there will be no more exile, but Israel will live in peace on its land.

HaKesav VeHaKabalah explains (*Devarim* 30:3) "Hashem your God will return (וְשָׁב) your captivity (שְׁבוּתְךָ)" in a similar fashion: Hashem will be pleased and content with your *teshuvah*, and even though it only comes because of your fear of Hashem's punishment, He will accept it, and from that time on, your life will be one of contentment.

The reason why, before mentioning *teshuvah*, the Torah tells us (ibid. v. 1), "It shall come to pass, when all these things are come upon you, the blessing and the curse," says *Or HaChayim*, is to stress that regardless of whether the *teshuvah* comes because of love ("blessing") or fear ("curse") of Hashem, Hashem will consider both as equally acceptable.

It would appear that the simple meaning of the text is that after you see that by keeping the *mitzvos* you receive a blessing, and when you transgress the *mitzvos* you are punished by a curse, you will then consider these matters carefully and do *teshuvah*, so that Hashem will ultimately gather in the exiles, and peace and tranquility will return, never again to be disturbed.

∽§ What the Redemption Will Be

As we mentioned earlier, according to R' Sa'adiah Gaon and *Rambam* the passage of "you will return" (*Devarim* 30:1-10) refers to the time of *Mashiach*. This is the source for the ultimate redemption of Israel.

Meshech Chochmah quotes *Yerushalmi Shevi'is*, where R' Yose bar Chanina refers the verses to the redemption at the time of Ezra, and according to this, the verse (*Devarim* 30:6), "Hashem your God will circumcise your heart and the heart of your descendants to love Hashem," refers to the fact that the *yetzer hara* of idolatry was abolished by *Anshei Knesses HaGedolah*, the Men of the Great Assembly. Thus we see that that view sees this *parashah* as referring to events which have already occurred. This, however, is the opinion of a single *amora*. The rest of *Chazal*, though, and the various commentators, regard this *parashah* as applying to the ultimate redemption. *Rambam* too, in his commentary on the Mishnah, Principle 12, states that "You will return" refers to the gathering in of the exiles at the time of *Mashiach*.

Avnei Shoham notes something interesting in *Rambam*. *Rambam* links the whole issue of *Mashiach* to "David" himself. In *Hilchos Melachim*, *Rambam* writes, "The King *Mashiach* will return the kingdom of David (not 'of the house of David')." Later, *Rambam* refers to David as "the first *Mashiach*" and to the *Mashiach* as "the last *Mashiach*." Further in *Hilchos Melachim*, *Rambam* writes, "If a king arises from the house of David, who studies the Torah and occupies himself with the *mitzvos* as David his father ..." This reference to David is in keeping with a verse in *Amos* (9:11), "In that day I will raise up the tabernacle of David that has fallen."

According to *Rambam*, at first a king will arise of the house of David, who will restore the monarchy as of old. Afterwards he will build the *Beis HaMikdash* and will gather in the exiles of Israel.

In reality, there are various opinions as to the order of the redemption in the future. According to *Yerushalmi Ma'aser Sheni* Chapter 5, the first step will be the building of the *Beis HaMikdash*, after which *Mashiach* will come. *Chinuch Mitzvah* 95 states that the Jewish people will be living in their land before the *Beis HaMikdash* is built. *Maharsha* on *Megillah* 17 says that the first stage of the redemption will be the gathering in of the exiles. *Tosafos Yom Tov*, on the other hand, *Ma'aser Sheni* Chapter 5, states that before *Mashiach* comes, the other nations will have a certain degree of control over us in *Eretz Yisrael*, just as was the case at the beginning of the Second *Beis HaMikdash* period.

All of the exact details will remain a mystery to us until the End of Days is upon us. Then we will know the true stages of our redemption.

Many commentators wish to find, within the verses regarding the redemption, a hint as to how it will occur. According to *Ran* (the same idea is also brought in Abarbanel), the Jews will find a certain relaxation of the pressure against them by the gentiles, and afterwards we will have the gathering in of the exiles.

Ha'amek Davar has an interesting description of the sequence of events, based on how he understands the verses. At first, there will be a reawakening of the Jews who live among major nations, as it states (*Devarim* 30:1), בְּכָל הַגּוֹיִם, "among all the nations," as opposed to בְּכָל הָעַמִּים, "among all the peoples." This awakening will be to return to *Eretz Yisrael*, as it states (ibid. v. 3), "Hashem your God will return your captivity." After the Jews living among the major nations move to *Eretz Yisrael*, "Hashem will gather you in from all the peoples" (מִכָּל הָעַמִּים — ibid.), namely, from all the other nations, regardless of size. This will be a slow process. *Ha'amek Davar* quotes *Ramban* on *Shir HaShirim* 8:12, "the thousand are yours, O Shlomo," that at first there will be a small degree of gathering in of the exiles, with the permission of the other nations. Afterwards, Hashem will again stretch out His hand, as it states (*Devarim* 30:3), "He will return and gather you in." After the people return to *Eretz Yisrael* from all the other nations, Hashem will punish those nations which persecuted the Jews, as explained in *Parashas Ha'azinu*, and as we see here (ibid. v. 7), "Hashem your God will place all these curses on your enemies."

Abarbanel finds in these verses a hint at the fact that Marranos and those who had been forcibly converted will return to Judaism and will move to *Eretz Yisrael*. Regarding the Marranos, we are told (ibid. v. 1), "You shall return to your heart," because they could not do this openly, whereas in regard to others it states (ibid. v. 2), "you will return." The Jews who remain faithful to Hashem's words will leave their captivity and their exile. Of them, it states (ibid. v. 3), "Hashem your God will return your captivity." The Marranos, though, do not feel the severity of this captivity, and in regard to them, the Torah states (ibid.), "He will return and gather you."

Vayeilech – וַיֵּלֶךְ

I.

Moshe in His Last Days

Our *parashah* deals with Moshe's last actions before he dies. The first thing he does is to inform the people of his death, which is imminent. He encourages and prepares them, telling them that they will inherit *Eretz Yisrael* under Yehoshua's leadership. Before all of Israel, Moshe appoints Yehoshua as the leader to succeed him. Hashem, too, corroborates this appointment, when He speaks to Moshe in the presence of Yehoshua.

The major emphasis of Moshe, the faithful shepherd, is to implant within the people the recognition that its existence depends on learning and observing the Torah. Moshe writes down the Torah, teaches and hands it over to the Levites, so that it will be placed in the *Kodesh HaKodashim* — "the Holy of Holies" — where it will remain. Two *mitzvos* are then given to the nation in order to ensure that the people will remain bound to the Torah: a) the *mitzvah* of *hakhel* (assembly) at the end of every *shemittah* cycle, when all the people are to be called together to hear specific parts of the Torah read to them. Even though this is a time-related *mitzvah*, women are obligated to keep it, and even the children must attend; b) the *mitzvah* for each person to write his own personal Torah scroll, which is deduced from the verse (*Devarim* 31:19), "Now write for yourselves this song."

Thus this *parashah* consists of words of encouragement which are meant to strengthen the people's faith in the fact that they will inherit the land, even though Moshe will no longer be present, and primarily to have the Torah become deeply rooted within the people, so that it should become the inheritance of all its classes.

✂ "Moshe Went"

The term, וַיֵּלֶךְ — "he went" — is discussed by the commentators. Abarbanel notes that two chapters earlier, in *Devarim* 29:1, we are told, "Moshe called all of Israel and said to them," the continuation of this being the beginning of *Parashas Nitzavim*, "You are all standing today before Hashem your God" (ibid. v. 9). That means that all of Israel were already there, and why should Moshe have needed to go to talk to them? *Ramban* answers that after Moshe completed what he had to say, all went to their tents. Now, before he died, Moshe went to the people to part from them.

Ibn Ezra says that Moshe went to each tribe individually, telling it of his impending death, and comforting the people by telling them not to fear, for Hashem would keep His word. It was at that time, says Ibn Ezra, that Moshe told each tribe its blessing, even though the text of these blessings appears only in the last *parashah* of the Torah, *VeZos HaBrachah*.

S'forno holds that after the covenant had been made, Moshe wanted the people to accept the covenant joyously, and not in mourning for his death. He therefore went to the tents of Israel, so as to inspire the people and to comfort them.

R' Samson Raphael Hirsch says that as the entire *parashah* is Moshe's will, he, who was the most humble man of all, did not bother the people to come to him, but rather went to them.

Various Chassidic works state that Moshe "went" and entered into the soul of each individual Jew. Each Jew has a spark of Moshe in him. This is what is seen in the end of this verse, "to all of Israel" (*Devarim* 31:1), namely that Moshe entered into the soul of each Jew. Furthermore, various Chassidic works state that the reason why "no man knew his burial place" (ibid. 34:6) is because Moshe's soul is stored away among the totality of Jewish souls.

Yehonasan ben Uzziel explains the words "Moshe went" as "Moshe went to the *beis hamidrash*." Many commentators wonder as to the origin of this statement. There is a beautiful answer to this question. *Rashi*, on the verse (ibid. 31:2), "I am no longer able to go out or come in," states that the wellsprings of wisdom were shut off to Moshe. He therefore went to the *beis hamidrash* to hear the Torah of others.

Baal HaTurim states that just before the words "Moshe went" the Torah mentions (ibid. 30:20), "the land that Hashem swore to give to your fathers Avraham, Yitzchak and Yaakov." Moshe went to tell

Avraham, Yitzchak and Yaakov that Hashem was keeping His promise, and was giving *Eretz Yisrael* to the Jewish people, by means of Yehoshua.

⋞ The Torah and Eretz Yisrael

The link between the Torah and *Eretz Yisrael* is expressed in our *parashah* when Moshe repeats the warning of the passage about the curses (*Devarim* ch. 28) and the troubles that will befall the nation if they do not observe the Torah, for Torah observance is the condition for inheriting *Eretz Yisrael*. But there is a major promise in our *parashah* that the Torah will not be forgotten by the Jewish people, even though Hashem knows the way the people will act "before I bring them to the land" (ibid. 31:21). He also knows that "you will surely become corrupted" (ibid. v. 29), but Moshe tells all of Israel "the words of this song until the end" (ibid. v. 30), and it is this song which is the witness to the words of Hashem that the Torah will always be the essence and root of Israel.

Moshe commands the Levites to place the Torah scroll in the *Kodesh HaKodashim*, next to the Ark of the Covenant (ibid. v. 25-26). The reason for the placing of one next to the other, says R' Ezriel Hildesheimer, is to guard the Torah from being "doctored" by any foreigners, so as to prevent people from making changes or forging things. This idea is also found in *Sifsei Kohen*, one of *Arizal's* disciples. He expresses this idea in almost the same words. Moshe made sure to guard the originality of the Torah, so that it should not be "doctored" by forgers. My friend R' Yosef Aaron Barnet נ"י also pointed out to me that the same concept is to be found in *Midrash Rabbah* on this *parashah*:

> R' Yannai said, "He (Moshe) wrote twelve Torah scrolls for the twelve tribes, and he placed one (other) in the Ark, so that if anyone wished to forge any matter, they [would refute him by] taking out the one in the *Aron*."

Together with his concern to guard the integrity of the Torah text, Moshe also informed Yehoshua that "you will inherit [the land]." Yehoshua would be the one to complete the conquest of the land. *Avnei Shoham* has a beautiful comment on this. The way Yehoshua inherited the land was through conquest, as explained by *Rambam* in *Hilchos Terumos* 1:8 and *Hilchos Beis HaBechirah* 10:16.

Rambam also explains there, why the first time that *Eretz Yisrael* was sanctified, at the time of Yehoshua, the sanctity remained only until the Jews were exiled after the destruction of the First *Beis HaMikdash*, while the *kedushah* — sanctification — of the land at the time of Ezra has remained to this day. The first *kedushah* was based on Yehoshua's conquest. Once that conquest was annulled by Nebuchadnezzar's conquest of the land, the *kedushah* was also annulled. The second *kedushah*, though, was brought about by the Jews'· occupancy of the land at the time of Ezra (i.e., by חֲזָקָה), and that *kedushah* did not lapse.

On this, *Kesef Mishneh* (on *Hilchos Beis HaBechirah*) asks: Didn't the Jews gain the right to a חֲזָקָה on the land after Yehoshua's conquest, by living on the land? Why then did the *kedushah* lapse with Nebuchadnezzar's conquest? Why should Yehoshua's occupancy with conquest be weaker than Ezra's occupancy without conquest?

The difference between conquest and חֲזָקָה (occupancy), though, is that conquest refers to the conquered nation, whereas חֲזָקָה refers to the land. It is obvious that one who conquers another nation takes possession of its assets. The ownership of those possessions, though, is based on the conquest, which is what caused one to have the חֲזָקָה in the first place. The second *kedushah*, though, was a result purely of the חֲזָקָה, and is not annulled.

◆§ The Mitzvah of Hakhel After Shemittah

In order to ensure that the Torah would be an integral part of Israel, Moshe announced the *mitzvah* of *hakhel*, which required the entire nation to come and hear the reading of passages of the Torah from the king. The purpose of this was "so that they will learn and fear" (*Devarim* 31:12).

According to *Chinuch*, the reason for *hakhel* is that as the foundation of the Jewish people is the Torah, it is fitting that it should be heard and taught when all the people are gathered together.

Rambam in *Hilchos Chagigah* states that the positive *mitzvah* of *hakhel* is to gather together all the people of Israel — men, women and children — at the conclusion of every *shemittah* year, and to read to them certain *parashiyos* of the Torah, so as to rouse the people to perform *mitzvos* and to strengthen their belief in the true religion, as it states (ibid. v. 10-12), "At the end of seven years, at the season of the *shemittah* year, at the *Succos* festival, when all Israel come ... gather together the people, the men, women and children, and your strangers who are within your gates." Afterwards, *Rambam* gives the various laws involved regarding when to read, how, and who are obligated to hear this reading.

According to Abarbanel, the time for this reading is on *Succos*, because that festival is after *Rosh Hashanah* and *Yom Kippur*, during which Israel all showed their subservience to Hashem's will. When all of Israel come to appear before Hashem in Yerushalayim on *Succos*, they will be cleaving to Hashem, and will appreciate the reading and learn to fear Hashem.

R' David Zvi Hoffmann states that even though the Festival of the Ingathering (i.e., *Succos*) marks the end of the work for the year, this is not true for *Succos* after *shemittah*, because the farmer has not worked for the entire year before *Succos*. This, then, is a reminder of how things were in the desert, and the people are now ready to receive the Torah anew, in fear and awe. *Kli Yakar* states that after *shemittah* the different classes of the rich and the poor have been erased. Thus there can be a true *hakhel* (assembly) and unity among the people.

Meshech Chochmah also sees the end of the *shemittah* year as being the most suitable time for absorbing the Torah, as Israel are totally free to serve Hashem. On the other hand, he sees the emphasis of the *mitzvah* in terms of an encouragement to the people to keep the Torah when they first begin their new six-year work cycle and are looking forward longingly to the next *shemittah* year. It is then that the people must be gathered, so that they will integrate the Torah laws into their everyday lives.

⋖§ The Parashah of the King

The Mishnah in *Sotah* 32 refers to the *parashah* of *hakhel* as the "*Parashah* of the King" (פָּרָשַׁת הַמֶּלֶךְ), as it was he who read the Torah from the beginning of *Devarim* to the *Shema* (*Devarim* 1:1-6:9). He then reads *Devarim* 11:13-22, and concludes [according to *Rambam*] with *Devarim* 14:22-28:69. *Chazal* tell us of King Agrippas, who received the Torah scroll from the *kohen gadol* and then proceeded to read it while standing. Then, when he reached the verse (*Devarim* 17:15), "you may not set a foreign man over you," he began crying [since he was not of Jewish descent]. *Chazal* then comforted him and told him, "Do not fear, Agrippas. You are our brother." Various *rishonim* state that the reading of the Torah at *hakhel* is the duty of the king.

It is interesting, though, that Josephus Flavius, in his *Antiquities of the Jews* IV, writes that it was the *kohen gadol* (High Priest) who read the Torah. And Josephus wrote of what he had seen with his own eyes. However, it is possible that, as Josephus lived at the time of

Agrippas II, who was far removed from Judaism, the reading of the Torah was given over at that time to the *kohen gadol*. The words of *Chazal* quoted above refer to Agrippas I, who appreciated the Torah.

Minchas Chinuch raises a question as to whether it is *halachah l'Moshe miSinai* — a Torah law handed down orally to Moshe at Sinai — that only the king reads the Torah, and where there is no king there is no reading. Thus, according to this view, the *mitzvah* was never observed until Shaul became the king. Alternatively, the *halachah* might be that the greatest man of the generation should read the Torah if there is no king.

Abarbanel and *Ralbag* hold that the duty to read the Torah in *hakhel* does not apply only to the king. *Ha'amek Davar* also holds that Moshe addressed the *kohanim* (*Devarim* 31:10) when giving this *mitzvah*, in order to indicate that if there is no king, the greatest person reads the Torah. That is also the opinion of *Tiferes Yisrael* in *Mishnayos Sotah*.

This also appears to be logical. The *mitzvah* of *hakhel* is one which is meant to implant Torah within Israel. If the reading of the Torah was assigned to the king, it was not meant to honor him, for that was not the purpose of the *mitzvah*. The king was the one to read the Torah so that he too would be obligated by what is written in the Torah, and so as to stress that he too is subservient to the Torah and accepts the yoke of the Kingdom of Heaven. If, however, there was no king, the reading of the Torah was meant to make the greatest leader and the people as a whole subservient to the Torah. And that was the aim of the *mitzvah* of *hakhel*.

◂§ "So that They Will Hear, and So that They Will Learn, and Fear Hashem"

The stress on "hearing, learning and fearing Hashem" is mentioned only in regard to the *mitzvah* of *hakhel*. This *mitzvah* includes men, women and children, converts, and even "their children who have not known" (ibid. v. 13). *Chazal* in *Chagigah* 3 tell us that the men come to learn, the women to listen, and the children come so as to give a reward to those who brought them. The question then arises: If children are not obligated to come, why do those who bring them earn a reward? *Sefas Emes* answers that the reward of those who bring them is the fact that by doing so, they draw their children closer to Torah. The parents who bring their children to the tents of Torah will be rewarded by raising children easily to the Torah path.

This idea is also to be found in *Akeidah*, who states that the reward of those who bring their children is "that they will learn" (ibid. v. 12).

Abarbanel too says that the reward of the fathers is that they will find it easier to educate their children, as the children have already become accustomed to hear the words of Hashem.

Chasam Sofer says that this holy place (*Beis HaMikdash*) has the capacity to implant purity (*taharah*) in one's heart, so that when these children grow up, they themselves will follow the proper path. Hashem thus wanted to reward those who bring their children to this level of *kedushah*. Here, *Chasam Sofer* dwells on explaining his well-known view that children should be taught Torah before they study any secular subject, when their hearts are still open to absorb the words of the Living God.

Books of *d'rush* (homiletics) cite a beautiful explanation of the statement by *Chazal* in *Chagigah* 3, that when R' Yehoshua heard the interpretation that "the children come so as to give a reward to those that brought them," he called it "a beautiful precious stone." *Yerushalmi Yevamos* states about R' Yehoshua: "I remember that my mother would bring my cradle to the synagogue, so that my ears should cleave to words of Torah." The reason why R' Yehoshua referred to that statement as "a beautiful precious stone" was that that very thing had happened to him, and he himself knew the great value involved of bringing infants to the *beis midrash*.

The reference here is evidently to infants who have not yet reached *gil chinuch*, an educable age, when the parents are Rabbinically obligated to train the child in *mitzvos* even though he is not yet *bar mitzvah*; and it is thus obvious that the verse, "that they should learn and fear," refers to the future — that is, these toddlers should "hear" now, so that when they reach *gil chinuch* they will "learn and fear." The question by *Chazal*, "why do the children (טַף) come?" also shows us that the reference is to children who are not of educable age. On the other hand, in regard to the Exodus from Egypt, we are told that there were 600,000 adult males "besides the infants" (מִטַּף — *Sh'mos* 12:37). As we know an adult male is anyone over the age of 13, the implication is that טַף refers to children under the age of 13, and not merely infants. טַף thus evidently includes children of educable age as well as infants. One must examine whether, when *Chazal* tell us "in order to give a reward to those who brought them," they might not be referring to children who have already reached an educable age (*gil chinuch*), for then the reward of the parents is for educating their children to do *mitzvos*.

II.

This Shirah

When the Torah tells us (*Devarim* 31:19), "now write this *shirah* (song)," the simple meaning of the verse is to write the song called *Ha'azinu* (ibid. 32:1-43), and that is the way *Rashi*, *Ramban* and various other *rishonim* explain the verse. According to this explanation, this command was only meant for that time, and not for all subsequent generations, or, as various commentators explain it, the stress is on the word "now," even before Moshe commanded Yehoshua.

According to *Or HaChayim*, the Jews were given three *mitzvos* in regard to this song: a) to write it, as it states, "and now write"; b) to teach it to the Jews, so that they would know its meaning, as it states (ibid. 31:19), "and teach it to *B'nei Yisrael*"; c) to "place it in their mouths" (ibid.), so that they would be able to read it properly.

According to *Rashi*, the purpose of the *shirah* is as a warning to *B'nei Yisrael*, to tell them that if a person sins, he will receive a grave punishment. *Rashi* explains the words, "so that this *shirah* will be a witness among *B'nei Yisrael*" (ibid.), that this is a warning by Hashem as to what will befall those who sin. This is the way various other *rishonim* also interpret this.

Oznayim LaTorah, though, states that the *shirah* is witness to the fact that the covenant between Hashem and His people will never be annulled. The Torah tells us (ibid. v. 20), "For I will bring them to the land ... and they will turn to other gods ... and will violate My covenant." There is thus reason to be afraid that Hashem will, *chas veshalom*, annul His covenant with us. But that is not what will happen: "This song will testify as a witness ... that it will not be forgotten from their seed" (ibid. v. 21). I promise you, says Hashem, that come what may, the Torah will not be forgotten by Israel, and there will always be remnants who will observe it and transfer it from father to son. Through the power of that Torah, My covenant with you will be upheld, and you will be redeemed.

We see this idea expressed in the end of the *shirah*, where, after talking of Hashem's "hiding His face," as it were (ibid. 32:20), it exclaims (ibid. v. 43), "Praise His people, O you nations: for He will avenge the blood of His servants, and will render vengeance to their adversaries, and will be merciful unto His land and His people." The *shirah* thus has both a warning before calamity strikes, and a promise that the Torah will not be forgotten by Israel, and as a result there will be an end to our troubles.

Because of the importance of the *shirah*, Ibn Ezra holds that when the Torah states, "And now, write *yourselves* this *shirah*" (ibid. 31:19), in the plural, it means that everyone who is discerning should write this for himself, in addition to the fact that Moshe wrote this in the Torah. By this means, there will be many more people who read it.

Abarbanel, too, says that the command was to Moshe, telling him to add this *parashah* to the Torah, after he had thought that the entire Torah was complete. The others were commanded to copy it and to allow as many people as possible to read it, because Moshe himself would not be able to complete this task.

Ramban, though, holds that the Torah commanded Moshe and Yehoshua to write down this *parashah*. Hashem wanted Yehoshua to become a prophet even before Moshe had died, and that was why He wanted him to be involved in the *shirah*. But it was only Moshe who wrote it, as it states (ibid. v. 22), "Moshe wrote this song the same day, and taught it to B'nei Yisrael." Throughout this time, Yehoshua stood at Moshe's side and both Moshe and he taught the *shirah* to the others, as it states (ibid. 32:44), "Moshe came and spoke all the words of this song in the ears of the people, he, and Yehoshua bin Nun."

Ha'amek Davar does not accept this interpretation. He is surprised at *Ramban's* view, as if Yehoshua had been commanded to take part in the writing of the *shirah*. It was written entirely by Moshe, as it states (ibid. 31:22), "Moshe wrote." According to *Ha'amek Davar*, there is a difference between writing the entire Torah and writing the *shirah*. Moshe told the entire Torah orally to the Jewish people, just as he had heard it from Hashem, and only afterwards did he write it. As to the *shirah*, Hashem warned Moshe to first write it and only then to teach it to B'nei Yisrael from the written text, as it states, "Moshe wrote this *shirah* ... and taught it to B'nei Yisrael" (ibid.). Moshe now pronounced a blessing on the reading of the Torah, as it states, "I will call upon the name of Hashem" (ibid. 32:3). Until that time, the *Shechinah* had spoken through Moshe's voice, and one does not pronounce a blessing on a miracle. Now, however, that the *shirah* had been written down and taught from the written text, it needed a blessing.

∾§ The Mitzvah to Write a Torah Scroll

Chazal in *Sanhedrin* 21 and in *Nedarim* 38, as well as in other places, explain the verse, "And now, write yourselves this *shirah*" (*Devarim* 31:19), as a positive *mitzvah*, namely, that everyone must write himself an entire Torah scroll. All those who list the 613 *mitzvos*, except for *Bahag* and R' Sa'adiah Gaon, include this as one of the 613 *mitzvos*. Those who hold one must write the entire Torah thus understand the word "*shirah*" (song) to mean the entire Torah. A number of commentators wonder how *Chazal*, and following them various *rishonim*, deduced this from the verse itself. We will bring a number of explanations below.

It appears that without a doubt this emerges from the fact that the word "write" in this verse appears in the plural form (כִּתְבוּ). As one cannot explain that Moshe was aided by someone else in the writing of the Torah, and since we do not find any reference to a command for all generations to write the *shirah* alone, the meaning of the word must be that it applies to all of Israel and to the whole Torah.

Ralbag explains *Chazal's* view and its source. He explains that we can see from the *parashah* that this is a reference to the entire Torah, and not merely the *shirah*. The Torah states (ibid. v. 22), "Moshe wrote the *shirah*," and thereafter it states (ibid. v. 24), "When Moshe finished writing the words of this Torah ... until the end." So too does it continue (ibid. v. 26), "Take this Torah scroll and place it next to the Ark of the Covenant of Hashem." Furthermore, we are told (ibid. v. 30), "Moshe spoke in the ears of the whole Congregation of Israel the words of this *shirah* until the end," and afterwards it states (ibid. 32:45-46):

> Moshe finished speaking all these things to all of Israel, and he said to them, "Set your hearts unto all the words which I testify to you this day, which you shall command your children to observe to do, all the words of this Torah."

From all of this, it is clear that "*shirah*" and "Torah" are identical. The *mitzvah* is to write an entire Torah scroll, which will include within it the *shirah*. The *mitzvah* is also to explain the Torah to Israel in addition to writing it, and to have it placed in the mouths of all of Israel.

Rambam in *Hilchos Sefer Torah* 7:1 states: "It is a *mitzvah* for each man to write a Torah scroll for himself, as it states (ibid. 31:19), 'and now, write yourselves this *shirah*,' namely, 'write yourselves the

Torah which has in it the *shirah*.'" In these words, *Rambam* attempts to bridge between the plain meaning and *Chazal's* halachic derivation (*drash*). What he thus does is to explain the word *shirah* as meaning literally "this song," and at the same time to explain that the Torah means to have us write the entire Torah, which includes the *parashah* of the *shirah*.

Rambam adds that "one does not write the Torah as separate *parashiyos*." It appears that what he intends to add by this is that one should not interpret the Torah to mean that one must write just the *parashah* of the *shirah* by itself, as the law is that one may not write separate *parashiyos* of the Torah.

Many of the *acharonim* discuss these words of *Rambam*. Could it not be that the *mitzvah* is to write just the *shirah* by itself, just as one is required to write certain specific *parashiyos* for *mezuzos* and *tefillin*, where we see that the prohibition against not writing separate *parashiyos* obviously does not apply?

Chasam Sofer in *Teshuvos Yoreh De'ah* 254 also finds the words of *Maharit*, *Yoreh De'ah* 3 surprising. *Maharit* asks a question on *Rif*, who states that the Torah may be written as separate parts. If that is so, asks *Maharit*, how do we know that "write yourselves this *shirah*" refers to the entire Torah? Could it not be that the Torah referred only to the *parashah* of *Ha'azinu*? It appears from this that *Maharit* holds that *Rambam's* view is accepted unequivocally. But, asks *Chasam Sofer*, is it not possible that the Torah really wanted to make the *parashah* of *Ha'azinu* an exception, as it did in the case of *sotah*, *mezuzah* and *tefillin*? *Chasam Sofer* says that he asked many wise scholars, and no one was able to answer the question. In his answer, he attempts to reconcile matters, but in a rather forced manner.

It appears, though, that *Rambam* adds the words, "one does not write the Torah as separate *parashiyos*," to the other proofs by the other *rishonim*. He too understood the meaning of the verses as did *Ralbag*, that one is not to understand the word *shirah* as referring only to the *shirah*, but to "the Torah which has the *shirah* in it." According to him, too, the language, "and now write," (in the plural) appeared to be difficult. Combining these reasons together with the law that one does not write isolated *parashiyos* of the Torah where the Torah does not clearly tell us differently — and here there is no express command to write *Ha'azinu* — *Rambam* justified the words of *Chazal* that the *mitzvah* is to write a Torah scroll.

Kli Chemdah notes that many *rishonim* deduced the law that one must write a Torah scroll from a *kal vachomer* (reasoning from minor to major): If one is required to write *Ha'azinu*, which testifies about the Torah, one is all the more obligated to write the Torah itself. *Rambam*, though, was unable to accept this view, for he holds in *Sefer HaMitzvos* that anything deduced by the 13 principles by which the Torah is expounded (including *kal vachomer*) is a rabbinic law, and not a Torah law. Therefore, if the Torah was referring only to the *shirah*, whereas the obligation to write the entire Torah is deduced from a *kal vachomer*, one cannot include the writing of a Torah within the 613 *mitzvos*. In addition, one can also ask how we know that this *mitzvah* applies to all generations, and not only to the generation of Moshe. The answer to this question must be that it is a *halachah l'Moshe miSinai*, an oral law given to Moshe at Sinai, that this *mitzvah* applies to all generations. However, as there is a rule that one cannot deduce a *kal vachomer* from a *halachah l'Moshe miSinai*, *Ramban* was forced to say that the verse refers to the entire Torah. In reality, this last answer is a difficult one, for if that is the case, how do the other *rishonim* deduce a *kal vachomer* from the *halachah l'Moshe miSinai*?

HaKesav VeHaKabalah says that he does not understand the hesitations by the *rishonim*. The whole matter appears to him to be a simple one. After Moshe had told the *shirah* to the people (*Devarim* 32:46), "he said unto them, 'Set your hearts to all the words which I warn you this day, which you shall command your children to observe to do, all the words of this Torah.'" It is clear from this that the purpose behind the writing of the *shirah* was so as to be a warning to observe the *mitzvos* of the Torah, and thus there is no need to warn us to write the entire Torah. After all, what good is a warning if one does not know what the Torah says and what its *mitzvos* are?

Further, *HaKesav VeHaKabalah* states that the Torah is known as "*shirah*" in a number of places. *Chazal* in *Chullin* 133, on the verse in *Mishlei* (25:20), "He sings songs to a bad heart," state that this verse refers to teaching Torah to a pupil who is not worthy. So too do *Chazal* tell us in *Chagigah* 12, on the verse (*Tehillim* 42:9), "Hashem will command His lovingkindness in the daytime, and in the night His song shall be with me," that the reason Hashem will command His lovingkindness in the daytime is because they spend the night learning His Torah. Thus we see the word "song" (*shirah*) means the Torah. And there are additional such references to the Torah as a "song." Thus we see that the way *Chazal* interpret the word *shirah* fits into the meaning of the verse, and when we are told to "write this *shirah*," it refers to the entire Torah.

One might think that there is clear proof to this from *Chazal* in *Nedarim* 38a, which then leads to the question of why *Rambam* found it necessary to bring proof from the fact that the Torah may not be written in separate *parashiyos*. In fact, *Sha'agas Aryeh* in his *teshuvos*, 34, asks that exact question on *Rambam* from *Chazal*. In *Nedarim*, we are told that R' Yose bar R' Chanina states that at first, the Torah was given only to Moshe and his descendants, as it states (*Sh'mos* 34:27), "write for yourself." On this, *Chazal* ask that later on it states (*Devarim* 31:19), "and now write yourselves this *shirah*." *Chazal* answer that the first verse, which was only directed at Moshe and his descendants, applies to all of the Torah, whereas the *shirah* alone was given to all of Israel. On this, the *gemara* asks further, that the Torah states (ibid.), "that this song may be a witness for Me against the children of Israel," which, as *Rashi* interprets it, means that the *shirah* stands as a witness and warning that Israel were commanded to learn the whole Torah (and not only the *shirah*). *Ran*, too, explains that if Israel were commanded to learn only the *shirah*, and not the whole Torah, what need is there for the *shirah* to be a witness and warning? — There would be nothing to be warned about. Thus we see the fact that the Torah refers to the *shirah* as a "witness" is proof that the word *shirah* refers to the entire Torah.

Chasam Sofer, though, in his *teshuvos* on *Yoreh De'ah* 254, states that this is no proof. Here, *Chazal* merely wanted to tell us that only Moshe and his descendants were obliged to observe the Torah. *Chazal* there ask quite properly, if that is the case, about what is the *shirah* meant to bear witness against Israel? It is, however, possible that all of Israel are obliged to observe the Torah, and yet it is possible that there is still a special *mitzvah* to write the *shirah* in itself. Then it could indeed serve as a witness to Israel as to the observance of the whole Torah, and a warning if it is not kept. One cannot, therefore, deduce from here if the *mitzvah* to write refers to the entire Torah or only to the *shirah*. Only if we explain this as does *HaKesav VeHaKabalah*, that after the Torah commanded us to write the warning it was obvious that we had to write the Torah itself, the obligation is clear without any doubts.

The simple explanation that this commandment refers to the entire Torah is that the Torah states, "and now write yourselves this *shirah*," in the plural form. According to all the commentators, the Torah does not clarify exactly what obligation this places upon the community as a whole, and especially as afterwards (ibid. v. 22) we are told that Moshe wrote the *shirah* by himself.

Abarbanel's and Ibn Ezra's interpretations that this refers to an obligation to copy the *shirah* is not that simple, for the *mitzvah* is for each person to write a Torah by himself.

◆§ The Writing of the Torah in Our Times

Tur in *Yoreh De'ah* 270 quotes his father, *Rosh*, that the *mitzvah* of writing a Torah scroll is in order to study and teach Torah as much as possible. Therefore, in earlier times, when people would learn from a written Torah scroll, they had an obligation to write a Torah scroll. "Nowadays, however, where a Torah scroll is written and is then placed in the synagogue to be read before the community, it is a positive *mitzvah* for every Jew who can afford it to write the five Books of the Torah, the Mishnah, *gemara*, and their commentaries."

Beis Yosef is surprised at *Rosh*. How can one annul a positive *mitzvah*, which is stated in the Torah, namely to write a Torah scroll? He concludes — and this he regards as *halachah* — that the opinion of *Rosh* is not meant to annul the obligation to write a Torah scroll, but to add that in our times the obligation extends to writing the Oral Torah as well.

It is interesting that the previous Gerer Rebbi and *Aperion* both explain the expression "and now" (*Devarim* 31:19) — "and now write yourselves this *shirah*" — along these lines. *Now* you are commanded to write only the written Torah, but in the future you will also be commanded to write the Oral Torah as well.

Chinuch, too, explains that the reason for the *mitzvah* of writing a Torah scroll is so as to increase study of the Torah among Israel, so that each person should have a Torah scroll in his possession. He concludes that even though there is a Torah obligation to write a Torah scroll, in our times we are commanded to buy and to write the other Torah works (Mishnah, *gemara*, commentaries and so on) as well, and it is proper for those who are God fearing to set aside a place in their homes for scribes, so that many books should be written.

Chasam Sofer, however, in *Yoreh De'ah* 254, states that it was unnecessary for *Beis Yosef* to try to read into *Rosh* the interpretation that the writing of the Oral Law is an added element to the obligation of writing a Torah scroll. *Rosh's* comment refers to the view of those who hold that we derive *halachos* from the reasons for the *mitzvos* (דְּרְשִׁינָן טַעֲמָא דְקְרָא). As the reason for writing the Torah scroll is so as to increase Torah study, *Rosh* added that in our times the main obligation is to write the interpretations of the Torah. The *halachah*, though, is in accordance with R' Yehudah, who does not deduce reasons for the *mitzvos* when this will result in a more lenient ruling. Here the more stringent ruling would be to include the writing of the other kinds of books as well. We do not, however, act more leniently and annul the *mitzvah* of the writing of the Torah, for this is a *mitzvah* just like any other.

Chasam Sofer, though, in *Orach Chaim* 52, asks why we do not recite a blessing on the writing of a Torah scroll in accordance with *Rambam* and most of the other *poskim*, who hold that even in our times there is a positive *mitzvah* to write a Torah scroll, "and not as *Rosh.*" It thus appears that *Chasam Sofer* understands *Rosh* to argue with *Rambam*, and that according to *Rosh*, there is no obligation to write a Torah scroll. This is surprising. After all, as we noted, *Rosh* only expands on the *mitzvah* so as to include the other types of books as well. But we don't have the right to annul a positive *mitzvah* written in the Torah. This requires further study. (R' Zvi Domb, the chief rabbi of Hod Hasharon, pointed out that in *Tur Yoreh De'ah* 270, *Perisha U'derishah* argues with *Beis Yosef's* interpretation of *Rosh*.)

There is also a need for further study regarding what *Rambam* writes in *Sefer HaMitzvos*: "If one is unable (to write a Torah scroll), he must buy one or hire someone to write it." According to *Chazal* and various *poskim*, the *mitzvah* is only to write the scroll, and one does not fulfill his obligation by buying one. *Chazal* in *Menachos* 30 state: "R' Yehoshua ben Levi said, 'One who buys a Torah scroll is like one who snatches a *mitzvah*, whereas one who writes it is as if he received it from Mount Sinai.' " *Nimukei Yosef* explains that one who buys a Torah scroll does not have as great a reward as one who writes one himself. *Rambam* (in *Mishneh Torah*) and the other *poskim* mention only the possibility of hiring someone to write a Torah scroll, but not buying one. *Minchas Chinuch* proves that *Ran's* view is that one does not fulfill the obligation by buying a Torah scroll, and that is the way *Rama* rules. It is thus surprising that *Rambam* in *Sefer HaMitzvos* mentions the possibility of buying a scroll.

Ha'azinu – הַאֲזִינוּ

I.

The Nature of the Song Ha'azinu

Ha'azinu is a majestic poetic piece, overflowing with strong images and full of feeling and lofty thoughts. Throughout the generations it has aroused the amazement of those who understand poetry. The *shirah* has seventy verses, and all agree that no other poem can compare to it in terms of its strong imagery and the depth of its concepts. It is also a poem in the modern sense of the term. But according to *Ramban* (on *Devarim* 31:19), it is known as a *shir* (song), "because Israel always say it with singing and music. It is also written as a song (in the Torah), because a song has breaks indicating when one pauses in the melody."

When *Ramban* refers to Israel saying the *shirah* "with singing and music," this is a reference to *Chazal* in *Rosh HaShanah* 31, that the Levites in the *Beis HaMikdash* would sing the *shirah* to accompany the *musaf* sacrifice on Shabbos. They would divide the *shirah* into six parts and each week sing another section of it. Thus they had a six-week cycle of singing the *shirah*. *Rashi* in *Rosh HaShanah* lists the divisions: (1) v. 1-6; (2) v. 7-12; (3) v. 13-18; (4) v. 19-26; (5) v. 27-35; (6) v. 36-43. According to *Rambam*, section 5 begins with v. 29 and the final section begins with verse 40 rather than verse 36.

S'forno regards this division by *Chazal* as a conceptual division in terms of the *shirah* itself. The first part is the introduction. The next part explains how Hashem wants history to develop for the benefit of man, and how Hashem wants to raise Israel to the highest heights, as will occur at the End of Days. The third part tells the history of Israel. Hashem always granted the Jewish people happiness and all the best, but they repaid Him bad for good. That is why they deserve a severe punishment. The fourth part describes Israel's fall, from the greatest heights to the lowest depths, to the extent that they were worthy of being, God forbid, utterly destroyed. The fifth part gives the reason why the Jewish people will nevertheless survive to the Redemption at the End of Days, in spite of their terrible sins. The last part describes the Redemption and the ultimate revenge against those who harmed the Jews.

Abarbanel, too, divides the *shirah* along similar lines, without referring to the words of *Chazal*. According to Abarbanel, the division by verses is a different one from that used by *Chazal*, but conceptually his division is like that of *S'forno*.

Rashash on *Rosh HaShanah* 31 asks a question on *Rashi*. *Rashi* states that until the fourth part, each part contains "six verses, and thereafter each contains eight verses." *Rashash* is astonished at this interpretation, for according to *Rashi's* division, the fifth part has nine verses. One who looks into *Rashi*, though, will see that all that *Rashi* wanted to note was that the first three sections have six verses each, and "thereafter eight verses" refers to the fourth part, for the fifth part has nine verses and the last again has eight verses. *Rashi* wanted to stress that after the first three parts there is no equal division of verses, as there was at the beginning. Only the first three parts have an equal number of verses, but those thereafter do not.

Rashash is also surprised at *Tur Orach Chaim* 428, who states that "they would read the *shirah* once, for the six days of the week." This implies, says *Rashash*, that they would read one portion of the *shirah* each day of the week, whereas *Chazal* state clearly that they read one portion each *Shabbos*. *Rashash* leaves this question open, and states that it needs extensive further study. *Orchos Chaim*, though, by the Spinka Rebbi quotes *Me'orei Or* p. 156b, "that it is a scribal error, and it [the text of *Tur*] should state once every six weeks." After studying this carefully, though, one need not say that this was a scribal error in the text of *Tur*. *Derishah* on *Tur* 428 explains that when *Chazal* referred to the saying of a section of the *shirah*, they used the term מוּסְפֵי דְשַׁבְּתָא, which we took to mean at the time of the *musaf* sacrifice each *Shabbos*. According to *Derishah*, though, this refers to the additional prayers said each day. The word שַׁבְּתָא can mean "week" or "Shabbos." Thus מוּסְפֵי דְשַׁבְּתָא could mean "the additional prayers of the weekdays." In the *Beis HaMikdash* there were *ma'amados* (groups of delegates who represented the people and took part as observers in the *Beis HaMikdash* services). *Derishah* states that "each day they (the *ma'amados*) would pray *musaf* (additional service) as well as *ne'ilah* (the fifth prayer service of the day, which outside the *Beis HaMikdash* is prayed only on Yom Kippur)." Thus, a different section of the *shirah* was said each day.

This view is also in keeping with that of *Rambam, Hilchos Klei HaMikdash* 6:4, that the *ma'amados* who were on duty in the *Beis HaMikdash* would say four prayers each day: *shacharis* (the morning service), *musaf* (additional service), *minchah* (the afternoon service) and *ne'ilah* (the closing service). *Ra'avad* disagrees with *Rambam*, but *Kesef Mishneh* negates *Ra'avad's* proof and proves that, according to *Rambam*, the *ma'amados* would say the *musaf* each day. According to this, one can quite easily explain that when *Chazal* and *Rambam* refer to מוּסְפֵּי דְשַׁבְּתָא, they are referring to the *musaf* of each weekday. This does not, though, necessarily mean that the Levites completed the *shirah* within a week. It might mean that throughout any given week the same section would be said each day. Only the following week would they continue with the next section. Thus, there was a six-week cycle during which the *shirah* was completed. *Tur* too, when he refers to "once for the six days of the week," is not disputing this fact, but is only coming to explain that, according to *Derishah*, the מוּסְפֵּי דְשַׁבְּתָא are the *musaf* prayers of each weekday, and not only those of *Shabbos*. There is thus no contradiction between *Chazal* and *Rambam*, but this is an explanation of what they said. This would seem to be the correct interpretation.

⇜§ The Shirah According to Ramban

Ramban regards the *shirah* as primarily a prophecy of what will happen to Israel from its earliest times to our times, and that is why we are told (*Devarim* 32:44), "[Moshe] spoke all the words of this *shirah* in the ears of the people." The reason the Torah mentions "*all the words*" is to teach us that this includes everything that would happen to us in the future. "Even though the *shirah* is so short, yet it contains many matters." In other words, the *shirah* is very condensed, and alludes to everything that will happen in the future. Indeed, Moshe explained the *shirah* orally to the people, setting forth everything that would happen to them, in all its details. *Ramban* is amazed at how clearly the prophecy is contained in the *shirah*, to the extent that he says:

Had this *shirah* been a single document written by astrologers, which tells us everything from the beginning to the end, it would have been worthy of belief, because everything in it has been fulfilled to this time, and nothing has been in error. How much more do we believe in and trust completely the words of God, by His prophet who was the most faithful in His house, for none will be like him either before or after him, may peace be upon him.

As to the nature of the *shirah*, *Ramban* states:

> This *shirah* is a true and faithful witness for us. It states clearly all
> that will happen to us. At first it mentions the kindness that
> Hashem showed us, from the time that He took us as His portion.
> It then mentions the favors which He did for us in the desert, and
> that He made us inherit the lands of large and mighty nations, and
> the great good and wealth and honor which He made us inherit
> there. Yet, because of all of this good [i.e., because they took pride
> in their wealth], they rebelled against Hashem and served idolatry.
> It then mentions (Hashem's) anger, until He finally sent pestilence
> and famine against them, and there was evil and the sword.
> Afterwards, He dispersed them in every direction and corner. It is
> well known that this is so, and it came true. Then the *shirah* states
> that in the end, Hashem "will take revenge against My adversaries
> and pay back those who hate Me" (ibid. v. 41). The reason for this
> is because they committed every type of evil deed against us due to
> their hatred of Hashem, for they hate Israel only because Israel do
> not follow in their ways, but remain with Hashem and observe His
> *mitzvos*, not intermarrying with them, not eating of their
> sacrifices, and despising their idolatries, as it states (*Tehillim* 44:23),
> "For Your sake we are killed all the day." Thus, it is because of
> their hatred of Hashem that they have done all these things
> against us, and they are His adversaries and those who hate Him,
> and it is fitting for Him to take vengeance on them.

From *Ramban's* words, we can see that he has a unique approach in
explaining the *shirah*, which differs from that of the other commentators. He does not see the *shirah* as a rebuke but rather as a detailed
prophecy of Israel's history, from the time that they entered *Eretz
Yisrael* for the first time until the ultimate redemption. At the end of the
shirah there is an explanation of why Hashem will punish the enemies
of Israel, even though, according to the *shirah*, they were messengers of
Hashem in punishing Israel for not obeying Hashem's commands.
Hashem used the hatred of the other nations only in order to refine
Israel and to return them to the proper path. But the hatred of the
enemies of the Jewish people was really a hatred of Hashem, more than
a hatred of Israel. They hated Israel through hatred of Hashem, not
because Israel did not obey Hashem's commands, but on the contrary,
because Israel linked their fate to the service of Hashem, and accepted
the Torah. It is the hatred of these enemies which will cause Hashem to
take revenge against them. At the end of his words, *Ramban* proves that
the vengeance of Hashem which is mentioned in the *shirah* refers to the

final redemption, for which we are still waiting to this day. As everything else in the *shirah* was fulfilled, that aspect will also be fulfilled.

Says *Ramban*:

> It is clear that this is a promise related to the future redemption, for in the Second *Beis HaMikdash* there was no manifestation of (*Devarim* 32:43) "Praise His people, O you nations," but instead they mocked them, saying, "What are these unfortunate Jews doing?" Many of the great Jewish leaders worked in the palace of the king of Babylon, and all were subservient to him. At that time, there was no "taking revenge on His enemies" (ibid.), nor did He "give atonement to His land and His people" (ibid.). The *shirah* also does not mention the conditions for *teshuvah* and serving Hashem as prerequisites for redemption [as the Torah states in the two *tochechos* which refer to the destructions of the First and Second *Batei HaMikdash*]. [The *shirah*] is simply a document that we will do bad but in the end we will endure. Hashem will punish us severely, but will not wipe us out, and will later have mercy on us, and will repay the (other) nations with His mighty and great sword, and will forgive our sins for His name's sake. Thus this *shirah* is a clear promise about the future redemption, refuting all the heretics.

This last section is a polemic against the Christians, who tried to explain these verses as having already taken place, and that, *chas veshalom*, there is no future for the Jewish people. *Ramban* proves that those events mentioned in the *shirah* have not yet come to pass, and therefore the *shirah* refers to the final redemption. *Ramban's* logic is like that of R' Akiva, who laughed when he saw foxes coming out of what had been the Holy of Holies, for, as R' Akiva stated, as the prophecy of the destruction had been fulfilled, the prophecy of the redemption would certainly be fulfilled as well. Thus, we have seen with our own eyes, that the first part of the *shirah* has been fulfilled with the Jews being chosen by Hashem, their ascent to the greatest heights, and afterwards the dreadful exile. And as we saw that, as promised by the *shirah*, we were not totally wiped out, we can therefore know for a certainty that Hashem's promise of vengeance against those who tormented the Jews will also come true, and "He will give atonement to His land and His people."

Abarbanel follows the same general drift in explaining the last part of the *shirah*, which deals with redemption. He finds in the *shirah* seven events which have not yet come to pass but which will come to pass. a)

It states here (ibid. v. 35), "To Me belongs vengeance and compensation," and (ibid. v. 41), "I will take revenge against My adversaries and pay back those who hate Me." It also states (ibid. v. 42-43), "I will make My arrows drunk with blood, and My sword shall devour flesh ... for He will avenge the blood of His servants." This prophecy was not fulfilled in either the Second *Beis HaMikdash* period or at any other time. b) Hashem's vengeance against the other nations and His redemption of Israel does not have a revealed time, as it states (ibid. v. 34), "Is this not laid up in store with Me, and sealed up among My treasures?" This is unlike the building of the Second *Beis HaMikdash*, which took place, as prophesied, seventy years after the first exile. c) Before the redemption, Israel will reach the lowest point of servility, as we see in the verse (ibid. v. 36), "There is none to save and strengthen them." That was not true during the Second *Beis HaMikdash* period, because at that time the Jews in Babylon lived in great wealth. d) At the time of the final redemption, the *zechus avos* — merits of our forefathers — will have ended, and that entails the danger of the destruction of the entire Jewish people, as it states (ibid. v. 26-27), "I said ... I shall cause their memory to cease from mankind [but refrained] ... lest they [the heathens] should say, 'Our hand is high, and Hashem has not done all this.' " This same concept is expressed in *Yechezkel* 20:8-9. e) *Techiyas ha'meisim* — "the revival of the dead" — will take place after the exiles are gathered in, as it states (*Devarim* 32:36,39), "When Hashem judges His people, and repents Himself for His servants ... I kill, and I revive." Likewise it is written in *Daniel* 12:1-2, "At that time ... many of those sleeping in the dust of the earth will awaken." And *Yeshayahu* (26:19) states that in that day, "Your dead will live." f) The redemption and atonement are not conditional upon *teshuvah* (repentance). Redemption will come regardless. This *shirah* is merely a document testifying about the bad things that will occur and that Hashem will punish us, after which He will repay the other nations and will atone for our sins. g) All the words of the *shirah* will be fulfilled. At this time, only the first parts have been fulfilled, but later, God willing, the rest will be fulfilled as well.

◄§ "Were It not that the Anger of the Enemy is Stored up Against Them"

The words in the verse of the *shirah* (*Devarim* 32:27) are unparalleled in their harshness. The terrible suffering endured by the Jewish people was not sufficient to punish them for their great sins. Had it been a matter of strict justice and no more, they would have been doomed to total extermination. The only reason this was not their fate was so that their enemies should not be able to boast that they had conquered Israel and its God. These frightening words express to us clearly everything that happened to us in the Holocaust. It is astonishing that *S'forno* explains the word אֲפָאֵיהֶם (*Devarim* 32:26 — אָמַרְתִּי אַפְאֵיהֶם, usually translated as "I said, 'I will scatter them into corners,' " from the root פֵּאָה — "corner") in a way that reflects our recent terrible history. He says:

> אָמַרְתִּי אַפְאֵיהֶם — I will leave a corner (פֵּאָה) of them, and will consume the rest, as I will do at the End of Days, since I have not achieved their perfection, neither at the giving of the Torah nor in *Eretz Yisrael*, nor in exile, as it states (*Yoel* 3:5), "In Mount Zion and in Yerushalayim will be a remnant, as Hashem has said, and in the remainder whom Hashem will designate."

S'forno states clearly that in the End of Days the Jewish people will face destruction, with only a corner remaining. *S'forno* also hints at Israel being saved in the land of its forefathers, as it states, "In Mount Zion and in Yerushalayim will be a remnant." These words were written hundreds of years ago, yet we have seen their realization in our days.

Ramban, though, explains אַפְאֵיהֶם to mean that, by Hashem's strict justice, He decreed that the Jews should be spread throughout the four corners of the world, and nevertheless they will not be destroyed but will remain alive for the sake of Hashem's great name. This is not because Hashem wants to show His great strength to the other nations, for all the nations are as nothing compared to Him and are of no importance to Him. Hashem, though, created man so that he will recognize His Creator, and he has the freedom to do good or evil:

> When all (the other nations) sinned of their own free will and denied Him, only this one nation remained for His name. He publicized the signs and wonders through them, for He is the God of gods and Lord of lords. By this He became known to all the nations. Now, if He would retract and destroy the memory (of the Jews), the nations would forget His signs and deeds ... and there would not remain any among them who would know His Creator, but only those who provoke Him. It was therefore appropriate for Him at the Creation to establish for Himself a nation for all time, for they are His servants who stood by Him in their exile, like servants, bearing the troubles and servitude.

Abarbanel interprets this in the exact opposite way. אַפְאֵיהֶם refers to a decree that Israel will congregate in but one corner of the world, so that their enemies will be able to destroy them in one fell swoop, so that no memory will remain of them. In His mercy, though, Hashem scattered the Jews among the different nations. Even though we have remained small in number, we will remain alive and capable of thought, and our memory will not be eradicated throughout this long and terrible exile we have suffered. The people of Troy were exterminated by the Greeks because they lived in one place. When, however, the Jews were destroyed by the king of England, other Jews remained living in peace in France. Then, when the king of France killed them, other Jews remained living peacefully in other places. Had they all been in one place, they would have been totally destroyed.

This is the essence of the *shirah* according to the *rishonim*. One may possibly add another explanation of this. One may say that the main motif of the *shirah* is that (*Devarim* 32:4), "The Rock, His work is perfect, for all His ways are judgment; a God of truth and without iniquity; just and right is He." Hashem wished to instill in us this awareness. We must realize that evil does not come from Him, but from our deeds. Hashem chose our nation to serve Him. He created and formed our nation in Egypt; "He is your father Who has acquired you, He has made you and established you"(ibid. v. 6). It was He who protected our nation in the desert, and brought us into *Eretz Yisrael*. The people turned away from Hashem, and that was what brought about the exile. We must realize this and examine our behavior. "If they were wise and understood this"(ibid. v. 29), they would eventually realize that, "where are their gods, their rock in whom they trusted"(ibid. v. 37)? Then they will know that "It is I, and there is no god with Me" (ibid. v. 39). After the people finally reach this understanding, Hashem will take mercy on them and He will take revenge on the other nations. Then Israel will realize the truth of the main point of the *shirah*, that "The Rock, His work is perfect, for all His ways are judgment." At that time, as we are told in the previous *parashah*, Israel will realize, and (ibid. 31:17) "on that day they will say, 'It is because my God is not in my midst that these evils have befallen me.'"

וזאת הברכה
Vezos HaBerachah

I.

Moshe's Blessing to the Tribes

There are commentators who endeavor to find a comparison and similarities between Yaakov's blessings to his sons before his death and Moshe's blessing to the tribes of Israel. There are certain similarities between the two blessings, such as Yaakov's comments about Shimon and Levi, that (*Bereishis* 49:5), "instruments of violence are in their habitations," which parallel Moshe's words (*Devarim* 33:8), "You tested Him at the Waters of Strife," and a number of other similarities mentioned by some of the commentators. (My brother-in-law R' Yitzchak Levi points out that this includes *Rashi* on *Devarim* 33:13.) Nevertheless, one who compares both texts will see that such similarities are purely coincidental. It is clear that Moshe's blessing is for the future, related to the impending inheritance of the land, whereas Yaakov's blessing related primarily to events which had occurred in the past, except for certain comments about some of the brothers.

In order to understand Moshe's blessing, it is important to mention the order in which the tribes inherited the land, as explained in the book of *Yehoshua*.

The tribes of Reuven, Gad and half of Menasheh went at the head of the other tribes to conquer the land. Afterwards, they returned and settled their land in Transjordan. Yehudah was the first tribe to conquer and settle its land west of the Jordan. The next was Yosef, while Binyamin settled between Yehudah and Yosef. The *Beis HaMikdash* was in Binyamin's territory. Shimon settled among Yehudah. Levi did not receive a portion. Afterwards, by lot, the tribes of Zevulun, Asher, Naftali and Dan were settled.

Moshe's blessing to the tribes was not exactly in this order. *Ramban*, Rabbenu Bachya and others explain the differences, but we cannot explain definitely Moshe's deep intentions in mentioning one tribe before another. The commentators attempt to find reference to the events which happened later, in Moshe's blessing. There are differences of opinion in these commentaries, but all share a common opinion that Moshe, in his blessings, was referring to the inheritance of the land.

⇜ "May Reuven Live"

Abarbanel, *Ba'alei HaTosafos*, *Ramban*, *S'forno*, the Gaon of Vilna, *HaKesav VeHaKabalah* and other commentators relate Reuven's blessing to the fact that it was the tribe which went at the head of the other tribes to conquer *Eretz Yisrael*. "May Reuven live, and not die; and may his people be a number" (ibid. v. 6). Moshe promised the tribe a simple life, and that "his people" would be "a number" — the same number would come back as left to go to battle, and they would not lose a single man. *Ramban*, Rabbenu Bachya and other commentators explain the word "not" as referring not only to "die" — but also to "a number" as if the Torah had written: "may his people not be a number" — i.e., they will be unlimited.

Rashi, quoting *Chazal*, states that the blessing to Reuven was to tell him that the incident with Bilhah (*Bereishis* 35:22) would not harm the tribe.

Abarbanel explains this simply. Reuven was in double danger at the time of the invasion of *Eretz Yisrael*: a) The wives and children had been left in Transjordan without any protection; b) the men of Reuven were at the head of the invasion force. Moshe's blessing was thus in the form of, "Long live the king." Hashem would help Reuven to withstand all the dangers.

⇜ The Tribe of Shimon

Shimon is not mentioned at all in Moshe's blessings. In *Yehoshua* 19:1, we are told that the second lot fell on Shimon, within the tribe of Yehudah. *Chazal* in *Sifri* tell us that when the Torah states in regard to Yehudah (*Devarim* 33:7), "bring him to his people," it refers to the tribe of Shimon, in accordance with what we are told in *Shoftim* (1:3), "Yehudah said to Shimon his brother, 'Come up with me in my lot.'" Thus, Shimon settled within Yehudah's inheritance.

Ibn Ezra, earlier, brings a view that Moshe did not mention Shimon because of the sin of Pe'or (*Bamidbar* 25:1-9). *Ramban* disagrees with this. Those who worshiped Pe'or were destroyed, and they were the members of various tribes, not only of Shimon. The reason Shimon is not mentioned, says *Ramban*, is that the Torah always mentions only twelve tribes. Yaakov too mentioned only twelve tribes, reckoning the two sons of Yosef — Ephraim and Menasheh — as one unit. Similarly, when the Torah mentions how the tribes pitched their tents in the desert, only twelve tribes are listed, including Menasheh and Ephraim, but excluding Levi. Thus, here the Torah leaves out Shimon, because it did not receive its own inheritance and settled within Yehudah.

⮜§ "May Hashem Hear the Voice of Yehudah"

According to various commentators, the above verse (*Devarim* 33:7) is a hint at the prayers of David and Shlomo, Asa before the Ethiopians, and Chizkiyahu before Sancheriv (Sennacherib). "Bring him to his people" (ibid.) — that he may return in safety after the wars. "Let his hands be sufficient for him" (ibid.) — this was in the battle of Yehoshaphat at Ramat Gilad (Gilead).

The expression, "this to Yehudah" (ibid.), means, according to Ibn Ezra and *Da'as Zekeinim MiBa'alei HaTosafos*, that the blessing to Reuven, "May Reuven live and not die," would also apply to Yehudah.

Many commentators explain this blessing as being related to various historic events. According to *Chazal*, Yehudah's bones rolled about in his coffin because he had pronounced excommunication upon himself (when he asked Yaakov to allow him to bring Binyamin down to Egypt — *Bereishis* 43:9), until Moshe's blessing.

Ramban, though, explains this according to the simple meaning of the text. The tribe of Yehudah were fighters, as we see in the verse (*II Shmuel* 1:18), "to teach the children of Yehudah the bow, as is written in *Sefer HaYashar*," and Yehudah was in the forefront of the battle to conquer the land. The blessing was therefore meant to offer the tribe encouragement and support.

Malbim explains that "bring him to his people" means that even those of Yehudah's soldiers who are not victorious will return home safely, without anyone in their ranks being missing.

⮜§ "Your Holy One"

Almost all the commentators agree, regarding the blessing of Levi (*Devarim* 33:8), that it is a song of praise of Levi's righteousness, for the *Urim* and *Tumim* (the sacred name enfolded in the breastplate of the High Priest — *kohen gadol*) that the *kohanim* — who are of this tribe

— would have, and for its steadfastness in regard to the Golden Calf. In fact, at the Golden Calf the members of the tribe even turned against their own mothers and other close relatives who had sinned.

Ramban explains this differently: The verse (ibid. v. 9), "Who said to his father and to his mother, 'I have not seen him,' " refers not to the sin of the Golden Calf, but to Shmuel the prophet, who left his parents at a very young age. "Whom you tested at Masah" (ibid. v. 8) — in other words, they were not among those who complained at Masah (*Sh'mos* 17:1-7). "May Hashem bless his wealth" (*Devarim* 33:11) — that is a blessing that they should not be harmed when they came into the *Mishkan* or *Beis HaMikdash* (*Ramban*), or refers to the presents that the Levites received of *ma'aser* (tithes) and *bikkurim* — "first fruits" (Ibn Ezra).

According to *Rashi*, *S'forno*, *Or HaChayim* and other commentators, the blessing of (ibid.), "let those that hate him not stand," is a hint to the victory of the *Chashmona'im* (Hasmoneans), where the Jewish forces were led by the *kohanim*, of the tribe of Levi.

A number of commentators state that the verse (ibid. v. 9), "Who said to his father and to his mother, 'I have not seen him,' " is meant to soften Yaakov's declaration (*Bereishis* 49:7), "may their anger be cursed, for it is strong." Zealousness is not always bad, and sometimes it is a positive virtue, worthy of praise.

Yosef Bechor Shor writes that, "May Hashem bless his wealth" (*Devarim* 33:11), reflects the fact, mentioned by *Chazal*, that the *kohanim* who performed the incense service in the *Beis HaMikdash* were blessed with riches.

According to the interpretation of *Chazal*, the verse "May Hashem bless his forces (חֵילוֹ)" means that Hashem should even bless the Levites' non-sacred things (חֻלִּין). Also, this verse teaches us that if a *kohen* who has been serving in the *Beis HaMikdash* finds out that he is the son of a divorced woman (and hence is not permitted to serve as a *kohen*, for he is a חָלָל), his previous service is nevertheless considered by Hashem to be desirable. This interpretation explains the verse as "may Hashem bless [the service of] his חָלָל."

☙ "He Dwells Between His Shoulders"

After having blessed Levi about the sacrifices, Moshe now goes on to bless Binyamin, in whose territory the *Beis HaMikdash* would be built, and afterwards blesses Yosef, for the *Mishkan* in Shiloh would be in his territory. The commentators state that as the *Beis HaMikdash* was more precious to Hashem than the *Mishkan*, Moshe mentioned Binyamin first. Most commentators explain that the meaning of the verse, "He dwells between his shoulders" (ibid. v. 12), means that the *Shechinah* — "Divine Presence" — would rest upon the *Beis HaMikdash* continually.

S'forno adds that the phrase, "He shall dwell in safety," in that same verse, refers to the fact that the tribe of Binyamin was not among the ten tribes which rebelled. *Chazal* said that "He shall dwell in safety" refers to the First *Beis HaMikdash*, while "He shall cover him the entire day" (ibid.) is a reference to the Second *Beis HaMikdash*, and "He dwells between his shoulders" refers to the future Third *Beis HaMikdash*.

Ralbag holds that "He dwells between his shoulders" is a hint at the first monarchy, that of Shaul, for Shaul was of the tribe of Binyamin.

◆§ The Nazir of His Brothers

The blessing of Yosef (ibid. vs. 13-17) is evidently the most exalted of all the blessings. It contains a blessing for Yosef's portion of the land, which will be excellent and filled with everything good. The blessing also praises Yosef as "the *nazir* ("the separated one") of his brothers," and there are also historical references to the tribe's actions. Thus, Yosef is referred to as "the firstborn of the ox" (ibid. v. 17), which many take as a reference to Yehoshua, as well as references to the actions of Ephraim and Menasheh.

The phrase, "the firstborn of the ox," is a cause of surprise among the commentators, for, after all, Yosef was not the firstborn. *Ramban*, though, says that the word בְּכוֹר, which is usually translated as "firstborn," can also mean someone who is prominent, as in the phrase (*Sh'mos* 4:22), "my son, my בְּכוֹר, Israel."

Akeidah and *Malbim* explain the word בְּכוֹר in its simple sense. Yosef was the head of the ten tribes, and took away the glory and majesty from the House of David.

Abarbanel sees a similarity between Moshe's blessing to Yosef and Yaakov's blessing to him (see *Rashi* on *Devarim* 33:13). Even the words used are similar. Yaakov too referred to Yosef as "the *nazir* of his brothers" (*Bereishis* 49:26). This refers to the later division between the tribes, which was led by the children of Yosef.

◆§ "Rejoice Zevulun in Your Going out"

The two tribes of Zevulun and Yisachar were mixed together in Moshe's blessings. "Rejoice, Zevulun, in your going out, and Yisachar in your tents" (ibid. v. 18). According to *Chazal*, Yisachar dwelled in the tents of Torah, while Zevulun supported Yisachar.

According to *Malbim*, there were a number of tribes which were joined together in common ventures. Yehudah and Binyamin had the monarchy and the *Beis HaMikdash*. Ephraim and Menasheh were also included together. The same applied to Yisachar and Zevulun.

Yosef Bechor Shor and various other commentators explain the verses in their simple sense. The people of Yisachar were shepherds, living in tents, while those of Zevulun were involved in trade, traveling along various trade routes to buy and sell different kinds of goods.

Zevulun was also given another blessing (ibid. v. 19), "the hidden treasures of the sand." Ibn Ezra states that the tribe's wealth would be so great that they would have to bury it in the sand. *Yosef Bechor Shor*, though, says that Zevulun would become wealthy from the grain that foreign ships would come to buy from it.

"There they shall offer sacrifices of righteousness" (ibid.). As Zevulun's territory would be a major trading center, the people of various nations would come there and would offer sacrifices to Israel's God. People would be afraid to undertake long and dangerous journeys, and would offer sacrifices at Mount Zion to ensure their safe passage.

Bechor Shor does not understand why Moshe mentioned Zevulun before Yisachar. *Rashi* and Abarbanel, though, state that Moshe mentioned their names in accordance with their inheritances, and according to the value of their land. According to *Chazal*, the reason Zevulun was mentioned first was that they engaged in trading and supported Yisachar, so that Yisachar could spend their time studying Torah.

✎§ "Blessed Be He that Enlarges Gad"

According to *Rashi*, *Ramban* and other commentators, the above verse (ibid. v. 20) refers to the enlargement of Gad in Transjordan, which was an empty territory with room for expansion. *Yosef Bechor Shor* states that grazing land is known as "land of broad spaces (מֶרְחָב)," as seen in *Hoshea* 4:16: "Hashem will pasture them like a sheep in broad spaces (בַּמֶּרְחָב)."

According to most commentators, the meaning of the verse (*Devarim* 33:21), "there the burial plot of the lawgiver is hidden," is that Moshe was buried in the portion of Gad. Abarbanel, though, says that the verse may be referring to the altar which was erected in Gad's portion after the conquest of the land, and as a result of which, the tribes almost declared war.

S'forno states that the phrase, "he performed the righteousness of Hashem, and His judgments with Israel," refers to the fact that it was there that the lawgiver clarified Hashem's justness to Israel, as Shmuel said to Israel when he argued with them (I Shmuel 12:7), "Therefore stand up, so that I may reason with you before Hashem, concerning all the righteousness of Hashem."

Gad showed His justness in fulfilling the promise made to Moshe in going out at the forefront in the conquest of Eretz Yisrael.

Ibn Ezra states that the reason Reuven is not mentioned in this regard is that the tribe of Gad had the mightiest warriors.

"Dan Is a Lion's Cub; He Shall Pounce from the Bashan"

According to the commentators, Dan lived near the border, and that was why he pounced like a lion. Abarbanel states that even though Bashan was part of Menasheh's inheritance, it was a place where lions camped, as we see in the verse (Tehillim 22:13), "the mighty ones of Bashan have surrounded me."

According to Ralbag and Or HaChayim, Moshe was referring here to Shimshon.

According to Rashi, "he shall pounce from Bashan" (Devarim 33:22) refers to the Jordan River, which descends from Dan.

⋞§ "Naftali Is Satisfied"

According to the commentators, Naftali's land was good, and its crops ripened there speedily. This was the first tribe to bring its bikkurim (first fruits to the Beis HaMikdash), because the land was full of Hashem's blessings.

"Take possession of the west and the south" (ibid. v. 23). According to Yosef Bechor Shor, this means that its inheritance was to the west and south of the Kinneret (Sea of Galilee).

Abarbanel notes a fine characteristic of this tribe, in that it was satisfied with its lot, and that is one of the finest qualities a person can have.

⋞§ "Asher Is Blessed with Children"

Asher is the only tribe whose blessing stresses its children. Rashi says that he does not understand why Asher received this blessing. Ramban holds that this blessing may be referring to what we are told in *I Divrei HaYamim* 7:40: "All these are the sons of Asher, distinguished heads of families, mighty warriors and outstanding leaders," which is not said about the other tribes.

Ramban and *S'forno*, though, explain the words בָּרוּךְ מִבָּנִים *(Devarim* 33:24) (which we translated above as "blessed with children") as meaning that the tribe would be one that the other tribes would all find acceptable. Thus it would be translated "blessed by the sons [of Yaakov]" and is parallel to the next phrase in the same verse, "acceptable to his brothers."

"Your locks are iron and brass" (ibid. v. 25). *Ramban* states that Asher's territory extended from Yafo (Jaffa) to Akko (Acre), which is the lock of *Eretz Yisrael*. The words, "and as your days, so shall your strength (דָבְאֶךָ) be," are interpreted to mean that Asher's land would be flowing with milk and honey, where the word דָבְאֶךָ is taken to mean זָבְאֶךָ, which is related to the word זָבַת — "flowing" — in a similar sentiment to "he dips his foot in oil" (ibid. v. 24).

The blessing of the tribes is the conclusion of Moshe's lofty final testament to the Jewish people, and Moshe, the master of all the prophets, ended it with a general blessing to the nation, and a stress on how praiseworthy Israel is. It was this nation which Moshe served his whole life, it was for them that he brought the Torah down from Heaven, and it was for the Jewish people that he had prepared the way to inherit *Eretz Yisrael* and to become deeply rooted in the Torah of Hashem. We are not able to fathom all of Moshe's intentions in his blessing. We can only attempt to give hypotheses, and sometimes we may even be able to find the true meaning.

II.

"There Never Again Arose in Israel a Prophet such as Moshe"

The last *parashah* in the Torah deals with Moshe's death, with his seeing the land just before he died, and with a description of how exalted a person he was — that there never arose another prophet such as Moshe. The commentators supply us with enough material here for a full book. We will only bring the briefest of summaries, from both *rishonim* and *acharonim*.

Seeing the land from afar was no less a miracle than the other miracles that were experienced. According to Abarbanel, this was impossible by natural means, because one cannot see an entire land from a distance. Abarbanel attempts to explain this in various ways. The most interesting of Abarbanel's interpretations are: a) Moshe's senses were different from ours; b) Hashem enhanced his vision. The fact is that even enhanced vision is not enough to be able to see all the details of the land, and especially when the land is divided up into tribes. Abarbanel therefore holds that Moshe saw before him a map of the land and of its form. Abarbanel has much more to say about this whole topic.

The commentators note that when the Torah links "you will see the land from afar but will not come there" (ibid. 32:52) this is not meant to be evil tidings and a punishment, but on the contrary — Hashem wanted to reward Moshe for his great desire to enter the land. The meaning of this verse is thus that as Moshe would not be entering the land, Hashem at least compensated him by letting him see it.

⋙ "Moshe Died There"

The description of Moshe's death, according to Abarbanel, Rabbenu Bachya, Ibn Ezra and various other commentators, came after Hashem told him to die, as detailed in the Torah (ibid. 32:50). The simple explanation, according to Rabbenu Bachya, is that Moshe fulfilled a positive *mitzvah* by dying. Abarbanel states that Moshe's death was not a natural one, but came through his clinging to Hashem.

There is a dispute among *tannaim* in *Bava Basra* 15 as to who wrote the last eight verses of the Torah, from "And Moshe died" until the end of the Torah. R' Yehudah (some say R' Nechemiah) asks: "Could Moshe have died and then written, 'And Moshe died'? Rather, Moshe wrote to that point, and from that point on was written by Yehoshua." R' Shimon, though, argues and states, "Can a Torah be valid if even a single letter is missing? Rather, until this point, Hashem spoke and Moshe wrote. From this point, Hashem spoke and Moshe wrote tearfully (בְּדֶמַע)."

What is the meaning of בְּדֶמַע? According to *Ritva*, until that point, Moshe would repeat all the verses that Hashem had dictated to him, but here he was unable to repeat them because of his tears.

The commentators who go furthest are Ibn Ezra and Rabbenu Meyuchas, who state that Yehoshua wrote the last twelve verses, from "And Moshe went up" until the end of the Torah. For once Moshe had gone up, he did not come down again.

Rabbenu Bachya disagrees. What is so surprising if Moshe wrote what happened to him? After all, he wrote all about the troubles that would come upon Israel, and then about the consolation that would follow, and this was centuries before these occurred.

Or HaChayim is also strongly against Ibn Ezra's view, and writes that "it is not fitting to write words such as these, for with my own ears I heard how people became entangled in them, and this leads to denying the Torah." But there are many that are astonished at *Or HaChayim*, for, after all, this view of Ibn Ezra is held by R' Yehudah in the *gemara*. It is true that Ibn Ezra expands the idea from 8 to 12 verses, but what difference does this make in the basic idea that a number of verses were written by Yehoshua?

Abarbanel too holds that Moshe wrote the whole Torah at Hashem's direction, including those *parashiyos* which dealt with the future.

There are commentators who hold that when the *gemara* states that Moshe wrote the last eight verses בְּדֶמַע — "with tears," it means that he used tears to write with, as opposed to the ink with which he wrote the rest of the Torah. This is *Rashba's* view. *Ein Yaakov*, though, rejects this view vehemently, for words written with tears for ink are invisible and illegible. Abarbanel therefore states that Moshe wrote everything with ink, but he wrote the last verse "with דֶמַע," namely, tearfully and sighing.

The Gaon of Vilna has an original interpretation of the word "דֶמַע." According to him, this is related to the phrase (*Sh'mos* 22:28) וְדִמְעֲךָ — "your *terumah*" (tithes of produce for the *kohen*). The root דמע means "mix." Tithes are called דֶמַע because they are mixed in with the other produce until one sets aside the *kohen's* portion. *Chazal* tell us that Hashem wrote the Torah two thousand years before He created the world. The meaning of *Chazal* is that the Torah had been written, but the letters were mixed and combined in a manner incomprehensible to man; later the letters and words were divided up as we have the Torah today. Here too, the letters of this section about Moshe's death were written in mixed fashion — בְּדֶמַע — whereas after Moshe's death the letters were divided into recognizable words.

We find another place in *Chazal* (*Menachos* 30) where this view is expressed. It states there, "R' Yehoshua bar Abba said in the name of R' Gidel in the name of Rav: 'Eight verses in the Torah an individual reads in the synagogue.'" *Rashi* explains that what this means is that one person must read all the eight verses together, and they cannot be divided among two or more people. That is also the way R' Yosef Karo rules in *Orach Chaim* 428:7. *Tosafos*, though, states that this is to teach us that, unlike the other *parashiyos*, the *chazan* does not need to help the reader.

R' David Zvi Hoffmann states that the use of the word "individual" in the quote of the *gemara* above is to be understood in the sense it is used in *Ta'anis* 10: "Whoever is worthy of being appointed the leader of the community is called an *individual*." The meaning of this *Chazal* is that as there are reasons to fear that people may mistakenly treat the last verses of the Torah without the proper respect due the entire Torah because Moshe did not write them, the person who reads them must be a *talmid chacham* — "scholar." R' David Zvi Hoffmann also found this stated in *Mordechai Halachos Ketanos* 955. Meiri, too, interprets the term "individual" as meaning the most distinguished member of the congregation.

Rambam, though, in *Hilchos Tefillah* 13:6 states:

> The eight verses at the end of the Torah may be read in the synagogue with less than ten people, even though all of it is Moshe's Torah, as given by Hashem. As they refer to the time after Moshe died, they are different (from the other verses) and therefore the *halachah* is different, and an individual may read them (i.e., without a *minyan*).

Ra'avad reacts by stating, "We have never heard of anything like this."

There is considerable debate about these eight verses, and just as there is a dispute among the *tannaim*, so there is also among the *rishonim*.

✥ No Man Knew His Burial Place

Akeidah explains at length the fact that Moshe died a natural death, whereas Eliyahu went up to the heavens in a storm. *Akeidah* says that man is composed of two parts, body and soul. There are three ways in which the two can be separated at death: a) For the wicked, the soul does not separate easily to go up to heaven, just as fire clings to a thorn bush. These souls are confronted by various destructive angels and must surmount all types of obstacles. b) In *tzaddikim*, the soul is stronger than the body, and there are even some that managed to subdue the body, but they did not free themselves from it entirely. *Radak* hints at this in regard to Eliyahu, when he states that when Eliyahu went up to the heavens, his clothes were burned by the fire of the heavenly spheres; namely, that his body was consumed. c) Moshe was higher than all of these. His body and soul separated totally, as we see in *Koheles* (12:7), "The dust shall return to the earth as it was, and the spirit will return to God Who gave it." The reason why no one knew where Moshe was buried, says Abarbanel, is that his body did not decay. The dust in his body merged completely with the earth. Abarbanel adds further that Moshe did not want people to be present when he died, because that would disturb his clinging to Hashem. The separation between the body and the soul was instantaneous, and there was no delay in the separation of the two parts.

Chizkuni holds that no one knew where Moshe was buried so that no other mortal would be buried in the vicinity, and also so that no one would be able to conduct a seance to evoke his spirit.

Ralbag gives three other reasons: a) so that people should not make Moshe into a god, as happened with the founders of other religions. b) Burial includes a certain element of humiliation, and Hashem wanted Moshe not to suffer that. c) Just as Moshe was separate from the others in his life, the same was true in his death. According to *Ralbag*, all three of these reasons are to be found in *Devarim* 34:6: a) "He buried him in the valley (בַּגַּי)" — with גֵּאוּת — "pride" — and not in a humiliating fashion. b) "Opposite Beis Pe'or" — hinting that they were not to make him a god, as was the case with the idolatry of Pe'or. c) "No man knew his burial place" — to show how great he was; just as he was separate from everyone in life, the same was true in death. Hashem touched him, and he died.

The words, "And he buried him," do not explain who did this, and this resulted in a dispute among *tannaim*. According to the simple meaning, Hashem buried him. According to R' Yishmael, though, the word "he" refers to Moshe, that Moshe buried himself. According to *S'forno*, "his soul that had separated" accomplished this, but Ibn Ezra explains this simply: Moshe went into a cave in the valley and closed himself up in it.

Meshech Chochmah quotes *Yerushalmi* at the end of *Yevamos*, which states that for three days a person's soul hovers over his body, and we are told in *Shabbos* that the soul goes up and comes down throughout the first twelve months after death. With Moshe, though, the link between the body and the soul was totally broken. When the Torah says "no one knew" (וְלֹא יָדַע), this means "no one recognized," implying that no one recognized Moshe after his death, because he ceased any contact with the place where he was buried.

Rambam has an interesting comment in his introduction to his commentary on the Mishnah. He has the following to say about Moshe's death: "He went up the mountain at noon on the seventh day of the month of *Adar* (*Sifri, Parashas Ha'azinu, Chazal* in *Megillah* 13), and the event occurred. From our point of view it is called 'death' because he was lost to us. But from his point of view it was called 'life,' because of the glory of the state that he rose to." So, too, do *Chazal* tell us in *Sotah* 13, that "Moshe our Teacher did not die, but went up and serves Above."

⊷§ No Prophet Arose in Israel like Moshe

Chazal and various commentators deal with the difference between Moshe's prophecy and that of the other prophets. Many are astonished at *Chazal's* comment that no prophet arose "in Israel" (*Devarim* 34:10) like Moshe, but such did arise among the other nations, that being Bilam. Was Bilam then as great as Moshe? Many different interpretations have been given of this. We will quote a few of these.

R' Chisdai Crescas states that prophecy is contained within nature. In the case of Moshe, though, it was above nature, and he did not need any preparation before receiving prophecy. In the case of Bilam, too, prophecy came through supernatural means, because of Hashem's supervision over His nation, Israel.

Abarbanel holds that Bilam had no connection with prophecy. He practiced witchcraft. Only because it was necessary was he granted the possibility of talking in Hashem's name, just as Hashem gave Bilam's donkey the power to speak. Israel had prophets, while the other nations had witchcraft. Moshe was the greatest of prophets among Israel, while Bilam was the head of the magicians. The entire *parashah* related to Bilam came to show how low he was.

HaKesav VeHaKabalah has an interesting, novel approach. According to him, "arose" (קָם) is related to the word הִתְקוֹמְמוּת, meaning to revolt, as in *Michah* 7:6: "Daughter rises up (קָמָה) against her mother." No prophet ever arose in Israel who had the audacity to claim to be as great as Moshe, but that did happen among the non-Jews, where Bilam acted as if he was on the same level as Moshe.

The Torah tells us that no prophet arose like Moshe, "whom Hashem knew face to face" (*Devarim* 34:10), and "with all the signs and wonders" (ibid. v. 11). The term "face to face" is explained in different fashions by various *rishonim*, as the Torah says, "My face shall not be seen" (*Sh'mos* 33:23). *Rambam* in *Moreh Nevuchim* 3:37 says that "face to face" parallels the verse, "He heard the voice speaking" (*Bamidbar* 7:89). Hearing Hashem's voice without any intermediary is known as "face to face." Even though Israel, too, heard Hashem's voice, their hearing was in the nature of hearing Hashem's speech through their senses, says Narbonne, but Moshe's hearing was beyond the senses. Israel reached that level only once, for the first two of the Ten Commandments.

Abarbanel says that Israel heard the voice only once, whereas Moshe always heard it. In addition, Moshe had attained the highest degree of prophecy.

Zohar notes that in regard to Israel the Torah uses פָּנִים בְּפָנִים (*Devarim* 5:4) — "face to face," whereas in regard to Moshe the Torah uses פָּנִים אֶל פָּנִים (*Sh'mos* 33:11). Israel saw Hashem in their own faces, whereas Hashem's face was directed toward Moshe's face.

Rabbenu Meyuchas has a similar approach. In the case of Moshe, the one face was directed toward the other, whereas in the case of the other prophets, they saw it only from the side, as in *Yechezkel* 1:28: "I heard a voice talking."

There are also many interpretations of the verse, "for all the signs and wonders" (*Devarim* 34:11). After all, didn't other prophets also show great signs and wonders, in one form or another? Why then is the Torah telling us that none arose like Moshe? *Rambam* in *Moreh Nevuchim* says that what was different in the case of Moshe was that the signs and wonders took place in the open, before all of Israel, whereas the signs and wonders of the other prophets only took place in front of limited numbers of people, as we see in regard to Elisha (*II Melachim* 8:4), "Tell me, I pray you, all the great things that Elisha has done."

Ramban, though, differs with this view. He asks whether, when Eliyahu stopped all the rain, this was not known to everyone. When Eliyahu appeared to Ovadiah, Ovadiah said to him (*I Melachim* 18:10), "there is no nation or kingdom where my lord has not sent to seek you." Similarly, the way the incident ended was known to everyone, because Eliyahu said (ibid. v. 19), "Now therefore send, and gather to me all Israel to Mount Carmel." The same was true when the sun stopped for Yehoshua. Wasn't this seen by everyone throughout the world? The *Tanach* itself (*Yehoshua* 10:14) says that "there was never a day like this before it or after it."

Ramban therefore states that the Torah is referring to the quality of the signs and wonders. There was never a day like that on which the Torah was given, either before or after it. By the same token, the miracles performed by Moshe lasted longer. Manna fell for forty years, and the pillar of fire stayed with Israel for those forty years. So too were there the miracles of the well and the quails, and the fact that the Jews remained in a desolate desert, full of snakes and scorpions, for forty years, yet lacked nothing.

Abarbanel says that the other prophets arranged for their miracles by praying, as it states, "Moshe and Aaron among His *kohanim*, and Shmuel among those who called His name." With Moshe, on the other hand, the miracles occurred simply because Hashem said they were to occur, for Moshe was constantly accompanied by Hashem's Presence. Even the greatest of miracles performed by the others could not compare to those performed by Moshe. Moshe lived for forty days and nights without food and water. Eliyahu was fed by an angel, and even he did not do totally without food.

Rivash has a novel interpretation. The other prophets prophesied to individuals. Eliyahu told a single woman that the oil and flour would not cease. Elisha imparted a blessing into the oil. And the same was true with the other prophets. Moshe, on the other hand, performed his miracles for the entire nation, and that is what the Torah meant when it said, "Before the eyes of all Israel" (*Devarim* 34:12). These miracles were for all of Israel. That was the way in which Moshe's spiritual height exceeded that of all the other prophets.

In conclusion, let us add a Chassidic morsel. *Tiferes Shlomo* states that Moshe wrote the *parashah* tearfully, not because he was told of his death, but because he was forced to write such lofty words of praise about himself, in spite of his great humility.

תושלב"ע